Frommer's®

D0959338

SCOTLAND'S
B E S T - L O V E D
DRIVING
T O U R S

Ⓦ Wiley Publishing, Inc.

Written by David Williams

First published 1992
Revised second edition 1996, published in this format 1998
Revised third edition published 2000
Revised fourth edition published 2003
Revised fifth edition published 2005

Edited, designed and produced by AA Publishing.
© Automobile Association Developments Limited 1998, 2000, 2003, 2005.
Maps © Automobile Association Developments Limited 1998, 2000, 2003, 2005.

Published by AA Publishing

Published in the United States by
John Wiley & Sons, Inc.
111 River Street, Hoboken, NJ 07030

Find us online at Frommers.com

Frommer's is a registered trademark of Arthur Frommer.
Used under license.

ISBN 0-7645-7798-0

Ordnance Survey®   This product includes mapping data
licensed from Ordnance Survey®
with the permission of the Controller of Her Majesty's
Stationery Office. © Crown copyright 2004. All rights
reserved. Licence number 399221

Color separation: Daylight Colour Art, Singapore

Printed and bound by G. Canale & C. S.P.A., Torino, Italy

A02026

CONTENTS

ABOUT THIS BOOK

This book is not only a practical guide for the independent traveller, but is also invaluable for those who would like to know more about the country. It is divided into four regions, each containing between five and seven tours which start and finish in the towns and cities which we consider to be the best centres for exploration. Each tour has details of the most interesting places to visit en route. Panels catering for special interests follow some of the main entries – for those whose interest is in history, wildlife or walking, and those who have children. There are also panels which highlight scenic stretches of road and which give details of special events, gastronomic specialities, crafts and customs. The simple route directions are accompanied by an easy-to-use map at the beginning of each tour, along with a chart showing intermediate distances in miles and kilometres. These can help you decide where to take a break and stop overnight, for example. (All distances quoted are approximate.)

Before setting off it is advisable to check with the information centre (addresses are given after the [i] symbol at the end of town entries) at the start of the tour for recommendations on where to break your journey and for additional information on what to see and do, and when best to visit.

Business hours

Banks: open Monday to Friday 9.30–5, but times do vary depending on the bank and the place. Some close for lunch.

Post offices: generally open Monday to Friday 9–5.30, Saturday 9–noon. Times and days vary from place to place.

Shops: are usually open Monday to Saturday 8.30–1.30, 3.30–7.30. Many are closed on Monday mornings, and food shops are often closed on Thursday after-noons. Times may vary in busy tourist areas.

Credit Cards

All major credit cards are widely accepted throughout Scotland.

Currency

The unit of currency is the pound (£), divided into 100 pence (p). Coins are in denominations of 1, 2, 5, 10, 20 and 50 pence, and one and two pounds; Scottish notes are in denomina-tions of £1, 5, 10, 20, 50 and 100. Bank of England notes are also legal tender, as well as euros, at the management's discretion.

Customs Regulations

For goods bought outside the EU, you can import, duty free, 200 cigarettes or 100 cigarillos or 50 cigars or 250g of tobacco; one litre of alcohol over 22 per cent volume or 2 litres of alcohol not

Shaggy Highland cattle

> **Tour Information**
> See pages 164–73 for addresses, telephone numbers and opening times of the attractions mentioned in the tours, including the telephone numbers of tourist offices.
>
> **Accommodation and restaurants**
> See pages 159–63 for a list of recommended hotels for each tour. Also listed are restaurants where you may like to stop for a meal.

over 22 per cent volume or fortified or sparkling wine, plus 2 litres of still table wine; 60ml of perfume, 250ml of toilet water and £145 worth of other goods. If goods are bought, duty paid, within the EU, you can import, additional tobacco, alcoholic drinks, gifts and other goods for personal use.

Emergency Telephone Number
Police, fire, ambulance, tel: 999.

Entry Regulations
Passports are required by all visitors, including citizens of EU countries. Visas are not required for entry into Britain by American citizens, nationals of the British Commonwealth and most European countries. Visa regulations can change – check before you travel.

Health
Inoculations are not required for entry to Britain. Health insurance is recommended for non-EU citizens.

Motoring
See pages 158–9.

Public Holidays
1–2 January: New Year
Good Friday/Easter Monday
First Monday in May: May Day
Last Monday in May: Spring Bank Holiday
Last Monday in August: Late Summer Bank Holiday
25–26 December: Christmas

Route Directions
Throughout the book the following abbreviations are used for Scottish roads:
A – main roads
B – local roads
unclassified roads – minor roads (unnumbered).

Telephones
Insert coins after lifting the receiver; the dialling tone is a continuous tone.
Useful numbers:
Operator – 100
Directory Enquiries – 118500 (BT), 118111 (One.Tel)
International Directory Enquiries – 118505 (BT), 118211 (One.Tel)
International Operator – 155

IDD code for Scotland – 44.
To make an international call, dial 00, then the country code, the area code, omitting the first zero, then the local number.

Time
The official time is Greenwich Mean Time (GMT). British Summer Time (BST) begins in late March when clocks are put forward an hour. In late October, the clocks go back to GMT. The official date is announced in the daily newspapers, and is always at 2am on a Sunday.

Tourist Office
Visit Scotland, 23 Ravelston Terrace, Edinburgh, EH4 3EU. Tel: 0131 332 2433.

SOUTHERN SCOTLAND

Southern Scotland is dominated by the grand mass of the Southern Uplands, the great band of hills that stretches right across the width of the country. For a long time it was easier to sail along the coastline than cross the hills, so the two coastal fringes were settled first. These narrow, fertile strips are still among the most populated parts of the region, with the best land devoted to cereals and herds of prime dairy cattle. Inland, the rolling uplands are home to the countless sheep which form the basis of the prosperous woollen and knitwear industries of the Borders.

The many castles and fortified houses found in the region are reminders of the centuries of border warfare that have shaped the history of the whole of southern Scotland. Cattle-raiding, pillaging, looting and burning were commonplace, but perhaps the most poignant reminders of those turbulent days are the great Border abbeys of Melrose, Kelso, Jedburgh and Dryburgh, which were mercilessly attacked and eventually destroyed by the English. Fortunately for us, their splendid ruins still survive to conjure up the past.

Boat showing the blue and white Ecosse flag in Eyemouth harbour

The region is much more peaceful now, and most of today's 'invaders' come armed with a bucket and spade or a set of golf clubs. The eastern side of the country, with its beaches, seaside resorts, fishing villages and busy mill towns, has been a tourist area for some time, with many of its best-known places made famous by the region's best publicist, Sir Walter Scott. The west coast's literary figure, Robert Burns, is highly regarded as 'a man of the people', and his special place in the Scots' heart can be judged by the number of memorials, plaques and statues that mark his journeys through the country.

The region can never match the grandeur of the western Highlands or the great museums and palaces of central Scotland, but it does offer a relaxed way of life in an area imbued with tradition. Its people are proud of that fact. They are keen not to lose the unique flavour of their local culture and any visitor who witnesses a Border town's rugby match will soon learn how independent the spirit is here.

The cycle museum at Drumlanrig Castle in Dumfries & Galloway

Tour 1

The journey along the Clyde coast is one of the finest in this part of Scotland, with glorious views over the Firth of Clyde to Arran and the smaller islands of the Clyde. With such views, it is no wonder that many Scots retire to this area. For the visitor, this scenery provides the backdrop to many places associated with Robert Burns, the national poet and the Scots' favourite literary figure.

Tour 2

Many visitors bypass this corner of the country, but there is a wealth of picturesque villages, historic buildings, sandy beaches and other attractions in this almost 'forgotten' land. The area is mainly agricultural and the great absence of industry and big towns has meant that many antiquities have been preserved and older building styles have survived. This is one of the warmest and driest parts of Scotland, factors that have helped foster agriculture – and palm trees!

Tour 3

The muddy creeks on the northern shore of the Solway Firth were havens to smugglers bringing contraband into Scotland. Given such a tradition, it comes as no surprise that the area's most famous figure was an exciseman – none other than Robert Burns, who spent his final years in the Dumfries area. The castles and granite towns of the coast contrast with large forests and rolling farmland inland.

Tour 4

Although the Clyde is normally thought of as an industrial river, the upper reaches are thronged with orchards and market gardens. Add a few castles and an impressive canyon and the Clyde Valley soon becomes one of the most surprising areas in this part of Scotland. The moors and hills above the valley are no less interesting and they have been home to Iron-Age people, Romans and farmers – and weekend gold prospectors!

Tour 5

The tour follows many important river courses as they wind their way through the hills of the Southern Uplands, the land of the shepherd and the forester. Although the area's population has never been large, it has certainly seen many visitors. Some were unwelcome as they came to raid and plunder; others,

the early tourists, came to sample the peaceful countryside and the delights of two of the country's most southerly spas.

Tour 6

The name of Sir Walter Scott is writ large in this area. He lived and worked here and also became one of Scotland's greatest novelists, to the extent that the Waverley novels gave their name both to a local railway line and to Edinburgh's main railway station. This is also the land of the ruins of the great Border abbeys, impressive medieval buildings that stand as monuments to man's craftsmanship – and powers of destruction.

Tour 7

The Border Country, of which this is part, has long seen the coming and going of armies and the number of castles found here is a measure of how dangerous an area this once was. Much of the coastline is rugged, and the cliff scenery quite spectacular, though in the north of the region the coastal scenery becomes gentler, giving way to fine beaches and grassy links that are ideal for golf. Inland, the rich agricultural district of the Merse supports many pretty villages, most of which nestle under the shelter of the Lammermuirs.

The Land
O' Burns

This tour starts in Ayr, once the chief port of western Scotland but now more famous for its associations with Robert Burns. And, indeed, throughout this tour the name of Scotland's most famous son keeps cropping up…

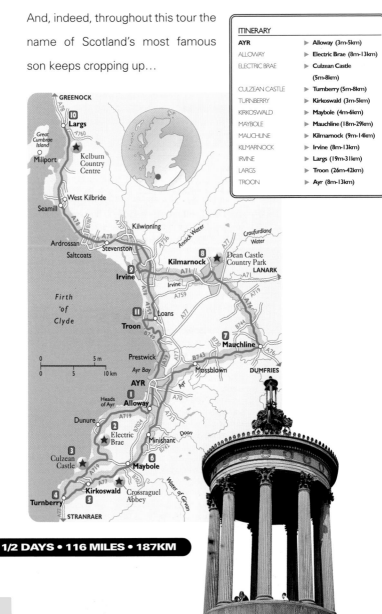

1/2 DAYS • 116 MILES • 187KM

The Burns Monument and Brig o'Doon in Alloway

ⓘ *22 Sandgate, Ayr*

▶ *Take the **B7024** from Ayr for 3 miles (5km) to the village of Alloway.*

SPECIAL TO...

There are a number of celebrated golf courses along the Clyde Coast. The links courses along the coast are ideally suited to the game, and are littered with bunkers. While most towns have courses, the most renowned ones are to be found at Ayr, Troon, Turnberry and Prestwick. They must surely rank as some of the most attractively located courses in Britain.

---

❶ Alloway, South Ayrshire
The Burns National Heritage Park was established here as this was where Robert Burns spent his early years. Burns was born in 1759 and he is regarded not only as Scotland's national poet but as one of her greatest literary figures. Although lionised by the predominantly Edinburgh-based literary celebrities of his day, he never abandoned his roots in the west and continued to work as a small farmer, and later as an exciseman. Like many great artists, he was never fully appreciated until well after his death, but now there are hundreds of Burns Societies all over the world, each year celebrating the poet's birthday (26 January) with such well-known favourites as *To a Haggis, Holy Willie's Prayer* and, probably his best-known work, *Auld Lang Syne.*

Opposite the park is the old ruined kirk where Burns' father is buried. This was a ruin even in Burns' day and it was here that Tam, in the poem *Tam o' Shanter*, saw warlocks, witches and Auld Nick (the devil). Also near by is the ancient and very beautiful Auld Brig o' Doon over which Tam escaped from the witches. Towering above the river is the Burns Monument, which is set in a very pleasant garden.

Burns was born in the little thatched cottage known as Burns Cottage. His father, William Burnes, built it around 1757 and it has been well preserved, not only as a memorial to the poet, but as a good example of local village architecture of the time. This type of two-roomed cottage is known as a 'but and ben', with the kitchen in the front room and the living room/bedroom at the back ('ben'). The neighbouring museum holds a vast amount of Burns memorabilia.

▶ *Continue on the **B7024** for a short distance. Just after crossing the River Doon, turn right at an unclassified road to Doonfoot. Turn left when the coastal road (**A719**) is met, 8 miles (13km).*

❷ Electric Brae, South Ayrshire
After the A719 passes Dunure and turns inland at Culzean Bay, the road goes 'up' the Electric Brae, a well-known and mind-boggling optical illusion. A car might appear to be travelling downhill, but drivers who come to a halt will find the car rolling backwards! On pleasant summer afternoons, there can be quite a queue of cars on this stretch of road trying to roll 'uphill'.

▶ *Continue on the **A719** for 5 miles (8km) to Culzean Castle.*

8 Culzean Castle, South Ayrshire

The present building is based on a medieval tower house that was later developed as a massive country house set within extensive parkland. It is now the National Trust for Scotland's most popular attraction and its country park has gardens, a nursery, a swan pond and a deer park.

In the late 18th century, Robert Adam started work on remodelling the house. The interior decoration has since been painstakingly restored to his original designs to the extent that this is now the Scottish showpiece of Adam's work. The most outstanding features are the magnificent Oval Staircase and the Round Drawing Room.

The extensive grounds, a continuing exercise in large-scale conservation, include woodlands, a walled garden, a swan pond and deer park.

Culzean Castle, commanding a fine position above Culzean Bay

BACK TO NATURE

The coastline of Culzean has many different things to look for and is certainly worth exploring. You may find agates on the pebble beach and the rock pools have a wide variety of life in them including sea anemones, sea urchins and butterfish. During the summer there are many seabirds, while during the winter great northern divers might be seen offshore.

▶ Continue southwards on the **A719** for 5 miles (8km) to Turnberry.

4 Turnberry, South Ayrshire
This famous golfing centre is dominated by the Turnberry Hotel. The golf course sometimes plays host to the British Open.

The remains of the castle, which stands by the lighthouse, may have been the birthplace of Robert Bruce. In 1307 Bruce

was lured across the Clyde from Arran by a mystic fire and defeated the English force that was occupying the castle, destroying the buildings in the process.

▶ Leave by the **A77** and follow it northeast for 3 miles (5km) to Kirkoswald.

5 Kirkoswald, South Ayrshire
Kirkoswald has a number of connections with Robert Burns as his mother's family came from the village. Burns' characters of Tam and Kate from the poem *Tam o' Shanter* came from

Kirkoswald and Souter Johnnie's Cottage is on the main road. This thatched house of 1786 was the home of John Davidson, the local 'souter' (local term for shoemaker), and is now a museum furnished in the style of Burns' day. Burns would have attended the old Kirkoswald Church, now a picturesque ruin within a graveyard in which the poet's grandparents and great-grandparents are buried.

▶ Continue on the **A77** for 4 miles (6km) to Maybole.

6 Maybole, South Ayrshire
Many substantial buildings line the narrow main street, the most striking of which is 17th-century Maybole Castle (not open). The castle is featured in the ballad *The Raggle Taggle Gypsies*, in which the King of the Gypsies, Johnnie Faa, persuaded a Countess of Cassillis to elope with him. Unfortunately he was caught and hanged, while the countess was imprisoned in the castle, in the room with the little oriel window that faces up High Street.

Maybole has a long history and its oldest building is the roofless Collegiate Church. Most of the remaining parts, although built in the 15th century, are in the style of the 13th and 14th centuries.

Crossraguel Abbey is met a little before Maybole. This relatively small Cluniac monastery (it only had 10 monks in the 15th century) was built in the mid-13th century. It was very badly damaged in the Wars of Independence (1296–1357) and had to be rebuilt. Although roofless, what walls remain indicate the scale of the establishment. The tall tower house is a particularly unusual building for an abbey.

The ruined Baltersan Tower is on the roadside between the abbey and the village.

▶ *Continue on the A77, then turn right at the B743 to Mauchline, 18 miles (29km).*

FOR HISTORY BUFFS

When driving along the road near Maybole, it is worth remembering that the asphalt or 'tarmacadam' surface was named after a local man, John Loudon MacAdam (1756–1836). He experimented with new ways of building roads by using a layer of large stones covered with layers of sucessively smaller ones. His ideas revolutionised road building in this country.

7 Mauchline, East Ayrshire
This little town is yet another in the area which has a number of associations with Robert Burns – not surprising, in view of the fact that he lived at the farm of Mossgiel, just to the north of Mauchline. The most outstanding building is the National Burns Memorial, which was constructed in 1896.

The church stands near the centre of the town and in its graveyard lie many people associated with Burns, including several of his children. Burns featured some of the locals in his poems, like the clockmaker John Brown ('Clockie Brown' in *The Court of Equity*), and a rogue cattle dealer called McGavin who was referred to as 'Master Tootie, alias Laird McGaun' in *To Gavin Hamilton, Esq.*

By the churchyard stands the Burns House Museum, where Burns and his wife set up house in 1788; this also has an interesting collection of local historical material.

Opposite the church stands Poosie Nansie's Inn, which provided the setting for *The Jolly Beggars*.

▶ *Leave by the A76 and follow it to Kilmarnock, entering the town by the A735.*

Dominating the town: the National Burns Memorial Tower at Mauchline, built in 1896

8 Kilmarnock, East Ayrshire
This industrial town, which is bigger than Ayr, built its affluence on the making of such diverse goods as whisky, carpets and various engineering products. Although much of the heart of the town has been changed by the building of modern shops, there are still some very fine buildings, many of them highly ornamented red or white sandstone structures, erected to reflect the wealth and aspirations of their builders.

The Dean Castle Country Park is on the northeast outskirts of the town. The attractive castle was a seat of the Boyds, lords of Kilmarnock, and was carefully restored in the 20th century. It houses a collection of arms, armour, tapestries and early musical instruments. The 200-acre (80-hectare) grounds offer many opportunities for walks.

Kay Park, which is on the eastern side of the Craufurdland Water, has as its centrepiece the tall red sandstone Burns Monument, which was erected in 1879. In 1786 Burns' first work was published and his *Poems chiefly in the Scottish Dialect*, usually known as the *Kilmarnock Edition*, brought him great fame – and the sum of £20.

FOR CHILDREN

The town's Galleon Centre offers many sporting facilities, including a crèche, a pool and an ice rink. Five miles (8km) east of Kilmarnock, along the A71, Loudon Castle Country Park has Britain's largest roundabout.

▶ *Leave by the* **A759***. On reaching the* **A71***, go to Irvine.*

9 Irvine, North Ayrshire
Irvine has many attractions, but the modern shopping centre, which crosses the River Irvine, dwarfs the old town and spoils Irvine's riverside location. The town prospered as a busy industrial centre and was Glasgow's main port before Port Glasgow was developed.

The Scottish Maritime Museum provides a fine introduction to this heritage. Among the exhibits are boats tied alongside the old harbour wall including a 'puffer' (a small cargo boat that served the west coast and its islands), the world's oldest remaining seacoaster and a number of other craft, including lifeboats. The museum has exhibitions and displays of various shipbuilding crafts. The prize exhibit is the Victorian engine-shop from Stephen's Linthouse yard in Glasgow, which has been re-erected here. This superb tall brick building is supported by the original cast-iron structure

The attractive exterior of Dean Castle – museum and country park

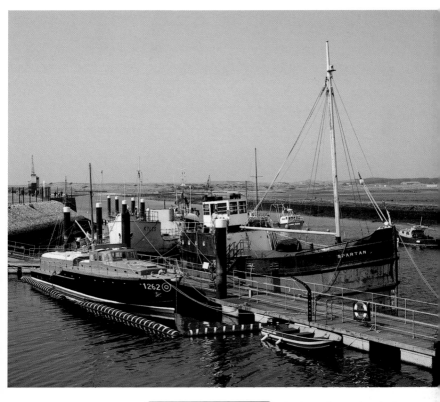

Boats moored at the Scottish Maritime Museum include a 'puffer'

that was quite revolutionary when it was constructed in 1872. But industrial museums are not just about factories and their products: they are about the people who made this possible, and the museum has restored a shipyard worker's 'room and kitchen' tenement house to what it would have looked like in 1910.

Harbour Street leads to the river mouth and the Pilot House, erected in 1906 with an automatic tide-signalling device which hoisted balls on top of the building to indicate the depth of the water.

The old part of the town is on the other side of the river. Robert Burns came here in 1781 to learn the trade of flax dressing (called 'heckling') and stayed at No 4 Glasgow Vennel, now a museum. He worked in a

FOR CHILDREN

Irvine's Magnum Centre is one of Scotland's most popular visitor attractions. It has a swimming pool, ice rink and facilities for sports such as squash, badminton, table tennis and golf practice.
The Clyde Coast is well known for its beaches, including Turnberry, Ayr, Prestwick, Troon, Irvine, Saltcoats and Ardrossan.

'heckling shop' at No 10; 'heck-lers' tended to be politically argumentative types, hence the modern usage of the word. Other places worth looking at include the conservation area of Hill Street, the Burns Club and Museum, and Cunninghame House, which houses the price-less Eglinton Trophy, 8 feet (2.4m) high and exquisitely

intricate, given as the prize for a famous mock-medieval tour-nament staged in 1839 at Eglinton Castle.

i New Street

▶ Leave by the **A737**, then join the **A78** (towards Greenock). Follow this to Largs.

10 Largs, North Ayrshire
This popular seaside town has a long and attractive promenade giving fine views of the Firth of Clyde. Largs has many distinc-tive sandstone buildings, espe-cially along its front. One unique structure that is hidden away and tends to be forgotten is the 1636 Skelmorlie Aisle, originally part of the parish church. Inside is an ornate Renaissance-style monument in the form of an archway, which has a mass of fine detail carved in locally quarried sandstone. Above it is a painted ceiling

The Land O' Burns

The round tower of Bowen Craig to the south of Largs, nicknamed The Pencil, commemorates the defeat of a Viking fleet here in 1263

which has survived remarkably well. The burial ground also contains the vault of a local family by the name of Brisbane, one of whose members, Sir Thomas Brisbane, gave his name to the state capital of Queensland, Australia.

At the southern end of the town, a walk along the coast leads to The Pencil, a tall monument that celebrates the Battle of Largs of 1263. A Viking fleet under King Haakon of Norway was driven ashore here and roundly defeated by the Scots, led by Alexander III. This battle ended the Vikings' occupation of Scotland and Vikingar is a major exhibition celebrating Scotland's Viking heritage.

A regular car ferry crosses over to Great Cumbrae Island. The island's 'capital', Millport, has a pretty location looking over to Little Cumbrae Island, and the beach is popular with families. Walking right round the island or across its top is a favourite outing and from the roadside Glaid Stone, at the summit of the island, there is a wonderful panorama over the Firth of Clyde.

i Railway Station, Main Street, Largs; 28a Stuart Street, Millport (seasonal)

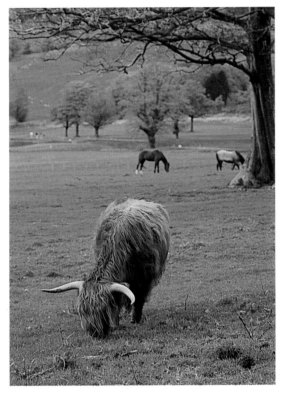

Although usually yellowish in colour, Highland cattle are sometimes red or black

▶ Return south along the **A78** past Irvine, turning off right on the **A759** to Loans and Troon.

❶ Troon, South Ayrshire
This is a pleasant seaside resort, with good beaches and renowned golf courses, one of which has hosted the British Open. The wide esplanade offers splendid views across the Firth towards the island of Arran. Troon developed as a port in the 19th century in order to ship out coal from the Kilmarnock coalfield. The quayside wagons were initially hauled by horses but in 1816 a Stevenson steam locomotive was used, showing how the railways could be used to transform the country's transport system.

The inner harbour has now been turned into a marina and there is a good viewpoint near it on top of the Ballast Bank. This tall artificial mound was built up over a long time partly by ballast unloaded from coal boats returning from Ireland.

▶ Leave by the **B749**. Turn right when the **A79** is met and follow this back to Ayr, 8 miles (13km).

SCENIC ROUTES

The journey along the Clyde Coast offers very fine views of the coast and the islands. On the southern part of the route, the view is dominated by the dome-shaped island of Ailsa Craig, often called 'Paddy's Milestone' as it lies halfway between Ireland and Clydeside. On the northern part of the route, the coastal road offers excellent views of the island of Arran.

RECOMMENDED WALKS

The parks in Ayr, Culzean and Kilmarnock all offer level walking that is eminently suitable for pushchairs and wheelchairs. There is also a large network of paths in Eglinton Park at Irvine, where walkers have opportunities to see swans, roe deer and mink.

Galloway &
The Covenanters

2 DAYS • 159 MILES • 255KM   Gentle scenery dominates this corner of the Scottish coast, while the mild weather ensures that plenty of people flock to its sandy beaches in the summer. Newton Stewart, the starting point on this tour, is a pleasant town on the River Cree, with few modern intrusions to spoil its charm.

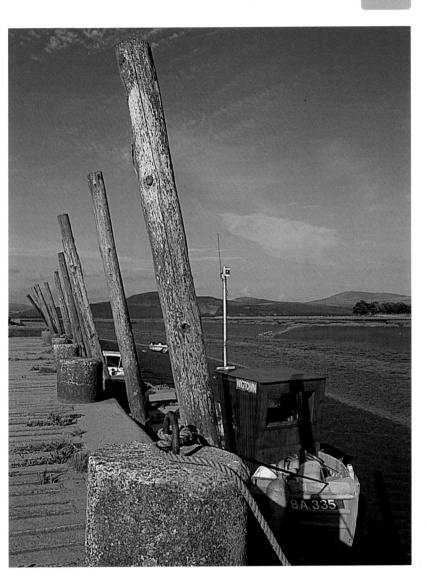

ℹ️ *Dashwood Square (seasonal)*

▶ *Leave by the **A714** and head southwards to Wigtown.*

❶ Wigtown, Dumfries and Galloway

This was formerly the county town of Wigtownshire, with an attractive central square lined by fine Georgian dwellings and an imposing civic building. Local government reorganisation sent it into decline, but its selection as Scotland's Book Town has reversed this. Many buildings on the square now house bookshops. Run down shops and hotels have been refurbished and a degree of prosperity has returned.

The tall monument seen on entering the town commemorates the local Covenanters who were executed for their beliefs. The best-known local martyrs were Margaret Wilson and Margaret MacLachlan, who

The quayside at Wigtown, on the estuary of the River Bladnoch

were executed by drowning in the River Bladnoch in 1685. The women's graves can be seen beside the parish church.

Just south of the town is Bladnoch Distillery, which offers tours and tastings.

▶ *Continue on the **A714**, then turn left on to the **A746** to Whithorn, 11 miles (18km).*

2 Whithorn, Dumfries and Galloway

Whithorn has been a notable goal for travellers ever since pilgrims started to visit its important religious buildings. The religious settlement dates from the 5th century when St Ninian established a mission, and this is the site of the first recorded Christian church in Scotland. Later, an important priory church was built but this was demolished during the Reformation and the prosperity of the village consequently declined.

Today, the old buildings are in ruins but a Romanesque doorway in what was the priory indicates the fine style of architecture in which they were built. Archaeologists have excavated the ground in front of the priory and have uncovered valuable evidence of the buildings that stood here. They have also unearthed hundreds of skeletons as they dug down through the ancient cemetery. These skeletons have provided fascinating clues to the life, health and death of the local people. The continuing investigations, known as the Whithorn Trust, have unearthed many interesting artefacts and these are now on display at the site's Discovery Centre, which is certainly worth a visit.

i *The Whithorn Trust (seasonal)*

▶ *Leave on the A746, then bear left at the B7004. Follow this to the Isle of Whithorn.*

3 Isle of Whithorn, Dumfries and Galloway

This picturesquely sited village is not in fact an island at all but does have a well-sheltered harbour which is frequented by fishing boats and many pleasure craft.

Just beyond the harbour is a grassy promontory with a look-out tower, and on a fine day Ireland, the Isle of Man, England and possibly even the hills of Wales can be seen. On the seaward side of the village

stand the remains of St Ninian's Chapel, which dates from the 14th century.

▶ *Return along the B7004, bear left along a minor road, then follow the A747 to Monreith, 9 miles (14km).*

SCENIC ROUTES

The coastal roads near the Isle of Whithorn and from Monreith to Glenluce have extensive views over the Solway Firth and the northern reaches of the Irish Sea. Keep binoculars handy in order to see the English and Irish coasts and the Isle of Man.

---

4 Monreith, Dumfries and Galloway

Just before the village is reached, a road (left) to the St Medan Golf Club leads to a memorial to Gavin Maxwell

(1914–69). This is in the form of a bronze otter – Maxwell was a writer and naturalist whose book about otters, *Ring of Bright Water*, was made into a film. A prehistoric spiral 'cup and ring' mark is plainly visible just below the memorial.

▶ *Continue on the A747, then turn left at the A75 (then right at the A747) to reach Glenluce, 16 miles (26km) away.*

FOR CHILDREN

Monreith Animal World, on the A747, keeps mainly small animals in large natural enclosures. There are goats, Shetland ponies, otters, beavers, reptiles, Highland cattle and a small Gavin Maxwell museum.

The picturesque harbour of the Isle of Whithorn

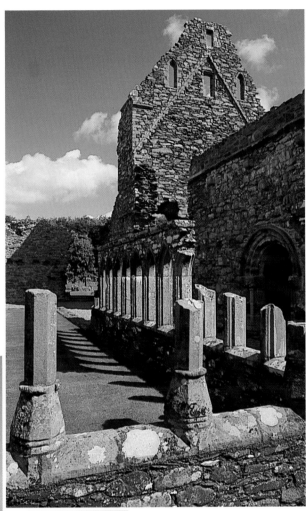

The remains of 12th-century Cistercian Glenluce Abbey

which has part of the original tiled floor still extant. One of the abbey's interesting architectural details that might be overlooked is the survival of the water-supply system, which still has the original jointed earthenware pipes and lidded junction boxes.

▶ *Rejoin the* **A75** *and head towards Stranraer. Bear left at the* **B7084**, *then follow the* **A716** *towards Drummore. Turn right at the* **B7065** *to reach Port Logan.*

6 Port Logan, Dumfries and Galloway
Port Logan is a planned village originally laid out in 1818, with a little pier that has an attractive lighthouse at its end. On the other side of Port Logan Bay, a small cluster of buildings marks the location of the Logan Fish Pond Marine Life Centre, one of the most surprising places in this corner of the country. This is a natural rock pool some 30 feet (9m) deep and 53 feet (16m) in diameter which holds mainly cod and pollack. It was established in 1800 as a fresh seawater 'larder' for nearby Logan House but is now a tourist attraction that will fascinate visitors especially as the fish will take food from the keeper's hand. Logan Botanic Garden lies beyond Port Logan Bay. This is an outstation of the Royal Botanic Gardens of Edinburgh and it has a marvellous collection of plants, especially in the well-sheltered walled garden.

5 Glenluce, Dumfries and Galloway
The village, developed as a staging post on the busy Stranraer to Carlisle road, is now a pleasant centre for exploring this corner of the southwest. For those who like adventure, Scotland's Outdoor Centre is close by, providing off-road driving, clay-pigeon shooting and many other activities.

Glenluce Abbey, to the northwest of the village, is an impressive ruined Cistercian monastery that was founded around 1190. Its best-preserved structure is the chapter house,

The warm Gulf Stream keeps the local climate exceptionally mild so many exotic plants such as tree ferns and palms are able to flourish here.

▶ *Return along the B7065 and A716 to Sandhead, then turn left at the B7042. Turn left at the A77 to reach Portpatrick.*

SPECIAL TO...

Galloway is a good farming area and many farms have fine herds of dairy cows. Much of the milk is processed in local creameries so look out for local cream, cheese and other dairy products. To keep children amused while driving along country roads, get them to look out for 'Belties', the distinctive black and white Belted Galloway cattle. The area's gardens benefit from the warmth of the Gulf Stream, hence the cabbage palms and other southern hemisphere plants growing here.

---

7 Portpatrick, Dumfries and Galloway

One of the most attractive of Scotland's small seaside resorts, Portpatrick has a well-sheltered harbour ringed by colourful stone-built houses and hotels. Portpatrick is the nearest Scottish harbour to Ireland and it was once an important base for ferries, fishing boats and troop ships, but today it is mainly pleasure boats that tie up in the harbour.

Although the village is far from the Galloway Hills, many walkers arrive here as this is the start of the Southern Upland Way, a long-distance walk of over 200 miles (320km) that stretches right across southern Scotland and ends at Cockburnspath near Dunbar. The Way begins at the back of the harbour.

The ruins of Old Portpatrick Parish Kirk stand behind the seafront houses and its most

Ferry departing for Ireland from Stranraer harbour

notable feature is its four-storey circular tower. This was probably both a belfry and a beacon for the harbour. Steps from the seafront lead southward to the 16th-century Dunksey Castle. This was built around 1510 but was a ruin less than two centuries later. The walk to the castle gives splendid views of the coastline, especially if the day is fine.

▶ *Return along the A77 and follow it for 9 miles (14km) to Stranraer.*

8 Stranraer, Dumfries and Galloway

Stranraer is the centre for shopping and services in this part of the country, and is also part of an important transport centre. It has a rail link direct to Glasgow, and a busy ferry service to Belfast and Larne in Ireland. Near the ferry terminal stands the North West Castle Hotel, the former home of Sir John Ross, who gained fame exploring the Arctic in search of the Northwest Passage, the sea route north of Canada, in 1817. Permanent displays on his exploits form part of the local history museum. Stranraer's

FOR HISTORY BUFFS

Castle Kennedy stands beside the village of the same name, east of Stranraer. It was built by the 5th Earl of Cassillis, a Kennedy, whose family in the 15th and 16th centuries was very powerful in this part of Scotland. Burnt down in 1716, the gaunt ivy-clad tower is surrounded by pleasant gardens, laid out by William Adam, in which there is a fine collection of rhododendrons and azaleas.

BACK TO NATURE

South of Bargrennan, a road goes left to the Wood of Cree Nature Reserve, which is under the care of the RSPB. The Wood of Cree is one of southern Scotland's best broadleaved woodlands and is sited by the marshy River Cree. Numerous birds may be seen, including the great spotted woodpecker and the tawny owl in the woods; snipe and water rail in the marshes; and tree pipit and redstart in the scrubland. The reserve has two marked walks: a woodland trail and a scrubland trail.

made from a fine-grained granite which was quarried for the making of curling stones. The island has a massive colony of gannets with over 10,000 pairs breeding there during the summer. Girvan's McKechnie Institute features exhibitions on the town and Ailsa Craig.

i *Bridge Street (seasonal)*

▶ *Leave by the **A714** and at Bargrennan turn left on to the unclassified road to Glen Trool.*

10 Glen Trool, Dumfries and Galloway
Glen Trool is one of Scotland's most scenic places, with access to the Merrick, the highest mainland peak in southern Scotland, and the Southern Upland Way. There is a visitor centre, and Bruce's Stone commemorates the famous king's victory over the English.

▶ *Return along the unclassified road to Bargrennan, then turn left on to the **A714** to return to Newton Stewart.*

main antiquity is the Castle of St John, which is right in the centre of town. This dates back to 1510 and was later used as a gaol. Its rooftop exercise yard gives a fine view of the local scenery. Inside there are displays on castle and prison life, and the Covenanters.

i *28 Harbour Street*

The wide, open beach of Girvan, with views to Ailsa Craig

▶ *Continue on the **A77** to Girvan.*

9 Girvan, South Ayrshire
Girvan is a little seaside town whose pretty, sandy beach is popular with families during the summer. It has a busy harbour, probably the best place from which to view the rugged island of Ailsa Craig. The island is

Queen of
the South

Dumfries' attractive setting on the banks of the River Nith has earned it the title 'Queen of the South'. This is the region's main town and its fine public buildings reflect the history and prosperity of the area. Inland from the 'granite towns' along this coast is a landscape dominated by farms and forests.

1/2 DAYS • 118 MILES • 193KM

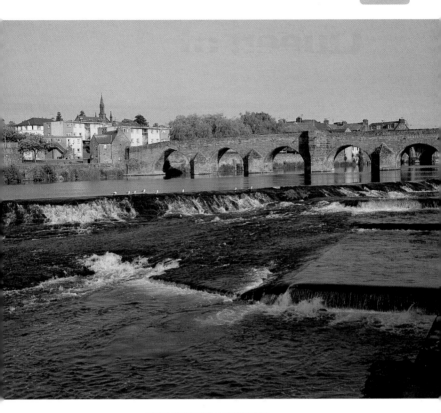

i *Whitesands*

▶ *Leave by the **A710** (the Solway Coast Road) and follow it to New Abbey.*

BACK TO NATURE

The National Nature Reserve at Caerlaverock, southeast of Dumfries, is managed to provide ideal feeding for thousands of birds that come here during the migrating season and the remainder of the year. Over 12,000 barnacle geese, plus many other birds such as pink-footed and greylag geese, whooper and Bewick's swans and various species of duck are regular visitors.
The centre has hides and an observation tower, and friendly, knowledgeable wardens lead free wildlife safaris.

FOR HISTORY BUFFS

Caerlaverock Castle was started in the 13th century and is the most important castle in the area. Unusually, it is triangular in shape and is protected by a double-towered gatehouse and a water-filled moat. Both the Scots and the English had a hand in reducing the walls, but substantial parts of the castle remain and there are some nice interior buildings.

⓿ New Abbey, Dumfries and Galloway
The village is best known for the ruins of Sweetheart Abbey, or New Abbey, founded in the 13th century as a Cistercian establishment. It is regarded as one of Scotland's most beautiful monastic ruins and, although roofless, it still has massive walls

Devorgilla's Bridge, crossing the River Nith, and Caul from the Whitesands

and a fine rose window. The abbey was founded by Devorgilla, wife of John Balliol, whose son became king of Scotland in 1292. After her husband died, Devorgilla carried his embalmed heart around with her until she died some 22 years later! She and the heart were buried in front of the high altar – hence the name of the abbey. Devorgilla also founded Balliol College in Oxford and named it after her husband.

The 18th-century corn mill in the village has been restored to working order and is open to the public. It is one of the finest mills of its type in Scotland. Just outside the village is Shambellie House, where the National Museum of Scotland has a museum of costume.

SCENIC ROUTES

The route between Dumfries and Dalbeattie follows the Solway Coast Heritage Trail, which affords excellent views over the Solway Firth towards England. The Solway has huge areas of mudflats and saltmarshes which are fascinating to see but also very dangerous, especially when the tide comes in.

▶ *Continue along the A710 for 19 miles (31km) to Dalbeattie.*

2 Dalbeattie, Dumfries and Galloway

Dalbeattie was established to exploit the local granite which was quarried at the nearby Craignair quarry. Many of the town's buildings are made from this bright grey stone which sparkles in the sunlight. While some of the stone was used locally, great quantities of it were exported to construct such buildings as London's Bank of England, Liverpool's Mersey Docks, the Eddystone Lighthouse off Plymouth and the Grand Harbour at Valetta, on Malta.

Dalbeattie makes a good base for further exploring the coastline.

BACK TO NATURE

The Colvend Coast, south of Dalbeattie, is one of the most attractive sections of shoreline in the region. There are fine beaches at Sandyhills Bay and secluded Rockcliffe, an oak woodland nature reserve at Southwick, and Rough Island bird sanctuary. At low tide, there are old 'smugglers' caves to explore around Portling and Port O'Warren.

▶ *Leave by the A711, then turn right at the A745 to Castle Douglas, 6 miles (10km).*

Threave Castle was built in the 14th century by Archibald the Grim

3 Castle Douglas, Dumfries and Galloway

The town was originally called Carlingwark after the local loch, but was renamed in 1792 by a Sir William Douglas after he had acquired the land. Castle Douglas was then developed into an important market town and its horse and cattle fairs helped attract the wealth that built the spaciously laid-out town centre. Now it's a 'Food Town' and major shopping hub.

The NTS's extensive Threave Garden is on the outskirts and it is particularly well known for its spring displays of nearly 200 varieties of daffodils. Threave Castle stands on an islet in the River Dee. Its four-storey tower was built in the 14th century and it is surrounded by an outer wall of about a century later. One rather unusual feature is that it has a near complete medieval riverside harbour.

i *Markethill Car Park, Castle Douglas; Threave Gardens (both seasonal)*

▶ *Leave by the B736 and turn left when the A75 is met. Turn left at the A711 and follow this to Kirkcudbright.*

4 Kirkcudbright, Dumfries and Galloway

Kirkcudbright's broad streets are a delight to stroll along as many old public buildings, such as the 17th-century Tolbooth, now an Art Centre, still stand. The mercat (market) cross of 1610 is on the Tolbooth steps. MacLellan's Castle, built in the late 16th century, stands near the harbour and dominates this part of the town.

The town has had a long and colourful history, including many connections with sea trading and piracy. In the late 16th century the pirate Leonard Robertson captured an English merchant vessel and sold its cargo to local lairds. When Queen Elizabeth of England complained to King James VI he promised to investigate the

[i] *Harbour Square (seasonal)*

▶ *Leave by the **A755** and turn left at the **A75**. Turn right at the **B796** to reach Gatehouse of Fleet.*

5 Gatehouse of Fleet, Dumfries and Galloway
This was once a prosperous spinning and weaving village but it is now more peaceful. There are numerous hotels, one of which, The Murray Arms, was where Robert Burns wrote *Scots Wha Hae*.

Cardoness Castle, outside the village, was built in the 15th century by the McCullochs in a prominent position above the Water of Fleet.

[i] *Car Park (seasonal)*

▶ *Return along the **B796** and turn right at the **A75**. Follow this towards Creetown. Turn right at a narrow signposted road to Cairnholy, 8 miles (13km).*

6 Cairnholy, Dumfries and Galloway
There are two monuments at Cairnholy. These were used well over 3,000 years ago as burial sites and for ceremonies

MacLellan's Castle, an impressive 16th-century building which dominates Kirkcudbright

matter, which he did by appointing a commission manned by the very lairds who had bought the stolen goods. Such was justice!

The Stewartry Museum has a good collection of local material and a section on John Paul Jones. He joined the Union navy and fought against the British during the American War of Independence; his daring exploits included attacks on the British coast. During a 'quiet' time he had the audacity to visit this area in secret. Broughton House, in High Street, was the home of E A Hornel and is run by the NTS as a museum dedicated to the artist, who died in 1933.

Tongland Hydroelectric Power Station stands on the River Dee, to the north of Kirkcudbright. This is just one of the power stations in the Galloway Hydroelectric Scheme and visitors are offered organised tours around the buildings. Downstream of the station is the attractive Tongland Bridge built by Thomas Telford in 1805.

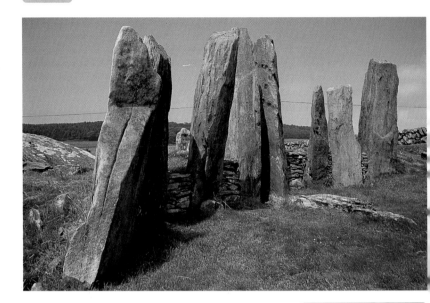

of some kind. Cairnholy I is particularly impressive, with its pillared façade and two tombs. The tombs would have originally been covered by a massive cairn of boulders but these were later removed, probably by farmers seeking easily obtained building stones.

▶ *Return to the* **A75** *and turn right. Leave the* **A75** *on the right at the signposted road to Creetown.*

7 Creetown, Dumfries and Galloway

Creetown is another 'granite town' with many of its buildings made of the local grey stone. The Gem Rock Museum is sited in a former school and has a marvellous collection of minerals, fossils and many other exhibits from all over the world. The Exhibition Centre features a display on life in Creetown with wartime memorabilia, as well as local history and nature, kiltmaking and arts and crafts. Carsluith Castle is on the left before entering Creetown. This started off as a rectangular tower in the 15th century but

Prehistoric chambered tomb at Cairnholy I

later additions gave it an L-shape and a balcony. It fell into ruins after 1748.

▶ *Rejoin the* **A75** *and turn right. Turn right at the* **A712** *to the Clatteringshaws Forest Wildlife Centre near Clatteringshaws Loch (Galloway Forest Park).*

8 Clatteringshaws Loch, Dumfries and Galloway

This artificial loch is surrounded by moorlands and conifers and is within the boundary of the Galloway Forest Park. The park is home to many animals and there are herds of wild goat and deer on the southern shore of the loch. The Clatteringshaws Visitor Centre has lots of information on the wildlife,

geology and history of the area and close by it is a reconstructed Romano-British hut from around AD 200–300, which is worth a look.

Close to the Loch is Bruce's Stone, a memorial to Robert the Bruce, the Scottish king who, so legend says, learned a lesson in persistence from a spider. This marks the spot where he allegedly rested after defeating English soldiers, commanded by Sir Aymer de Valence, at the battle of Glentrool.

Near the centre, the Raiders' Road goes off to the right through the forest and follows an old cattle rustlers' route. Different breeds of deer may be seen here and you may be lucky enough to see otters; buzzards, sparrowhawks and ravens can also be spotted.

▶ *Continue on the **A712** for 6 miles (10km) to New Galloway.*

9 New Galloway, Dumfries and Galloway
This quiet little village stands above the Water of Ken, a 9-mile (14.5-km) loch, created by the Hydro, and now both scenic and recreational.

▶ *Leave by the **A712**, then turn left at the **A713** to reach St John's Town of Dalry.*

10 St John's Town of Dalry, Dumfries and Galloway
The main street in this pleasant village is lined with white-washed cottages, at the top of which can be seen a peculiar little stone seat known as St

The Robert Bruce memorial by the shores of Loch Trool in the Galloway Forest Park

John the Baptist's Chair. There is no evidence that he ever sat upon it, but one of Sir Walter Scott's acquaintants found the legend intriguing enough to try and take it away. The Southern Upland Way follows the main street and passes the chair on its long coast-to-coast journey between Portpatrick and Cockburnspath. The church, which was erected in 1831, has several interesting gravestones. The most notable one is the horizontal Covenanters' stone (to the Auchencloy Martyrs) in the corner of the churchyard, inscribed with the story of their shooting by Claverhouse.

▶ *Leave by the **A702** and follow it for 11 miles (18km) to Moniaive.*

11 Moniaive, Dumfries and Galloway
Moniaive is best remembered for being the birthplace of James Renwick, the last Covenanter, who was hanged in Edinburgh in 1688. A monument commemorating him has

been erected at the edge of the village.

To the east, beyond Kirkland, stands Maxwelton House, the birthplace and home of Annie Laurie, about whom a famous ballad was composed. The original song was written around 1700, although a later version was penned in 1835. The house was built on to a 14th-century castle.

▶ *Continue on the **A702**, then turn right at the **B729**. Turn right at the **A76** to return to Dumfries.*

SPECIAL TO...

The relaxed style of living in the area has attracted many craftsmen and women. The amazing variety of crafts includes engraving, pottery and jewellery-making as well as more unusual ones like the production of embroidered landscapes, willow furniture and even clogs.

1/2 DAYS • 119 MILES • 190KM

- **9** Bothwell Castle
- David Livingstone Centre
- Strathclyde Country Park
- **8** Blantyre
- Motherwell
- **7** Hamilton
- Chatelherault Country Park
- Larkhall
- Avon
- Crossford
- **10** Craignethan Castle
- **LANARK**
- EDINBURGH
- **6** Strathaven
- **New Lanark**
- **1** Falls of Clyde
- Discover Carmichael Visitor Centre
- **2** Biggar
- KILMARNOCK
- 711m ▲ Tinto
- Coulter
- Glespin
- **5** Douglas
- Lamington
- Muirkirk
- Crawford-john
- AYR
- 593m ▲ Cairn Table
- Abington
- Duneaton Water
- KILMARNOCK
- Leadhills
- CARLISLE
- **3** Wanlockhead 725m ▲ Lowther Hill
- **Sanquhar** **4**
- Mennock
- DUMFRIES
- Nith

0 — 5 m
0 — 5 — 10 km

Seeking Gold

This tour starts in Lanark, home to another Scottish hero, William Wallace, who is thought to have lived in nearby Castlegate before being caught up in the struggle against the English. A statue of him now stands above the door of the 18th-century Church of St Nicholas. Lanark makes a good base from which to explore the surrounding hills and valleys of the Clyde Valley.

ⓘ *Horsemarket, Ladyacre Road*

▶ *Follow the local signs from the market for 1 mile (2km) to the village of New Lanark.*

> ### RECOMMENDED WALKS
>
> From New Lanark, it is possible to walk up the Clyde Gorge to the dam at the waterfall of Bonnington Linn. This magnificent gorge, formed about 12,000 years ago after the last Ice Age, has a number of fine waterfalls, notably Corra Linn. The water is used to power a hydroelectric power station, but on certain holiday weekends the station is closed down and the falls are at their most impressive.

❶ New Lanark, South Lanarkshire

The village, a World Heritage Site and a major tourist attraction, is set in the magnificent wooded gorge of the Clyde. It was founded during the 18th century by David Dale, who harnessed the power of the Clyde, and by 1820 the cotton mills supported a population of 2,500. But it was Dale's son-in-law, Robert Owen, who made New Lanark famous as a model community.

A pioneer of social reform, Owen established an enviable standard of living for his workforce and their families, with benefits such as reduced hours of work, free medical care, education and cultural activities for all. The buildings were well constructed and spacious (for that time) and he took on pauper apprentices and housed and educated them. He also built the Institute for the Formation of Character. His ideas, including his refusal to use child labour, were revolutionary, and it astounded other mill owners that his mills were efficient and profitable.

Fewer than 200 people live here now, many of them

The dramatic Falls of Clyde, well worth a walk from New Lanark

employed in the award-winning heritage sites. These include a restored millworkers' house, a period-style shop, Robert Owen's house, various exhibitions and working textile machines, and an audio-visual ride, The New Millennium Experience.

▶ *Return to Lanark, then leave by the **A73**. Turn left at the **A72** and the **A702** and follow this to Biggar, 13 miles (21km).*

> ### FOR CHILDREN
>
> The Discover Carmichael Visitor Centre lies between Lanark and Biggar. As well as numerous animals and outdoor activities, there is also a collection of wax models of historical Scots figures. Biggar Little Theatre has a complete Victorian theatre in miniature which is used for puppet plays. There is also a puppet exhibition and a chance to try your hand at outdoor Victorian games.

2 **Biggar,** South Lanarkshire
Biggar's main street is even wider than Lanark's, a fact that may have encouraged the saying 'Lanark's big, but Biggar's Biggar!'

For such a compact place, Biggar has a remarkable number of interesting places to visit. The oldest is Boghall Castle, now a ruin but once a substantial fortification that was besieged by both Regent Moray and Oliver Cromwell. The most unusual building in the village houses the Biggar Gasworks Museum, the only surviving rural gasworks in the country, built in 1839.

The Gladstone Court Museum (off High Street) contains a number of replica shops, a schoolroom, a bank and a post office, scenes which portray life in Victorian Biggar. Further down the street can be seen the small footbridge called the Cadgers Brig. Legend has it

Scotland's only surviving rural gasworks houses the Biggar Gasworks Museum

that William Wallace crossed this in 1297 disguised as a cadger (a pedlar) to spy on the English army that was camped near by.

On one of the higher parts of the village stands St Mary's Church, founded in 1545, and the last pre-Reformation church

in Scotland. Opposite this is the Moat Park Heritage Centre, which has displays covering 6,000 years of history in Clydesdale. Behind it lies a small valley in which runs the Biggar Burn and this can be followed upstream to Greenhill, a farm that was relocated here, stone by stone, from

Wanlockhead lead mine – once a major mining centre but now closed down, although it's possible to take a tour of Loch Nell Mine

south of Tinto. This is a Covenanting museum, with relics and mementoes of the 17th century.

i *155 High Street (seasonal)*

▶ *Leave by the **A702**, going southwest, and follow this to Abington. Turn off at the **B797**, which leads to Wanlockhead, 20 miles (32km).*

3 **Wanlockhead,** Dumfries and Galloway
Sitting at an altitude of 1,533 feet (467m), this is Scotland's highest village. With neighbouring Leadhills, Wanlockhead was once a major lead mining centre, hence all the piles of debris that have been left here. Lead was probably mined here in Roman times, but the modern history of the mines started in about 1675 and the industry managed to keep going until the 1950s. Gold has also been excavated in the area; the largest piece found was nearly 7oz (200g) in weight and is now in the British Museum. Goldpanners sometimes come to the district to try their luck and skill in winning a few flakes from the streams.

A number of buildings associated with the mines, complete with mining equipment, have been preserved as the Museum of Leadmining, and these include the Pates Knowes Smelt Mine, Wanlockhead Beam Engine, Loch Nell Mine (guided tours), miners' cottages and the miners' library. The history of the mines and of the district is told in the Visitor Centre.

i *Welcome Break Service Area, M74 northbound, Abington*

RECOMMENDED WALKS

Wanlockhead is on the Southern Upland Way and the Way's route can be followed from the village to the summit of Lowther Hill. The strange-looking 'golf ball' building on top of the hill houses radar equipment.

▶ *Continue on the B797 and turn right at the A76 to Sanquhar.*

4 **Sanquhar,** Dumfries and Galloway

Although there is a great deal of agricultural land around Sanquhar, it has the air of an industrial town, and lies on the edge of the district's coal mining area.

The ruins of Sanquhar Castle lie on the outskirts. The castle was built by the Ross family but sold to the Douglases of Drumlanrig in 1639. One of that family, the 1st Duke of Queensberry, built the mansion of Drumlanrig but spent only one night there and then retired to Sanquhar Castle.

The finest building in the village is the Tolbooth, a splendid Georgian building topped by an octagonal cupola, a clock tower and a weathercock. A double-sided staircase leads to a first-floor entrance.

The busy main street boasts the oldest post office in the world (1763) and a tall granite obelisk erected to commemorate the two Sanquhar Declarations. These were issued by the Covenanters in defiance of Charles II and James VII (II of Great Britain).

▶ *Continue on the A76 and turn right at the B740. Turn left at an unclassified road before Crawfordjohn; this road leads to Glespin, Douglas and Muirkirk. When this road meets the A70, turn right and follow it to Douglas, 19 miles (31km).*

5 **Douglas,** South Lanarkshire
The village is named after the Douglas family, the most famous member of whom was the 'Good' Sir James, so-called by the Scots because it was he who attempted to carry out Robert the Bruce's wish to have his heart taken to the Holy Land. Unfortunately he never got there, as he was killed in Spain. The English, however, knew him as 'Black Douglas' because he was such a ferocious fighter. His most barbaric act took place here in 1307 when he destroyed his own castle, then occupied by English troops. In a gruesome act that became known as the 'Douglas Larder', he made a great pile of

Crumbling stonework marks the site of the Castle of Sanquhar all the food in the captured castle, poured on all the wine, killed all his prisoners and threw their bodies into the mix and set fire to it!

The 14th-century St Bride's Church, which has an attractive 16th-century octagonal clock tower, has a mausoleum in which lie the remains of the Good Sir James. The clock tower is the oldest working town clock in the country and was supposedly a gift from Mary, Queen of Scots in 1565. However, don't set your watch by its chimes because they sound three minutes before the hour, keeping faith with the Douglas family motto 'Never behind'.

▶ *Return along the **A70** and continue on it to Muirkirk. Turn right at the **B743** and follow this to Strathaven.*

6 **Strathaven,** South Lanarkshire
Strathaven is the site of the 15th-century Avondale Castle. Beside it stands the Town Mill

which continued to grind flour until as recently as 1966, but now serves as the local theatre and arts centre. The town built its prosperity on the weaving industry and the John Hastie Museum contains displays on weaving and ceramics together with mementoes of the Covenanting times and the Radical Rising of 1820, one of whose leaders was a local man, James Wilson.

▶ *Take the **A723** for 7 miles (11km) to Hamilton.*

7 **Hamilton,** South Lanarkshire
Although Lanark was the county town of the former Lanarkshire, Hamilton became its administrative centre and its fine public buildings reflect its importance. The town's Muir Street Museum, which is housed in a 17th-century coaching inn, has a very good transport section.

The parkland lying between the town and the motorway used to be the site of

Formerly the Duke of Hamilton's hunting lodge, Chatelherault is today an impressive country park

Hamilton Palace, which had to be demolished in 1927 as the extensive coal mine workings that honeycomb the land had weakened its foundations. However, the splendid 19th-century Adam-built Hamilton Mausoleum still stands here. When having a look around, it's worth noting the fine cupola and ornate carvings. Inside the building its 15-second echo is the longest of any building in Europe, a fact that put paid to its original purpose as a chapel. William Adam also designed the Duke of Hamilton's hunting lodge, Chatelherault, and this magnificent building overlooks the district. The wooded gorge of the River Avon is impressive and beyond it are the remains of Cadzow Castle and some very ancient oaks.

ℹ️ *Road Chef Services, M74 northbound*

▶ *Leave by the A724 and follow this to Blantyre.*

8 Blantyre, South Lanarkshire
Blantyre was the home of the explorer David Livingstone and the David Livingstone Centre

relates his exploits, which included the 'discovery' of the Victoria Falls and Lake Nyasa. The centre is based in the row of 18th-century tenements where he was born, and includes an animated display in the Africa Pavilion, an art gallery, themed garden, African playground and riverside walks.

▶ *Return along the A724, turn left at the A725 and join the B7071 to Bothwell. Bothwell Castle is signposted from the town.*

9 Bothwell Castle, South Lanarkshire
The outstanding castle, which stands on a rocky promontory above the River Clyde, was partially completed before the outbreak of the Wars of Independence and was twice besieged and deliberately dismantled to deny it to the English. Later rebuilding in the late 14th and 15th centuries turned it into an impressive structure and the castle's donjon has walls 15 feet (5m) thick.

▶ *Return along the B7071, heading towards Hamilton. Follow the A724, then the A72 to Crossford. In the*

Painting from the David Livingstone Centre, showing the explorer being attacked by a lion

village, a signposted road on the right leads to Craignethan Castle, 13 miles (21km).

10 Craignethan Castle, South Lanarkshire
Craignethan Castle, a stronghold of the Hamiltons, was built in the 15th and 16th centuries when developments in artillery had made the defence systems of many castles obsolete. Its new defensive strategies included a caponier, a low chamber constructed across the defensive ditch that allowed the defenders within to protect the vulnerable base of the castle walls.

▶ *Return to Crossford and turn right. Continue on the A72 for the 6-mile (10km) return to Lanark.*

Taking
the Waters

Water is an important feature of this tour, which, for some of the way, follows the course of the Tweed, one of Scotland's greatest trout and salmon rivers. The tour starts in the village of Moffat, which in the 17th century gained importance as a spa after the discovery of suphurous springs there.

1/2 DAYS • 120 MILES • 194KM

ITINERARY		
MOFFAT	▶	**Dawyck Botanic Garden** (26m–42km)
DAWYCK BOTANIC GARDEN	▶	**Broughton** (5m–8km)
BROUGHTON	▶	**West Linton** (14m–23km)
WEST LINTON	▶	**Peebles** (14m–23km)
PEEBLES	▶	**Innerleithen** (6m–10km)
INNERLEITHEN	▶	**Galashiels** (12m–19km)
GALASHIELS	▶	**Yarrowford** (13m–21km)
YARROWFORD	▶	**St Marys Loch** (11m–18km)
ST MARYS LOCH	▶	**Grey Mare's Tail** (9m–14km)
GREY MARE'S TAIL	▶	**Moffat** (10m–16km)

i Unit 1, Lady Knowe (seasonal)

BACK TO NATURE

Scotland has a number of spa towns and Moffat has always been one of the most popular. The water is rather sulphurous – one writer compared it to a 'slightly putrescent egg'! Nevertheless, it has attracted many sufferers afflicted with lung infections, dyspepsia, rheumatism and other disorders. The waters flow from the local greywacke rock, a type of limestone. The wells are signposted from the village, and are worth visiting.

▶ Leave by the **A701** and turn right at the **B712** to Dawyck Botanic Garden.

1 Dawyck Botanic Garden, Scottish Borders

This outstation of the Royal Botanic Garden in Edinburgh was developed from the gardens laid out around Dawyck House during the last 300 years. Some of the conifers stand 130 feet (40m) high. Daffodils are the main attraction in the spring, while autumn colour is provided by magnificent beeches and maples. Many unusual rhododendrons and narcissi can be found here. Plants are on sale in the conservatory shop.

▶ Return along the **B712** and turn right at the **A701**. This leads to Broughton.

2 Broughton, Scottish Borders

The John Buchan Centre is dedicated to the life and work of the novelist whose best-known novels were *The 39 Steps* and *Greenmantle*. Apart from spy stories, he also wrote biographies of historical figures such as Sir Walter Scott and Oliver Cromwell. He later became Lord Tweedsmuir and was Governor-General of Canada until his death in 1940. Nearby Broughton Gallery is housed in a building designed by Sir Basil Spence to resemble a 17th-century fortified tower, and sells paintings and crafts by living artists.

▶ Continue on the **A701** and turn right at the **A72**. Turn left at the **A721** and right at the **A702**. Follow this to West Linton.

3 West Linton, Scottish Borders

West Linton was once busy with cattle drovers bringing their beasts over the Pentland Hills on their way to buyers in England, but today it is a peaceful little place, pleasant for exploring the narrow streets.

The village was famous for its stonemasons, who became the chief gravestone carvers in the area. Gifford's Stone, a bas-relief on a wall in the main street, shows the stonemason James Gifford and his family. Opposite it is another of his works, the Lady Gifford Well, which was carved in 1666.

▶ Leave by the **B7059**. Turn right at the **A701** and left at the **B7059**. Turn left at the **A72** for Peebles.

Strolling in the tranquil and restful Dawyck Botanic Garden

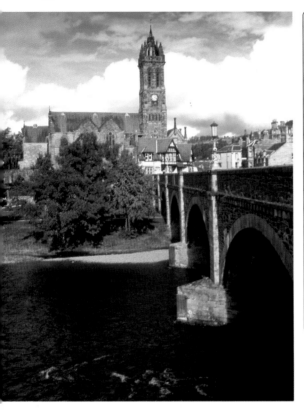

RECOMMENDED WALKS

There is great scope for walking in this area and many parts of the Southern Upland Way provide well-marked paths that are straightforward to follow. For those who can organise transport at the end of the walks, the Way offers pleasant outings on the eastern shore of St Marys Loch, from the loch to Traquair and from Traquair to Galashiels (via cairns known as the Three Brethren).

Peebles is the start of the Tweed Walk, where a choice of circular walks of different lengths allows walkers to pass Neidpath Castle and follow the river upstream, visiting various points of interest; contact the Tourist Information Centre for further details.

4 **Peebles,** Scottish Borders
This is certainly one of the Scottish Borders' most impressive towns, with an attractive position beside the River Tweed and a fine array of buildings along both sides of the main street. It developed under the protection of a royal castle and its modern prosperity came from tweed and knitwear. The Chambers Institute in High Street was given to Peebles by the publisher William Chambers, who was born here. It dates from the 16th century and houses the Tweeddale Museum and Gallery, featuring local history, contemporary art exhibitions and the 'Secret Room', with its 62-foot (19m) long plastercast of a frieze from the Parthenon in Athens. Plasterwork is also the theme of the Cornice Museum of Ornamental Plasterwork along Innerleithen Road. It re-creates

The parish church in Peebles overlooks the River Tweed

a plasterer's workshop of around 1900, and visitors can get kitted out in apron and wellington boots to try their hand at the craft. At the top of High Street, the 15th-century mercat cross stands in the middle of the road.

One of the town's oldest buildings is the Old Cross Kirk, built in the 13th century on the order of King Alexander III after the discovery of a 'magnificent and venerable' cross.

Neidpath Castle stands to the west of Peebles. This substantial five-storeyed building was built in the 14th century by the Hayes family and sits on a steep rocky crag overlooking the River Tweed. South of the town are Kailzie Gardens and its art gallery.

i *Ladyknowes*

View along Peebles' busy broad main street

The dining room at Traquair House

▶ Continue on the **A72** for 6 miles (10km) to Innerleithen.

5 Innerleithen, Scottish Borders

The town's wells, which were associated with St Ronan, became very popular in the 19th century, helped enormously by Sir Walter Scott's novel *St Ronan's Well*. The poet James Hogg also played a role in publicising the village as he helped organise the St Ronan's Games from 1827 to 1835. The wells can still be visited and are found by following Hall Street and St Ronan's Terrace. This is the oldest spa in Scotland and the present pump-room was built in 1826. The NTS has taken Robert Smail's Printing Works in the High Street under its care. This fascinating little print shop was started in 1840, when the original press was water-powered. Visitors can try typesetting by hand, and see the machines in action.

The history of Traquair, just over a mile (2km) south, goes back to Roman times when it was a town of similar importance to Peebles. Today it is best known for nearby Traquair House, the country's oldest and most interesting continuously inhabited house. Attractions include an 18th-century working brewery which produces three rich dark ales – sample them in the brewery shop, a maze, craft workshops and extensive grounds, but the most famous feature of the house are the wrought iron 'Bear Gates' at the end of the driveway. These were closed in the 18th century by the 5th Earl, who promised they would not be reopened until another Stuart king was on the British throne.

▶ Continue on the **A72** for 12 miles (19km) to Galashiels.

6 Galashiels, Scottish Borders

Galashiels gained early importance when it was a hunting seat for the Scottish kings. But its real growth came when woollen mills diverted Gala Water to power their machinery. This is now a busy town and one of the main centres of the Borders' textile industry. The story of the mills is told in the Lochcarron Cashmere Wool of Scotland Visitor Centre; tours round these mills show the entire process of tartan manufacture.

The town's most historic building is Old Gala House, which was founded around 1583; it has a fine painted ceiling of 1635. The mercat cross, which marks the centre of the old town, stands near Gala House and was erected in 1695. As all the public business of the medieval town was conducted here, this is one of the places involved in the town's Braw Lads Gathering, the annual festival during which the boundaries of the town are ridden round on horseback.

The local war memorial is in the form of a statue of a

SPECIAL TO...

Many of the towns have a justly famous reputation for producing high-quality knitted goods and many of the mills have their own shops where bargains can be found. Although it might be thought that the word 'tweed' (meaning the cloth) comes from the river of the same name, that is not so. The word is said to have originated in 1832 from a one-time misreading in London of the word 'tweel', which was the name given locally to one of the types of cloth.

---

mounted Border 'reiver'. Although these men have become romanticised figures of legend, they were basically cattle thieves and their activities gave rise to the word 'blackmail' for payment as an 'insurance' that livestock would be safe from theft.

Spools of wool ready for the loom at the Lochcarron Cashmere Wool of Scotland Visitor Centre

---

[i] 3 St John Street (seasonal)

▶ *Leave by the A7 (to Selkirk). Turn right at the B7060, then left at the A707 at Yair Bridge. Continue on this road which becomes the A708 near Selkirk. Follow Ettrick Water and then Yarrow Water on the A708 to Yarrowford, a distance of 13 miles (21km).*

7 Yarrowford, Scottish Borders

The scattered village of Yarrowford lies by Yarrow Water, about which William Wordsworth wrote no fewer than three poems! Downstream of the village lie three buildings that are of interest: Newark Tower, Foulshiels and Bowhill.

The name Newark Tower signifies that it is the 'new work' which was erected to replace an unsuitable 'auld work'. It was constructed some time before 1423 as a royal hunting lodge in what was known as Ettrick Forest. The term 'forest' in this case does not necessarily imply that the whole area was wooded, but that special laws governed its

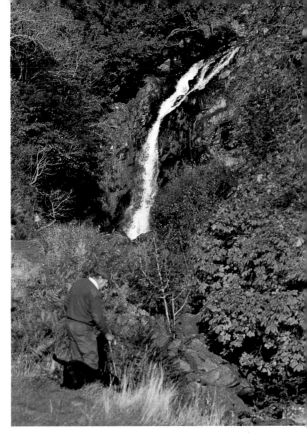

The aptly named Grey Mare's Tail waterfall

use as a playground for the king and his entourage. However, the forest was inhabited not only by wild animals; it made a splendid hiding place for thieves, until the king decided to chase them as well! In the 16th century, James V replaced 10,000 deer with an equal number of sheep, greatly increasing the importance of sheep farming and the woollen industry in the area. In conjunction with this step, many trees were felled – thus destroying the oak, birch and hazel forest that had prospered here since the end of the Ice Age.

Foulshiels, now a ruin, was the birthplace of Scots explorer Mungo Park who travelled in West Africa between 1795 and 1796 in search of the source of the River Niger. His exploits were described in his book *Travels in the Interior of Africa*, but his second trip into these uncharted lands led to his death.

Bowhill House and Country Park features a very large country mansion built in the early 19th century. It has an outstanding collection of French furniture as well as a large collection of paintings by Old Masters including Van Dyck, Canaletto and Gainsborough.

▶ Continue on the **A708** to the southern end of St Marys Loch.

8 St Marys Loch, Scottish Borders

This is one of the largest lochs in southern Scotland and it is a popular place with walkers, boating enthusiasts and anglers. At the southern end of the loch stands a monument to the local poet James Hogg. He was a good friend of Sir Walter Scott and the two of them, along with other literary figures, spent convivial evenings in the nearby Tibbie Shiels Inn.

▶ Continue on the **A708** for 9 miles (14km) to the car park at the Grey Mare's Tail waterfall.

9 Grey Mare's Tail, Dumfries and Galloway

Just a short distance from the roadside, the Tail Burn tumbles 200 feet (60m) over the waterfall known as the Grey Mare's Tail. A path runs up the eastern bank of the burn offering different views of the waterfall and the opportunity to explore Loch Skene. Leaflets warn about the dangers of leaving the path. The burn joins attractive Moffat Water, whose valley the road follows towards Moffat. The valley is a magnificent textbook example of a glacial valley, with its U-shape formed as the glacier smoothed the mountainsides.

▶ Continue on the **A708** for 10 miles (16km) in order to return to Moffat.

Walter Scott
Country

Much of the countryside explored in this tour was the inspiration behind Sir Walter Scott's *Waverley* novels: the ruined abbeys of Melrose, Dryburgh and Jedburgh; the Eildon Hills. It is only fitting, therefore, that this tour should end with a visit to Scott's home.

1/2 DAYS • 116 MILES • 187KM

ITINERARY		
MELROSE	▶	**Dryburgh Abbey** (6m-10km)
DRYBURGH ABBEY	▶	**Jedburgh** (13m-21km)
JEDBURGH	▶	**Hawick** (12m-19km)
HAWICK	▶	**Hermitage Castle** (16m-26km)
HERMITAGE CASTLE	▶	**Langholm** (17m-27km)
LANGHOLM	▶	**Eskdalemuir** (14m-23km)
ESKDALEMUIR	▶	**Ettrick** (12m-19km)
ETTRICK	▶	**Selkirk** (18m-29km)
SELKIRK	▶	**Abbotsford** (5m-8km)
ABBOTSFORD	▶	**Melrose** (3m-5km)

The heart of Robert the Bruce is buried within the imposing ruins of Melrose Abbey

i Abbey House (seasonal)

▶ Leave Melrose by the B6361 and turn left at the A68. Cross the River Tweed, then turn first right and first left. Head towards Dryburgh following the B6356. Turn right after passing Scott's View and continue to Dryburgh Abbey.

SCENIC ROUTES

As the B6356 makes its way to Dryburgh, there is a wonderful view of the River Tweed and the Eildon Hills at a spot known as Scott's View. Sir Walter Scott passed this way on many occasions and always halted here to enjoy the view, describing it as the 'grandest and most extensive panorama in the Borderland'. When he died his funeral cortège made its way past here to his final resting place at Dryburgh Abbey and his horses, without being commanded to, stopped quite naturally at the viewpoint.

❶ Dryburgh Abbey,
Scottish Borders

Much of the abbey's substantial ruins date from the 12th and 13th centuries and they occupy a wonderfully peaceful position on a horseshoe bend of the River Tweed. Founded in 1150, the abbey suffered at the hands of the English raiders but nevertheless remains the most complete of the Border abbeys. The grave of Sir Walter Scott can be found in the north transept. A short woodland walk leads to a massive 19th-century statue of the Scottish patriot Sir William Wallace.

To the northwest of the abbey (and reached via the B6404) stands the very attractive Smailholm Tower. This was erected in the 16th century as a defensive structure, which explains why the few windows it has are very small. There is a marvellous panoramic view from it and ships approaching Berwick once used it as a landmark as it was so conspicuous. During medieval times this area was often attacked by English forces and tall towers were needed to spy on the movements of the enemy and to warn others of the approach of an attacking force. This is why the parapet wall has a watchman's seat and a recess for a lantern, in accordance with an Act of Council in 1587 which stated that castle owners must 'keep watch nyght and day, and burn baillis (bales) according to the accoustomat ordour observit as sic tymes upoun the borderis'. At one time it was owned by Sir Walter Scott's grandfather and Scott used to visit here as a boy; he later featured the tower in *Marmion*.

▶ Return to the **B6356** and continue following that road. Turn right at the **B6404** and enter St Boswells. Turn left at the **A68** and follow it to Jedburgh.

2 Jedburgh, Scottish Borders
The town's location close to the border meant that it was forever being attacked by the English, and its castle was often under siege by the ancient enemy. The locals, fed up with all this harassment, managed to persuade the Scottish parliament to pull the castle down in 1409, thus relieving them of the task of having to fight the invaders to defend it! The

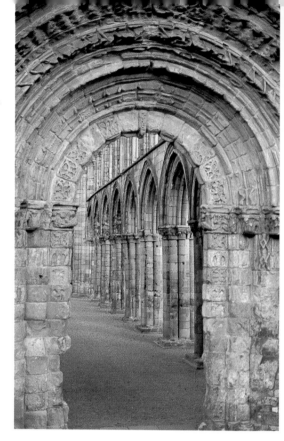

present building occupying the site is still called the 'castle' but it was built in the 19th century as a gaol and is now used as a museum.

The other major building in the town is Jedburgh Abbey, founded as a priory in 1138. After various attacks by the English, the building was destroyed by them between 1545 and 1546. However, the abbey walls still soar skywards and the tower stands as it did when rebuilt in 1504 to 1508. Mary, Queen of Scots visited the town in 1566 and stayed in the Spread Eagle Hotel in High Street, which is claimed to be the oldest continually occupied hotel in the country. A fire here forced Mary to leave and she stayed at what is now the Mary, Queen of Scots' House, a fine 16th-century fortified house.

ⓘ *Murray's Green*

Jedburgh Abbey was founded in the 12th century and colonised by monks from Beauvais in France

> ### BACK TO NATURE
>
> Just north of Jedburgh, Harestanes Countryside Visitor Centre offers walks, a wildlife garden and pond, and traditional craft demonstrations. Melrose's Priorwood Garden, which is run by the NTS, specialises in flowers for drying. A variety of plants are grown and dried here and advice on this craft is always available. The orchard has a wide variety of apple trees, arranged to illustrate the history of the fruit. Nearby Harmony Garden has herbaceous and mixed borders, vegetable and fruit areas and lovely views. The monks of Melrose Abbey established their orchards at Gattonside, just over the Tweed from the abbey.

Priorwood Garden, where a large variety of plants are grown especially for drying

▶ *Leave by the B6358, then join the A698 to Hawick.*

8 Hawick, Scottish Borders
Hawick is the largest and busiest of the Border towns. Its numerous woollen mills have brought it much prosperity since frame knitting was introduced here and commercialised in 1771. When mechanisation came to the industry, production changed from hose to fine underwear, which as the advertisements of the day put it, 'enjoyed the patronage of many of the crowned heads of Europe!' Peter Scott & Co offer mill tours, and at nearby Trowmill tours of Wrights' weaving flat are available.

Many of the mills stand by the River Teviot, which provided their original source of power. The river also flows past Wilton Lodge Park, in which stands the museum and art gallery, which has displays on Border history, the knitwear industry and natural history.

ℹ️ *Drumlanrig's Tower (seasonal)*

▶ *Leave by the B6399. Just after Hermitage, turn right at the unclassified road signposted to Hermitage Castle.*

4 Hermitage Castle,
Scottish Borders
This must be one of the grimmest-looking castles in Scotland, with its very small windows and the high arch that joins the east and west towers together. It's also sited on an isolated expanse of moorland, well away from any settlement.

In 1566, when she was holding court at Jedburgh, Mary, Queen of Scots heard that her lover Bothwell was lying wounded in the castle. She rode the 20 miles (32km) at a furious speed, stayed for a couple of hours then returned, an exertion that cost her a 10-day fever.

▶ *Return to the B6399 and turn right. Turn right at the B6357 and enter Newcastleton. Within the village, turn right at the minor road to Langholm and turn left when you join the A7, 17 miles (27km).*

5 Langholm, Dumfries and Galloway
This small town sits at the confluence of the Esk, Ewes and

6 Eskdalemuir, Dumfries
and Galloway

There is a settlement at
Eskdalemuir (at the junction of
the Langholm and Lockerbie
roads), but the name is more
commonly applied to the tract
of moorland near the upper
reaches of the White Esk. To
be correct, it used to be a great
moorland, but the land is now
given over to huge conifer
plantations.

The Romans built an
important road here, some 24
feet (7m) wide, and this eventually led to *Trimontium*, near
Melrose. The most intriguing
group of modern incomers were
Tibetan Buddhist monks who
left their country in 1959 and
settled here in Johnstone
House. The community that
they founded flourished and
they later built one of Scotland's
most remarkable buildings, the
Samye Ling Temple, a colourful
four-storey structure. This is the
largest Buddhist temple in
western Europe and numerous
examples of Tibetan art can be
seen inside.

The meteorological station
at Eskdalemuir is sited further
along the road. This was originally founded in 1908 to
continue the terrestrial magnet-
ism measurements formerly
made at Kew (in southeast
London). To broaden the scope

Wauchope Waters. There is a
fine view of it from the summit
of Whita Hill (to the east), on
top of which there is a monument to Sir John Malcolm. Close
to the start of the path to the
monument, there is a rather
interesting (or bizarre, depending on your taste) monument
dedicated to the modern Scots
poet Christopher Murray Grieve,
who wrote under the pen-name
Hugh McDiarmid.

Another of Langholm's sons
was the great engineer Thomas
Telford, whose famous designs
include the Caledonian Canal,
the Menai Straits Bridge and St
Katharine's Docks in London.
Many roads and bridges in
Scotland are also his. Telford
started his working life as a
stonemason, and an archway, an
early example of his own handi-
work, can be seen beside the
town hall. A memorial to him is
sited at Bentpath, on the road to
Eskdalemuir.

▶ *Leave by the **B709** and follow
it to Eskdalemuir.*

of scientific research in this
area, a seismological station has
been established near by.

▶ *Continue on the **B709** to
Ettrick.*

7 **Ettrick,** Scottish Borders
The collection of houses and
farms at Ettrick is found where
the B709 meets Ettrick Water at
Ramseycleuch. The poet James
Hogg was born here and a tall
sandstone memorial at his birthplace can be found on the roadside by following Ettrick Water
upstream. Hogg is one of the
Borders' most famous characters
and was affectionately known as
the Ettrick Shepherd. His
poetry was first published in
1794 and he went on to write
countless poems, articles and
books. Ettrick's church is
further upstream and this is
where Hogg is buried. Beside
his headstone is one inscribed
'Here lyeth William Laidlaw
the far-famed Will o'Phaup who
for feats of frolic, agility and
strength had no equal in his
day'. This gentleman was
Hogg's grandfather and he was
the last man in Ettrick to speak
to the fairies. There is a James

Hogg Exhibition at Aikwood
Tower, further along on the
B7009. The tower also hosts art
exhibitions, and is set in lovely
medieval-style gardens.

▶ *Continue on the **B709**. Turn
right at the **B7009** to enter
Selkirk.*

8 **Selkirk,** Scottish Borders
The town occupies a hilly site
where a Tironensian abbey was
founded around 1113. The
abbey was eventually moved to
Roxburgh and then to Kelso, so
Selkirk never developed as a
religious centre like the other
Border towns which had their
splendid abbeys. As the town
grew it became famous for its
shoemaking, to the extent that
its burgesses were given the
name 'souters' (Scots for 'shoe-
makers'). This trade died out
and Selkirk's modern prosperity
is based on the woollen mills
beside Ettrick Water.
  The triangular marketplace
is dominated by a statue of Sir
Walter Scott. Behind is his
Courtroom, with displays on
Scott, James Hogg and Mungo
Park, an audio-visual presentation and Scott's bench and chair

Sir Walter Scott's romantic
creation, Abbotsford

from his time as Sheriff of
Selkirkshire.
  The local museum in
Halliwell's House is to the west
of the marketplace and is
reached through a narrow lane.
The museum has an excellent
display of local material including the reconstructed interior of
an old ironmonger's shop.
  To the east of the marketplace, and past the statue of the
explorer Mungo Park, is the
Flodden Memorial, dedicated to
the local men who perished at
the Battle of Flodden in 1513.
The statue is of a man called
Fletcher, reputedly the only
Selkirk man out of 80 to return
from the battle, carrying a
captured English standard.

[i] *Halliwell's House (seasonal)*

▶ *Leave by the **A7** towards
Galashiels. Turn right at the
B6360 to reach Abbotsford.*

9 **Abbotsford**, Scottish
Borders
Sir Walter Scott bought the site
on which he built Abbotsford in

1811. The house took a long time to complete as he kept adding bits on, eventually ending up with a great variety of styles. Basically, it is of Scots baronial style but he included a 16th-century door from Edinburgh's Tolbooth, a copy of a porch at Linlithgow Palace and even medieval gargoyles. He was, apparently, no less a romantic in his architectural taste than he was in his writings. The house also contains wonderful memorabilia, such as a gun belonging to Rob Roy, and a cup which Bonnie Prince Charlie carried around with him.

Scott was a lawyer and served as Sheriff in Selkirk. He assiduously collected and wrote down the oral tradition of the old Border tales that had been handed down through the generations, thus ensuring that many of them were preserved. He also began to write his own material and started to make a reputation for himself as a poet and then as a novelist. His best-known works include *Kenilworth*, *Redgauntlet* and

Abbotsford interior

Ivanhoe. Unfortunately, the financial collapse of a publisher landed him with huge personal debts of about £114,000 which he tried to work off; sadly his exertions led to his untimely death in 1832.

► *Continue on the **B6360** and turn right at the **A6091** for 3 miles (5km) for Melrose.*

The beautiful walled garden at Abbotsford

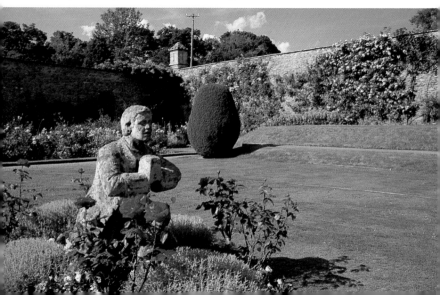

The Border
Country

Few cities match Edinburgh's city centre: Princes Street and its gardens; Edinburgh Castle; the Royal Mile, with its medieval 'lands', or blocks of flats; the Palace of Holyroodhouse, and the elegant Georgian architecture of New Town. The best view of all the city's treasures is from Arthur's Seat, a volcanic hill 823 feet (251m) above sea level.

2 DAYS • 148 MILES • 239KM

Princes Street at sunset

i 3 Princes Street

▶ Leave by the **A1** and turn left at the **A198** to reach Gullane.

❶ Gullane, East Lothian
Gullane is renowned as a golfing centre, with a number of courses including a championship course at nearby Muirfield.

Further east, the centre of the old village of Dirleton, claimed to be the most beautiful village in Scotland, is dominated by the grand Dirleton Castle, which dates back to the 13th century. Perched on top of a rocky platform, it has massive towers and was defended by a moat at least 50 feet (15m) wide.

▶ Continue on the **A198** for 5 miles (8km) to North Berwick.

❷ North Berwick, East Lothian
This seaside golf resort is dominated by the nearby 613-foot (187m) North Berwick Law, which offers fine views over the town and the coast.

By the harbour, the Scottish Seabird Centre is an award-winning wildlife centre and one of Scotland's five star attractions. Its vantage point overlooking the sea and the islands of the Forth make it the ideal place to see and find out about the wide variety of wildlife that inhabits the area. Depending on the time of visit, you may see whales, dolphins and grey seals, as well as a number of seabirds, ranging from puffins to guillemots.

i Quality Street

▶ Continue on the **A198** and turn left at a signposted minor road to Tantallon Castle, 3 miles (5km).

❸ Tantallon Castle, East Lothian
This grim-looking 14th-century castle stands in a spectacular clifftop position, with three sides protected by the sea and the fourth by thick walls. Two great sieges took place here: the first ended by negotiation (the attackers ran out of gunpowder!) and in the second, General Monk attacked it for 12 days in 1651, damaging the towers. This is the best place on the mainland to view the Bass Rock. The island has huge numbers of gannets breeding there and the colony is so important that the birds' scientific name *Sula bassana* comes from the island.

Whale jaw crowning the top of Berwick Law

▶ *Return to the **A198** and continue southwards. Turn right at the **B1407** to enter Preston.*

4 Preston, East Lothian
On the outskirts of the village stands the charming 18th-century water-driven Preston Mill. Originally a meal mill, the unusual design of its kiln has similarities with an English oast house. The buildings are constructed of orange sandstone rubble and roofed with traditional east coast pantiles. A short walk leads to the Phantassie Doocot, a dovecot which once housed some 500 pigeons.

▶ *Leave by the **B1047** and turn left on to the **B1377**. Turn left at the **A1**, then left at the **A1087** to Dunbar.*

5 Dunbar, East Lothian
This popular seaside resort is now a rather peaceful place, a far cry from the turbulent times when its castle was of some importance. The castle was eventually sacked by Cromwell

in 1650 and its walls torn down, the stones being used to improve the harbour. The remains sit forlornly by the harbour entrance. The attractive harbour is home to a busy fishing fleet and to the local lifeboat station. John Muir, the conservationist, was born in Dunbar in the mid-19th century.

i *143 High Street*

▶ *Continue on the **A1087** and turn left at the **A1** to Cockburnspath.*

6 Cockburnspath, Scottish Borders
The position of this village, which is so close to the border, has meant a turbulent and rather troubled history. This was an important stopping point for horse-drawn coaches (a mode of travel which peaked in the 19th century) and the layout of the village and its marketplace owes much to this time. The parish church is worth a look; it has a fine tower in the middle of the west gable and an unusual sundial on the southwest corner.

The mercat cross is the finishing point of the Southern Upland Way, the long-distance footpath that starts at

Portpatrick, over on the west coast. By following the Southern Upland Way from its terminus, you will find yourself by a group of houses at Cove, below which is the picturesque Cove Harbour. The harbour is reached by going through a tunnel cut into the cliff; this was made in the 18th century and was connected to cellars probably used for curing and barrelling fish, and possibly by smugglers.

Preston's Phantassie Doocot, once home to over 500 pigeons but now home to considerably fewer

▶ Continue on the **A1** and turn left at the **A1107**. At Coldingham, turn left at the **B6438** and follow this to St Abbs.

7 St Abbs, Scottish Borders

This neat little fishing village is now a resort, often busy with divers who come to explore the local bays.

Nearby Coldingham has an ancient priory. Founded in 1098 by King Edgar, the 13th-century priory church was built on a site that had a religious house way back in the 7th century. Life could hardly have been peaceful for those who stayed here during the frequent outbreaks of hostil- ities, as the monks were subject to the English king and the priors to the Scots king!

▶ Return along the **B6438** to Coldingham and turn left at the **A1107**. Turn left at the **B6355** for Eyemouth.

8 Eyemouth, Scottish Borders

This busy fishing port has regu- lar fish markets which are worth visiting. This is home to a large fleet and the local people have been connected with fishing for a very long time. The town's saddest day came on 14 October, 1881 when a sudden gale blew up and 129 local fishermen were drowned, some of them in full sight of their families on shore. The local museum tells the story.

ⅰ Auld Kirk, Manse Road (seasonal)

▶ Return along the **B6355**, then follow the **A6105** to Duns.

Tapestry from Eyemouth museum, showing the 1881 fishing tragedy

The picturesque little harbour at St Abbs

9 Duns, Scottish Borders

This long-established village, with its well-built stone houses, makes a useful stopping point for touring this part of the Borders. Duns was the home town of the world motor-racing champion Jim Clark, who died in a race in Germany in 1968; a small museum has mementos of his short but fascinating life. A short drive away from Duns is the mansion Manderston, with formally laid-out gardens and a marble dairy, both of which are worth a tour.

▶ Leave on the **A6112** for 12 miles (19km) to reach Coldstream.

🔟 Coldstream, Scottish Borders

Coldstream stands on the banks of the River Tweed, which at this point marks the border with England. The river is crossed by a magnificent seven-arch bridge and on the Scottish side a toll house was the east coast equivalent of Gretna Green, a place where marriages could take place with the minimum of delay. Like many Border towns, Coldstream has a wealth of well-built houses. The Market Square is a little off this street and is the location of the Coldstream Museum, telling the story of the town and the Coldstream Guards regiment.

Outside Coldstream stands the Hirsel Homestead Museum comprising a museum, craft centre and walks in the estate.

> ⓘ *Town Hall, High Street (seasonal)*

> ▶ *Leave by the **A697** and turn left at the **A698** to reach Kelso.*

⓫ Kelso, Scottish Borders

Kelso has one of the most attractive town centres in the Borders, with a huge open square. The town stands at the confluence of the rivers Teviot and Tweed and from the fine bridge which crosses the Tweed there is a good view of Floors Castle, a huge mansion built by William Adam between 1721 and 1725, offering glittering excesses of fine French furniture, porcelain and paintings. Kelso Abbey was once the Borders' greatest abbey but only the west end of it stands today. It was founded here in 1128 but its position on the 'invasion route' meant that it suffered frequent attacks. North of Kelso, Mellerstain House is one of Scotland's finest Robert Adam mansions.

> ⓘ *Town House, The Square*

> ▶ *Leave by the **A6089**. Turn left at the junction with the **A697** and left at the **B6362**. Follow this to Lauder.*

⓬ Lauder, Scottish Borders

This attractive town has a wide main street in the middle of which stands the Tolbooth. This was originally built in 1318 and the ground floor was used as a gaol up to 1840. Lauder's parish church is an interesting structure in the form of a Greek cross with an octagonal steeple and four arms; it is dated 1673. Impressive Thirlestane Castle, close to the town, houses the Border Country Life Exhibitions.

The village of Earlston lies only a few miles south of Lauder. This was Ercildoune in medieval days and the home of Thomas the Rhymer who lived during the 13th century. His ability to see into the future was reckoned to be a gift from the Queen of the Fairies with whom it was believed he stayed for a number of years.

> ▶ *Take the **A68** north to Pathhead, then turn left at the **B6367** to Crichton Castle.*

⓭ Crichton Castle, Midlothian

Crichton was at one time the home of the Earl of Bothwell, the ill-fated third husband of Mary, Queen of Scots. The ruins of this substantial structure stand on the edge of Middleton Moor and above the Tyne Water. It dates from the 14th century and one architectural curiosity is a Renaissance-influenced wall erected in the late 16th century. This is an arcade of seven bays topped by diamond-patterned stone-work and is unique in the country. Crichton's church is a fine building which was restored in 1896.

> ▶ *Return along the **B6367** to Pathhead. Turn left and follow the **A68** to Edinburgh.*

The surviving ruin of Kelso Abbey, showing fine Norman detail

---

FOR CHILDREN

There are a number of good beaches, notably at Gullane Bay. Indoor swimming pools are located in Kelso, Duns, Dunbar and Eyemouth and there is an outdoor one at North Berwick. Pony trekking is available at Earlston, Ford (near Pathhead) and Westruther (east of Lauder). You can get close to puffins, gannets, seals and dolphins at the Scottish Seabird Centre in North Berwick.

CENTRAL SCOTLAND

The great firths of the Clyde, the Forth and the Tay have narrowed the middle of Scotland to a thin neck of land only 30 miles (48km) wide. This is where the majority of the Scots live, in an area that is rich with history. Bronze-Age cemeteries, medieval castles, battlefields and architectural follies all have their statements to make about their builders' views of the world and how they lived – and died.

Much of the region's history has been bloody. Land- and sea-borne invaders attacked, plundered and wrought destruction. But many invaders stayed and left their mark, often introducing foreign influences that have added to the common heritage of the modern Scottish nation. The Celts, Vikings, French and the peoples of the countries washed by the Baltic and the North Sea have all contributed to the country's history, but it has been the English who, despite being the 'auld enemy', have in so many ways changed the country – and also radically influenced how the Scots see themselves today as a nation.

Black Mount and the Rannoch Moors, seen from the River Bá

Central Scotland's modern prosperity was based on the Industrial Revolution and many would argue that this was where that important period of history began. One of the world's first major ironworks, the first major use of efficient steam engines, the world's biggest shipbuilding industry – all of these were based right here.

Although the manufacturing industry has declined, the outstanding engineering marvels of Scotland are now today's tourist attractions in their own right. Eighteenth-century ironworks, 19th-century canals and the world's most famous railway bridge – spanning the Firth of Forth – are all showpieces of an industrial nation's genius for design. The region can also boast many architectural gems: the rich legacy of Victorian buildings in Glasgow, the grand country houses designed in Scots baronial style and the distinctive cottages of farmer and fisherman all display a very Scottish flavour. Glasgow itself has enjoyed regeneration in recent years, and now takes its rightful place as one of Europe's most lively and interesting cities. But it is the quality of life that matters more than bricks and mortar and one of the greatest attractions of the populated areas is their closeness to the hills and glens of the Highlands. The hills are never far away and even Glasgow, the country's industrial 'capital', has the Campsie Fells only a few miles from its centre.

Tour 8

Although this route is only a couple of hours' drive away from the industrial heartland of Scotland, it nevertheless encompasses some superb Highland scenery. The highly indented coastline, backed by 3,000-foot (900m) high hills, provides a backdrop to some fascinating places like the 5,000-year-old cairns at Kilmartin, medieval castles and the picturesque setting of Crinan Canal.

Tour 9

The Cowal Peninsula is made up of a group of narrow peninsulas shaped like a grasping hand trying to grip the northern shore of the island of Bute. The narrow, twisting roads of Cowal give ever-changing vistas over the sea lochs and the great estuary of the Firth of Clyde, the busy waterway that linked the local communities before the arrival of the railway and the motor car.

Tour 10

The 'border' between the Highlands and the Lowlands is studded with lochs gouged out of the landscape by long-lost glaciers. Some of the country's best-known lochs are found here, and today's visitors follow in the footsteps of the 19th-century tourists, eager to sample the 'wild' scenery so vividly romanticised by Sir Walter Scott.

Tour 11

This historic corner of Scotland has an abundance of important buildings that armies fought over for centuries. Abbeys, grand palaces and austere castles were the prizes sought by the warring parties, and Stirling, the 'gateway to the Highlands', was the jewel in the crown that invaders tried to capture and that the Scots defended to the last. The battle sites excavated here testify to the lives sacrificed in the centuries of turmoil. But some places can often evade change and the small coastal town of Culross retains a rich legacy in its preserved buildings that time just passed by.

Tour 12

A rich agricultural area, Strathmore provides the background to this tour which skirts the southern limits of the Grampian Highlands. Prosperous farming communities, busy east-coast fishing ports and the industrial town of Dundee all add their interest. In many ways this area is one of Scotland's 'hidden gems', as it is often missed by visitors who are more intent on heading straight for the Highlands.

Tour 13

Although never a separate legal entity, Fife earned the title 'Kingdom of Fife' through the influence of its ancient abbey in Dunfermline and later its medieval university in St Andrews. Cut off from the rest of the country by the great firths of the Forth and the Tay, it has a character that is very different from the rest of Scotland. This is most evident in its traditional architecture, especially the small white stone buildings with their pantiled roofs that are such a common feature in the many picturesque fishing villages of the East Neuk.

The cantilevered Forth Rail Bridge at dusk

Argyll
Coast & Castles

Oban is still a thriving fishing port and the gateway to the Inner Hebrides. From Oban the tour winds along the dramatic coastline and then goes inland to the heart of the Highlands and Glen Coe, site of Scotland's most infamous massacre.

ITINERARY

OBAN	▶ Easdale (16m -26km)
EASDALE	▶ Kilmartin (29m-47km)
KILMARTIN	▶ Crinan (7m-11km)
CRINAN	▶ Lochgilphead (7m-11km)
LOCHGILPHEAD	▶ Crarae Garden
	(14m-23km)
CRARAE GARDEN	▶ Auchindrain (5m-8km)
AUCHINDRAIN	▶ Inveraray (6m-10km)
INVERARAY	▶ Loch Awe (15m-24km)
LOCH AWE	▶ Glen Coe (36m-58km)
GLEN COE	▶ Ballachulish (4m-6km)
BALLACHULISH	▶ Castle Stalker
	(14m-23km)
CASTLE STALKER	▶ Scottish Sea Life
	Sanctuary (13m-21km)
SCOTTISH SEA LIFE	▶ Loch Etive (6m-10km)
SANCTUARY	
LOCH ETIVE	▶ Oban (5m-8km)

2/3 DAYS • 177 MILES • 286KM

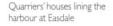

FOR CHILDREN

An animal-based attraction is the Oban Rare Breeds Farm Park with its collection of pigs, sheep and cattle.
The Argyll Wildlife Park near Inveraray boasts many animals including wildcats, badgers, wild boar and deer.

BACK TO NATURE

Oban Bay can be seen from the town's harbour. Look for common seals, black guillemots and eiders. There is a nature trail at nearby Glen Nant 10 miles (16km) northeast via the B845, south of Taynuilt.
Look for wood warblers, redstarts and roe deer in the woodlands

Quarriers' houses lining the harbour at Easdale

i   *Argyll Square*

▶ *Head south on the **A816**, then turn right at the **B844** which leads to Easdale (16 miles/26km).*

❶ Easdale, Argyll & Bute
The village of Easdale lies on the island of Seil, connected to the mainland by the humped bridge known as the 'Bridge over the Atlantic'.

Easdale was a slate quarry-

ing centre and the rows of quarriers' houses look much as they did in the 19th century when a ferocious sea broke into and flooded the workings; the industry never recovered. The folk museum tells the story.

▶ *Return along the **B844** and turn right at the **A816** and follow this to Kilmartin.*

❷ Kilmartin, Argyll & Bute
The area around the small village of Kilmartin has some of Scotland's most outstanding large cairns. West of the village is the massive Bronze-Age Glebe Cairn and southwest of the village are the three Nether Largie Cairns. The cairns were used as tombs from around 5,000 years ago, with bodies or cremated remains interred in stone-clad cells ('cists') within the cairns. A little further to the southwest lie the two Temple Wood Stone Circles.

Kilmartin church's graveyard contains many celebrated sculptured gravestones, including the Poltalloch Stones, and others can be seen inside the church.

Kilmartin House contains an award-winning museum, with a superb audio-visual presentation.

The 16th-century fortified house known as Carnassarie Castle can be seen on a hill just before the village.

Stone circle at Temple Wood, near Kilmartin

▶ *Continue on the A816, then turn on to the B8025 to meet the Crinan Canal. Turn right at the B841 to Crinan.*

3 Crinan, Argyll & Bute

The Crinan Canal was opened in 1801 so that boats could avoid the cruel seas around the Mull of Kintyre. This was a great boon to fishermen as the short-cut was only 8½ miles (14km) long compared to the sea route of 130 miles (200km). The advent of steamships dealt the canal a severe blow, but the canal is still in use today and is often busy with pleasure craft.

▶ *Return along the B841, which follows the canal. Join the A816 and follow it to Lochgilphead, 7 miles (11km).*

4 Lochgilphead, Argyll & Bute

The town developed as an administrative centre for the region and also because of the trade brought by the canal. A popular attraction today is a visit to the local Highbank Pottery.

i *Lochnell Street (seasonal)*

▶ *Leave by the A83 for 14 miles (23km) to Crarae Garden.*

5 Crarae Garden, Argyll & Bute

The garden was founded in 1912 in a steep-sided gorge and today has a rich collection of rhododendrons, magnolias,

Inveraray Castle, obviously modelled on the romantic French châteaux

azaleas and many other trees and shrubs from around the world. The warmth of the Gulf Stream and an annual rainfall of 75 inches (190cm) help ensure that the garden delights visitors throughout the year, especially in early summer (for the rhododendrons) and in autumn.

▶ *Continue on the A83 for 5 miles (8km) to Auchindrain, just beyond the village of Furnace.*

6 Auchindrain, Argyll & Bute

Queen Victoria visited this little Highland township in 1875 and was impressed enough to record it in her diary. Today, the

houses, barns, smiddy (traditional term for blacksmith) and other buildings have been preserved as an open air folk-life museum to show how people have lived here through the centuries.

▶ *Continue on the A83 for 6 miles (10km) to Inveraray.*

7 Inveraray, Argyll & Bute

This neat and well-planned village on Loch Fyne has been a royal burgh since 1648, but its 'modern' planning dates back to the middle of the 18th century, and the exteriors of the houses have hardly changed since then.

The large parish church, in the middle of the main road, dominates the centre. It was built at the turn of the 18th century with a central dividing wall so that services in Gaelic and English could be conducted simultaneously.

The fascinating Inveraray Jail Museum consists of the former courthouse (with actors in period costume) and two prisons. The older of the two was erected in 1820 as the Argyll County Prison and the newer one was built to 'modern' standards in 1849. The cells feature displays explaining the harshness of prison life and the appalling conditions the prisoners were kept in. Near the gaol

'Let's be havin' yer' – Jail Museum at Inveraray

are the 'lands', rows of houses reminiscent of some old Edinburgh houses. Neil Munro, author of the Para Handy tales, was born close by.

Down at the pier, the *Arctic Penguin* is now a floating museum of maritime history, with exciting hands-on displays and on-board cinema. It has exhibits on Scottish pirates, the Highland Clearances and the Victorian era.

Inveraray Castle stands a short distance away from the village. The present building is mid-18th-century and replaces a castle built by Colin Campbell in about 1415. This is the home of the Dukes of Argyll, the chiefs of Clan Campbell, and it has many exhibits relating to the clan's history.

[i] *Front Street*

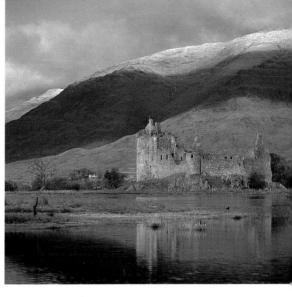

RECOMMENDED WALKS

There are many walks in Argyll suitable for family outings, for example on the western shore of Loch Awe. The Crinan Canal towpath also provides pleasant walks, with lots to see when boats are passing through the locks.

SPECIAL TO...

Fresh seafood is a speciality of the region. Crabs, prawns and lobsters should be available in many restaurants and Loch Fyne is famous for its herrings. Herrings were once given the alternative name of 'Glasgow Magistrates' as the quality of those sold in the city had to be approved by the magistrates. Indeed, the city used to give barrels of these delicious fish to people who rendered the city a great service!

▶ *Leave by the A819 and turn left at the A85 for Loch Awe.*

8 Loch Awe, Argyll & Bute
Loch Awe is dominated by the massive Ben Cruachan, a mountain with a pump storage hydro-electric power station inside it. Visits into the heart of the mountain start from the visitor centre (west along the A85). At the head of the loch stands the imposing ruin of Kilchurn Castle, a Campbell stronghold

The Three Sisters in Glen Coe, Scotland's most infamous glen

built in the 15th and 17th centuries. It was abandoned in the 18th century and in 1879 a hurricane blew down the top of the tower that can be seen lying in the courtyard.

The intriguing St Conan's Church sits below the south-eastern slopes of Ben Cruachan. This was started in 1881 and

Winter sun on the hills around Kilchurn Castle on the banks of Loch Awe

added to over the next 50 years. It has elaborate carvings, including fragments from Iona Abbey, rich woodwork and a rare mixture of styles.

▶ *Return eastwards along the A85, then bear left at the B8074 towards Bridge of Orchy. Turn left at the A82 and follow it across Rannoch Moor to Glen Coe.*

9 Glen Coe, Highland
Glen Coe itself is regarded by many Scots as the country's finest glen and whatever the weather, the scenery is dramatic.

The visitor centre near the foot of the glen has displays on the district and tells one of Scotland's most tragic stories, the Glencoe Massacre of February 1692. In 1691 William III offered a pardon to the warring clans on condition that they took an oath of allegiance to the crown by 1 January, 1692. The local MacDonald chief reluctantly made his way to Fort William just before the deadline, only to be told that he should go to Inveraray. He did so, but arrived a day after the deadline. The regiment in Glen Coe, under the command of a Campbell, were billeted with the MacDonalds for 10 days. A message was sent to them, which had the King's private

approval, and at a given signal, without warning, the Campbells rose up and slaughtered 38 of their hosts, supposedly because of the failure to take the oath. About 300 people escaped into the hills, but the atrocity was never forgotten. A restored cottage with a heather-thatched roof houses a museum of local history. It shows life in this area over the past three centuries, with exhibits ranging from domestic and agricultural history to the story of the Jacobites.

ⓘ *NTS Visitor Centre (seasonal)*

Golden sunset silhouetting romantic Castle Stalker

▶ *Continue on the A82 past the village of Glencoe to Ballachulish.*

🔟 **Ballachulish,** Highland
This was once Scotland's main slate producer and in the 1880s, the quarries' peak of production, 600 men produced 16 million slates a year. This ended in 1955 but the massive quarries can still be seen.

Steps under the Ballachulish Bridge lead to a memorial to James Stewart who was hanged here in 1752 for the murder of Colin Campbell, a government official. He was undoubtedly a scapegoat convicted by a partisan court and Robert Louis Stevenson used this terrible miscarriage of justice in his novel *Kidnapped*.

ⓘ *Albert Road (seasonal)*

▶ *Continue on the A82, then follow the A828 to the village of Portnacroish for Castle Stalker.*

Ⅱ Castle Stalker, Argyll & Bute
This romantically set rectangular keep (not open) is perched on a low rocky platform at the mouth

BACK TO NATURE

One of the most notable sights in many parts of western Scotland, particularly Argyll, is the rhododendron, a plant introduced in the 18th and 19th centuries. Its ability to colonise poor ground, together with its dense foliage that inhibits light reaching smaller plants, often makes people regard it more as a weed than an exotic plant to be nurtured.

Feeding the seals at the Scottish Sea Life Sanctuary in Oban

of Loch Laich. It was built in the 13th century, and in 1689 it was exchanged for an eight-oared galley during a drunken spree, when the owner was clearly not in full control of his senses!

▶ Continue on the **A828** for 13 miles (21km) to the Scottish Sea Life Sanctuary, near Barcardine.

12 Scottish Sea Life Sanctuary, Argyll & Bute
Scotland's west coast is famous for its important fishing grounds so it is entirely appropriate to have the Scottish Sea Life Sanctuary here. Crabs, lobsters, rays and a huge shoal of herring are just some of the creatures on view. There are also seals and the sanctuary provides a refuge for abandoned seal pups. Make sure you are there for one of the feeding times.

▶ Continue on the **A828** to Connel where the road crosses the mouth of Loch Etive, 6 miles (10km).

Fishing boats, car ferries and yachts make Oban one of the busiest harbours in Scotland

13 Loch Etive, Argyll & Bute
Just under the Connel Bridge are the unusual Falls of Lora, a tidal waterfall where the direction of the falls depends on whether the tide is going in or out. To the east stands the village of Taynuilt. This was

once one of Scotland's iron-smelting centres and the impressive Bonawe Furnace has been conserved to show something of what an 18th-century ironworks looked like; however, you will have to forget the peace and quiet of the countryside to imagine all the dust, dirt and smoke it must once have produced.

▶ At Connel, join the **A85** and return to Oban.

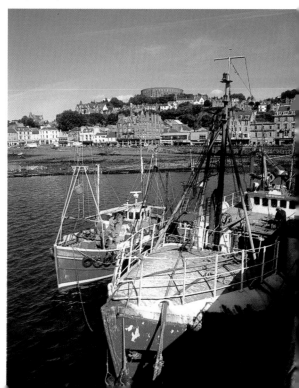

'Doon the Watter'

The town of Paisley grew up around its abbey, founded in 1163, and is best known for its shawls featuring the distinctive teardrop-shaped Paisley pattern. From Paisley the tour explores the sea lochs and green-clad mountains of the Cowal Peninsula.

2 DAYS • 132 MILES • 213KM

ITINERARY

[i] Glasgow International Airport, Paisley

▶ *Leave Paisley on the **A726** (to Greenock and Erskine Bridge). Join the **M8** and head towards Greenock, then take the **M898/A898** to the Erskine Bridge (toll) over the River Clyde. Head west along the **A82** (towards Crianlarich) then bear left on to the **A814**.*

0 Dumbarton, West Dunbartonshire

A modern industrial town owing its historic importance to its prominent position on the northern shore of the River Clyde, Dumbarton was the capital of the ancient kingdom of Strathclyde and it has had a royal castle since medieval times. Dumbarton Castle stands on Dumbarton Rock overlooking the river and much of the present fortification dates from the 16th to 18th centuries. The hilltop behind the castle gives a superb view of the area.

Dumbarton is now an important whisky distilling

The river port of Dumbarton, now more famous for its whisky distilling than for its shipbuilding

centre but it used to have a flourishing shipbuilding industry. Although few ships are built on the Clyde these days, one important structure that remains is the Denny Tank, which has been preserved by the Scottish Maritime Museum. This was used for experiments: models of proposed ships were towed along the 330-foot (100m) tank in order to show how the full size ship might perform at sea.

[i] Milton A82 northbound

Dumbarton Castle and the 18th-century Governor's Mansion above the River Clyde

▶ *Leave Dumbarton by the **A814** and follow it along the coast for 8 miles (13km) to Helensburgh.*

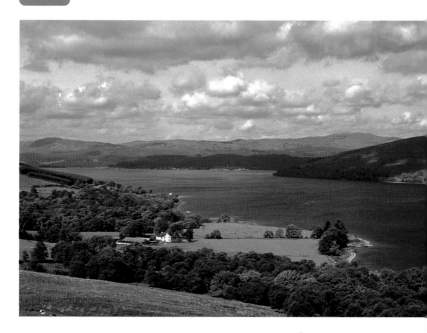

Loch Fyne – one of Scotland's best known sea lochs

2 Helensburgh, Argyll & Bute

Helensburgh's grand architecture dates back to the late 18th century when it was built as a planned dormitory town for Glasgow, to which it was connected by regular sailings. The town's long promenade gives a pleasant walk and by the seafront is a tall granite obelisk commemorating Henry Bell, designer of the world's first seagoing steamship, *The Comet*.

The recent revival in interest in the work of the outstanding Scottish architect and designer Charles Rennie Mackintosh makes a trip to Hill House one of the town's main attractions. This mansion was built at the beginning of the 20th century for the publisher Walter Blackie and remains an outstanding example of modern Scottish domestic architecture. The exterior design and the household furnishings reflect Mackintosh's individual style.

John Logie Baird, pioneer of the television, came from Helensburgh and a memorial bust to him is in the town's Hermitage Park. After leaving Helensburgh, the route passes the huge complex of the Clyde Submarine Base.

i *Clock Tower, The Pier (seasonal)*

▶ *Continue along the **A814** for 17 miles (27km) to Arrochar.*

3 Arrochar, Argyll & Bute

The little village of Arrochar sits at the head of Loch Long and below the hills often referred to as the 'Arrochar Alps'. These rise steeply from the shore and provide wonderful walking and climbing, especially 2,891-foot (881m) Ben Arthur, which is usually known as The Cobbler.

Loch Long has been associated with seafarers for many centuries. The most notable naval exploit was in 1263 when the Viking King Haakon landed at Arrochar. He had his boats hauled 1½ miles (2km) over the strip of land to Tarbet and then sailed over Loch Lomond to attack inland settlements!

To the west of Arrochar, the A83 climbs steeply up Glen Croe to the well-named 'Rest and be Thankful', at 803 feet (245m). Below this can be seen the earlier military road which was built after the 1745 Jacobite uprising in order to 'pacify' (meaning 'subdue') the Highlands.

ℹ️ *Pier Road, Tarbert*

RECOMMENDED WALKS

Experienced walkers will head for the Arrochar Alps, but there are other walks of varying grades in the Argyll Forest Park, which lies in the area of lochs Long, Goil and Eck. Information can be obtained from tourist information centres.

▶ *Leave Arrochar on the **A83** to Campbeltown. Turn left at the 'Rest and be Thankful' on to the **B828**, then join the **B839** to reach Lochgoilhead.*

❹ **Lochgoilhead**, Argyll & Bute

At the head of Loch Goil, this village is popular with visitors for its excellent walking and sailing.

Five miles (8km) down the western shore of the loch stands the ruin of Carrick Castle, destroyed by fire in 1685. The structure dates at least from the 15th century and was probably used by James IV when he came to this area, known as Cowal, to hunt wild boar.

▶ *Leave Lochgoilhead by the **B839** and follow this to the shore of Loch Fyne. Turn left on to the **A815** just before the shore.*

❺ **Loch Fyne**, Argyll & Bute

This long sea loch is set among beautiful ranges of green-clad mountains. Apart from the little village of Strachur, where there is a blacksmithing museum and craft shop, the district's settlements are small and scattered and many of the houses are used as retirement homes.

South of Strachur stands Castle Lachlan, home of the chief of the MacLachlans. During the Clearances the local people were moved out of their homes and settled in the village of Newton, which the chief built between the castle and Strachur. This is now a sleepy hamlet, and many homes are used only at weekends. The 18th-century Clearances, when landowners moved thousands of people off the land to make way for more profitable sheep farming, led to depopulation of the area. However, the importance of sheep has diminished greatly and much of the poorer land has been given over to extensive conifer plantations.

The easy route to and from 'Rest and be Thankful'

BACK TO NATURE

The sea lochs around Cowal are home to many seabirds including gulls, cormorants and ducks. Keep a sharp look out for seals from the shore of Loch Fyne. Of all Cowal's lochs, Loch Striven is probably the quietest and least touched by agriculture.

▶ *Follow the **A815** to Strachur. Keep to the lochside by joining the **A886** and later bear right on to the **B8000** to Kilfinan. Follow this to Tighnabruaich.*

❻ **Tighnabruaich**, Argyll & Bute

Both Tighnabruaich and neighbouring Kames grew during the heyday of steamship navigation on the Clyde. This is a popular sailing centre and many yachts can be seen in the narrow waterways around the northern coast of Bute. Just north of Tighnabruaich is one of Scotland's most famous viewpoints – across the narrow strait known as the Kyles of Bute.

FOR CHILDREN

Cowal is an area for outdoor activities with sailing at Tighnabruaich and ponytrekking at Lochgoilhead and Inellan (south of Dunoon). Alternatively, Helensburgh Pier Family Amusement Park has rides for all ages.

▶ *Leave Tighnabruaich by the **A8003**. Turn right at the **A886** and then left at the **B836**. Turn right on the **A815** for Dunoon.*

❼ **Dunoon**, Argyll & Bute

Dunoon has built up a reputation as one of the most popular stopping places for people sailing 'Doon the Watter', as the Glaswegians say, and its picturesque pierhead buildings have welcomed countless visitors. As befits a seaside resort, it has a long promenade and colourful Castle Gardens. Here you will find the excellent Castle House Museum, with furnished Victorian rooms and other exhibits.

Near the pier stands a statue of Robert Burns' 'Highland Mary', who was born in the town. This was Mary Campbell, who was betrothed to Burns but died. Burns tried hard to cover up their relationship, probably because it complicated his life with his future wife, Jean Armour.

The Cowal Bird Garden is always delightful, and a good wet-weather attraction is the Dunoon Ceramics tour.

Dunoon is world famous for its Cowal Highland Gathering, which takes place on the last Friday and Saturday in August. The Gathering was started in the 1890s and today it attracts

Younger Botanic Garden – woodland gardens on a grand scale

FOR HISTORY BUFFS

Eight miles (13km) south of Dunoon stand the ruins of 15th-century Castle Toward. This was a stronghold of the Lamont clan, but in 1646 it was surrounded by a force of Campbells. Although the Lamonts accepted and signed a truce they were seized and taken to Dunoon where they were summarily executed and their bodies thrown into mass graves. This bloody act is commemorated by a memorial on Tom-a-Mhoid Road near Castle Hill.

competitors from many countries as it hosts World Championship Highland dancing. Pipe bands from near and far compete and some 20,000 visitors have been known to throng the main street for the parade.

The Younger Botanic Garden is at Benmore, just 7

SPECIAL TO...

The development of steamships in the 19th century led to the 'discovery' of Cowal by visitors keen to go 'Doon the Watter' (the River Clyde) from Glasgow to the smoke-free countryside. Many wealthy Glasgow merchants built villas in the Cowal villages and decanted their families there during the summer months. Cruising on the Clyde is now an increasingly popular pastime and cruises from places such as Dunoon and Tighnabruaich are available. One ship to look out for around Cowal is the PS *Waverley*, the world's last sea-going paddle steamer. It is based in Glasgow and operates many summer cruises, calling at piers on both sides of the Firth of Clyde.

miles (11km) north of Dunoon on the A815. This outstanding garden is an outstation of

Edinburgh's Royal Botanic Garden; it has magnificent rhododendrons and an impressive avenue of tall redwoods that was planted here in 1863.

ⓘ *7 Alexandra Parade*

▶ *Take the Caledonian MacBrayne ferry from Dunoon to Gourock. Alternatively, take the Western Ferries' ferry from Hunter's Quay (just north of Dunoon) to a point a little southwest of Gourock; then head towards Gourock on the A770.*

8 Gourock, Inverclyde
Gourock is a pleasant coastal town that boasts excellent views of the Clyde, notably from Lyle Hill above the southeastern side of Gourock Bay. On top of the hill is a monument to Free French sailors who sailed from here and died during World War II's Battle of the Atlantic.

To the east of Gourock are the industrial towns of Greenock and Port Glasgow. Greenock was a shipbuilding centre and once an important embarkation point for emigrants leaving Scotland for new lives in North America or Australasia. The Custom House Museum explores the Customs and Excise service, including a display on one of its former employees, Robert Burns. The town's most famous son was the engineer James Watt, whose invention of the condensing steam engine, the first efficient use of steam power, paved the way for the Industrial Revolution. The McLean Museum has a display on James Watt among its collections.

Port Glasgow gained its present name in 1688 when it became the city's port as ships could not progress further upstream (its previous name had been Newark). The city's 16th-century castle still stands by the shore, although it is rather overshadowed these days by the many industrial buildings all around it.

ⓘ *7a Clyde Square, Greenock*

▶ *Leave Gourock by the coastal road (the **A770** which joins the **A8** at Greenock) and bear right on to the **A761** to Bridge of Weir, via Kilmacolm. After Bridge of Weir, continue on the **A761** for 1½ miles (2.5km) after the local railway station, then turn sharp right at a signposted minor road to Kilbarchan.*

9 Kilbarchan, Renfrewshire
In the 18th century the village of Kilbarchan was an important centre where wool, linen and cotton were hand woven. A weaver's cottage of 1723 has been preserved at The Cross by the NTS. This continued to be used for weaving until 1940 and it has a 200-year-old loom on which weaving demonstrations are now given.

Hand-woven tartans are still made today at Kilbarchan

▶ *Rejoin the **A761** (to Paisley, via Linwood), then turn left on to the **A737** to return to Paisley.*

SCENIC ROUTES

The nicest part of this tour is on the A8003, when the narrows of the Kyles of Bute are seen. If you are lucky you may see a ship negotiating the passage past the Burnt Islands. The true narrows are opposite Colintraive, whose name means 'straight of swimming', dating from the times when cattle drovers used to swim their beasts across here.

Rob Roy
Country

WASHING
THE
FLEECE

This tour includes Loch Lomond and the Trossachs, Scotland's first national park, and Loch Tay – but starts in Glasgow, one of Britain's most exciting cities. It is certainly worth spending a few days in Glasgow: its museums and galleries are among Britain's finest and the city is well endowed with green spaces.

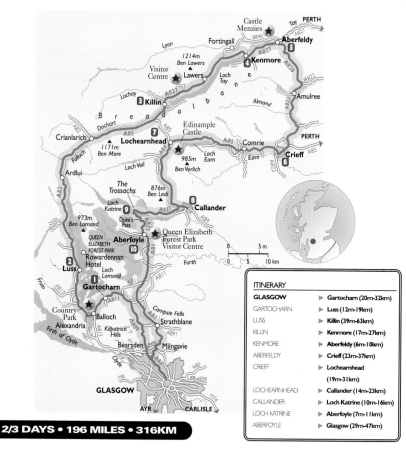

2/3 DAYS • 196 MILES • 316KM

ITINERARY		
GLASGOW	▶	**Gartocharn** (20m-32km)
GARTOCHARN	▶	**Luss** (12m-19km)
LUSS	▶	**Killin** (39m-63km)
KILLIN	▶	**Kenmore** (17m-27km)
KENMORE	▶	**Aberfeldy** (6m-10km)
ABERFELDY	▶	**Crieff** (23m-37km)
CRIEFF	▶	**Lochearnhead** (19m-31km)
LOCHEARNHEAD	▶	**Callander** (14m-23km)
CALLANDER	▶	**Loch Katrine** (10m-16km)
LOCH KATRINE	▶	**Aberfoyle** (7m-11km)
ABERFOYLE	▶	**Glasgow** (29m-47km)

ⓘ *11 George Square, Glasgow*

▶ *Leave by the **A81**, then the **A809** and turn left at the **A811** to reach Gartocharn.*

❶ Gartocharn, West Dunbartonshire

This small village gives a good introduction to Scotland's most-loved loch, Loch Lomond. Although Gartocharn doesn't actually sit on the lochside, there is a superb view of it from the hill behind, Duncryne. For little effort this is a vantage point that gives views towards the loch, 3,194-foot (974m) Ben Lomond on the east shore and the Luss Hills, which rise from the western shore.

The area around the loch was one of the last places to lose its glaciers at the end of the Ice Age and the smooth, U-shaped glacial valleys in the Luss Hills are obvious features of this type of landscape. The careful observer will notice a change

between this glacially eroded highland landscape and the smoothly sculpted hillocks around Gartocharn's farmland. This change in scenery marks the geological divide between the Highlands and Lowlands. Further along the road, at Balloch, is the National Park Gateway Centre at Loch Lomond Shores.

ⓘ *Drymen Library, The Square, Drymen (seasonal)*

▶ *Continue on the **A811** and turn right at the **A82**. Follow this northwards, turning right at an unclassified road sign-posted to Luss, a distance of 12 miles (19km).*

❷ Luss, Argyll & Bute

The delightful little lochside village of Luss has many

Contestant giving his best at the World Pipe Band Championships in Glasgow

Majestic Loch Lomond as seen from Duncryne Hill

exceptionally picturesque cottages. The National Park Centre is located here, and the renowned Thistle Bagpipe Works are close by. Further north, a ferry operates from Inverbeg across the loch to Rowardennan.

Kenmore church and boats on Loch Tay

RECOMMENDED WALKS

Hillwalkers will find plenty of good hills near a number of villages. Crainlarich has two interesting pairs of hills in Beinn a' Chroin and Beinn Tulaichean, and Ben More and Stob Binnein. Killin has Ben Lawers and the group of hills called the Tarmachans. Lower hills further south include Ben Venue, Ben Ledi and Ben An. The forests, especially around Aberfoyle, offer many walks, though views of the hills and lochs may be restricted at times by the trees. The Queen Elizabeth Forest Park Visitor Centre at Aberfoyle is run by Forest Enterprises, and many marked paths start from here. Other walks include parts of the West Highland Way (which follows the eastern shore of Loch Lomond), to the Bracklinn Falls (near Callander) and to the Falls of Moness (near Aberfeldy).

► *Rejoin and continue on the A82, then turn right on to the A85 at Crianlarich. Turn left at the A827 to Killin (39 miles/63km).*

BACK TO NATURE

The rich flora on Ben Lawers attracts many botanists, both amateur and professional, to this remarkable mountain. The hill is rich in lime and other minerals which provide the nutrients needed by the Arctic/Alpine species that grow here. Cliff edges, which are out of reach of sheep and deer, support such plants as roseroot, angelica and wood cranesbill, while shady crevices host oak fern and wood anemone. Birds are not too common on the higher slopes but look out for buzzards and kestrels, with occasional sightings of golden eagles and peregrines. Mountain hares can be seen on the high ground.

3 **Killin,** Stirling

Killin attracts hill walkers for the many fine hills in the district, the best known of which is Ben Lawers, at 3,984 feet (1,214m). The NTS has established a visitor centre on the western flank of the mountain.

The River Dochart flows past the village before debouching into Loch Tay. Before reaching the village it tumbles over the wide Falls of Dochart, which are quite fearsome when the river is in spate. Overlooking the falls is the fascinating Breadalbane Folklore Centre.

i *Breadalbane Folklore Centre (seasonal)*

► *Continue on the A827 for 17 miles (27km) to Kenmore.*

4 **Kenmore,** Perth & Kinross

On the shores of Loch Tay, Kenmore has been developed as a small resort and watersports centre. Beside the village is

SCENIC ROUTES

Much of the route is through fine scenery, with perhaps the best parts being along the shores of lochs Lomond and Tay for views of the lochs and their mountains.
Another fine stretch is through the pretty Sma' Glen (between Aberfeldy and Crieff) where the River Almond winds its way through the hills.

he ornamental gateway to aymouth Castle (private). Part f its park has been developed as golf course. To the north lies he quiet settlement of ortingall, reputedly the birth-lace of Pontius Pilate. A yew ree in the churchyard is said to e over 3,000 years old.

▶ *Continue on the **A827** for 6 miles (10km) to Aberfeldy.*

Aberfeldy, Perth & Kinross This pleasant touring centre tands beside the splendidly rnate bridge which General George Wade built in 1733 at his important crossing of the River Tay. Wade was responsible or some 250 miles (400km) of

military roads in the Highlands between 1726 and 1735, as part of the government's attempt to gain control over the region. This network included 40 stone bridges, of which this is the best known, and at the time it was the only bridge over the Tay. The Black Watch Memorial, which stands quite close to the bridge, was erected in 1887. The regiment was enrolled into the British Army in 1739 and took its name from the men's dark tartan, chosen to differentiate them from the Guardsmen or Red Soldiers.

Aberfeldy lies in a belt of good agricultural land and the water mill is one enduring reminder of how the local grain was processed. This was originally built in 1825 and has been restored to allow it to produce stoneground oatmeal. To the northwest of the village, at Weem, stands Castle Menzies, home of the chief of Clan Menzies. The present castle, constructed to a Z-shaped design, was built in the 1570s, and has been restored by the Clan Society.

ⅰ *The Square*

▶ *Leave by the **A826**. Turn right at the **A822**, then right at the **A85** and follow this into Crieff.*

6 Crieff, Perth & Kinross Crieff is a traditional Highland resort and one that offers much to the visitor wanting a base to explore the countryside. The visitor centre has its own pottery offering factory tours, and the local Glenturret Distillery, founded in 1775, has a visitor centre and tours round the premises.

West of Crieff, on the A85, is Comrie, a pretty village surrounded by wooded crags.

ⅰ *High Street*

▶ *Continue on the **A85** for 19 miles (31km) to Lochearnhead.*

7 Lochearnhead, Stirling Lochearnhead, at the western end of Loch Earn, was developed when the railway was built through Glen Ogle. The line's route can be followed through the glen – look out for the massive boulders that have tumbled down the hillside and must have threatened the trains that chugged up the steep incline. Near the village, where the Burn of Ample meets the loch, stands Edinample Castle, which was built in 1630.

Crieff's local Glenturret Distillery

▶ *Leave by the **A84** and follow it for 14 miles (23km) to Callander.*

8 **Callander,** Stirling
This is one of Central Scotland's busiest little resorts as it is a favourite stopping place for many visitors.

The town stands by the banks of the River Teith and has many good walks near by.

Serious walkers head for Ben Ledi, which dominates the local scenery at 2,882 feet (879m), or the rather higher Ben Vorlich, at 3,231 feet (985m), which stands between Callander town and Loch Earn.

Much of the town was laid out in the 18th century as a planned village with its centre at Ancaster Square, which now houses the Rob Roy and Trossachs Visitor Centre. Rob Roy MacGregor (1671–1734) was a most intriguing character and the hero of Sir Walter Scott's novel *Rob Roy*. The story of Rob Roy's life is intertwined with legend and Scott's artistic licence. However, he did represent the last flings of Gaeldom

against the encroaching 'civilisation' of the Highlands by English and lowland Scottish 'culture' as well as naked economic and political might. At the end of the 17th century the king, William of Orange, was determined to subdue the Highlanders and even took the step of proscribing the name MacGregor. Rob Roy then used his mother's clan name of Campbell and allied himself with his kinsman, the Duke of Argyll, in feuds with the Duke of Montrose. When Montrose chased him out of his home, he turned his hand from cattle-

The summit of Ben Ledi, viewed from Duke's Pass

dealing to reiving (cattle-raiding), earning a reputation as the Scots' equivalent of Robin Hood, stealing from the rich landowners and giving the money to destitute Highlanders.

i *Rob Roy and Trossachs Visitor Centre, Ancaster Square (seasonal)*

▶ *Return along the A84 and then turn left at the A821. After passing the Trossachs Hotel, follow the signs (right) to Loch Katrine.*

9 Loch Katrine, Stirling
The loch lies in the heart of the area known as the Trossachs, though the name is properly given to the little pass between lochs Achray and Katrine. Its fame as a beauty spot stemmed from Sir Walter Scott's description of it in the poem *The Lady of the Lake*; Dorothy Wordsworth and others also described its charms. The road between the loch and Aberfoyle is known as the Duke's Pass, as it was built in the 19th century by the Duke of Montrose to cater for the ever-increasing number of visitors, drawn here after reading Scott's work.

The loch is one of the main sources of Glasgow's water and the 1855 scheme to pipe this very pure water the 35 miles (56km) to the city was a massive feat of civil engineering. Today, visitors can cruise on the *Sir Walter Scott* across the waters of the loch and sail under the slopes of Ben Venue.

▶ *Return to the A821 and turn right. Follow the A821 to Aberfoyle, 7 miles (11km).*

10 Aberfoyle, Stirling
Aberfoyle is a tourist centre by the River Forth hemmed in by a huge conifer plantation, much of it within the Queen Elizabeth Forest Park. The 'Clachan at Aberfoyle' was one of the settings used by Scott in *Rob Roy*

Local attraction to be sampled at Aberfoyle

(a clachan is a hamlet). The village's Scottish Wool Centre features many varieties of sheep bred in Scotland.

i *Trossachs Discovery Centre, Main Street (seasonal)*

A steamer trip on the *Sir Walter Scott* provides a splendid view of Loch Katrine

▶ *Continue on the A821 and the A81. Follow this back to Glasgow, 29 miles (47km).*

FOR HISTORY BUFFS

To the east of Aberfoyle lies the Lake of Menteith, one of only a handful of 'lakes' in Scotland. On one of the lake's islands, Inchmahome, stands the Priory of Inchmahome, founded in 1238. Mary, Queen of Scots was sent to the island at the age of five, prior to sailing to France in 1547. The island can be reached by ferry from the Port of Menteith.

Abbeys,
Battlefields & Castles

This tour covers many of the historic sights which make up Scotland's bloody history. Strategically positioned on the eastern route into the Highlands, Stirling saw two great battles during the Wars of Independence – in 1297 at Stirling Bridge and in 1314 at Bannockburn.

1/2 DAYS • 91 MILES • 148KM

i *41 Dumbarton Road; Castle Esplanade; M9/M80 Junction 9 Pirnhall Motorway Service Area (seasonal)*

FOR CHILDREN

The Blair Drummond Safari and Leisure Park is to be found to the northwest of Stirling, on the flat agricultural land of the Carse of Stirling. The most fascinating part of the park is the drive round the main enclosure, where you can observe wild animals such as lions, zebra and deer roaming around at very close quarters; don't be surprised if you find there are monkeys clambering all over your car!

▶ *Leave by the **A9** and follow it for 1 mile (2km) to Causewayhead.*

❶ Causewayhead, Stirling
This small village is dominated by the Abbey Craig, upon which is perched the 220-foot (67m) high Wallace Monument, erected in tribute to Sir William Wallace, victor of the Battle of Stirling Bridge. The top of the monument gives an outstanding view of the district. Close to the village in a meander of the Forth stands the ruined Cambuskenneth Abbey, founded around 1147.

▶ *Continue on the **A9**. Just before Dunblane, turn right at a roundabout at the end of the **M9** and follow the **B8033**. Take a signposted road on the left into the village, 5 miles (8km).*

❷ Dunblane, Stirling
The cathedral, which is situated near Allan Water, was founded around 1150 and its presence raises the status of what is essentially just a village to that of a small city. The story of the cathedral and Dunblane is told in an interesting little museum that stands

Costume pageant at the Queen Mary Gardens, Stirling Castle

Panoramic view of the ramparts of Stirling Castle and the Church of the Holy Rude

opposite the cathedral. To the west lies the quiet village of Doune. Its main attraction today is the fine medieval castle.

i *Stirling Road (seasonal)*

Bird's-eye view of the impressive stronghold of Castle Campbell, Dollar

[i] Mill Trail Visitor Centre, Alva

▶ Leave by the **B913** and turn right at the **A977**. Turn right at the **A876**, heading towards Kincardine Bridge, turn left just before and follow an unclassified road along the coast to Culross.

4 Culross, Fife

Culross, frozen in time, is possibly Scotland's most remarkable town. During the 16th and 17th centuries, it prospered by trading in coal and salt with ports across the North Sea, but when this failed, the town declined. Fortunately it never really changed during the industrial development of the succeeding centuries, so although it is quite small it preserves many of the features that have been lost in other ancient towns. The NTS has played a major part in conserving this unique place, especially through its 'Little Houses Scheme', and today numerous buildings can be visited, whisking you back through the centuries. Cobbled streets and white-painted buildings with pantile roofs help to produce an air that is so very different from any other Scottish town and the virtual completeness of the medieval character of Culross has attracted many television and film companies to locations here.

The town's main building, the Palace, was never in fact a royal mansion at all, but the home of the local laird, George Bruce, and was originally built between 1597 and 1611. The title deeds describe it as 'the Palace of Great Lodging in the Sand Haven of Culross'. Among the other fascinating buildings here, visitors should look out for the Town House, the Study, the House of the Evil Eye and the abbey.

▶ Continue on the unclassified road, then turn right at the **B9037**. Join the **A994**, which leads to Dunfermline (7 miles/11km).

SCENIC ROUTES

The journey through Glen Eagles and Glen Devon is the most scenic part of the tour, with the road making its way through the heart of the Ochils. Two misconceptions about Glen Eagles should be explained: firstly, the name means 'churches' and not 'eagles' and secondly, the golfing hotel of Gleneagles is not here but near Auchterarder.

▶ Return to the **B8033** and turn left. Join the **A9** and head towards Perth. Turn right at the **A823**, then right at the **A91** in order to enter Dollar.

3 Dollar, Clackmannanshire

This neat little town lies in a sheltered position at the foot of the Ochil Hills and one of its chief attractions is the wooded Dollar Glen, through which a path runs to Castle Campbell. This stands on a promontory overlooking the confluence of two streams, intriguingly named the Burn of Sorrow and the Burn of Care. Until 1490 it was called Castle Glume, hence it is sometimes referred to as the 'castle of gloom'.

Dollar is one of the Hillfoot towns, small mill towns which gained prosperity through the woollen industry. A mill trail links these communities and guides visitors through the district. The Mill Trail Visitor Centre at Alva is the focal point of this trail and it has displays explaining the history of the local woollen industry.

5 Dunfermline, Fife
Dunfermline was built around a substantial Benedictine abbey which was constructed in the 12th century. Apart from the abbey church, there are the ruins of the monastery's domestic buildings and the palace, which was often used as the abbey's guest house. The abbey church was a favoured place with the Scottish kings and it superseded Iona as their place of burial. The great warrior King Robert the Bruce was buried here but it was only in 1818 that this fact was known for certain. During some restoration work, a skeleton, dressed in what may have been royal robes, was discovered and it was noticed that the breast bone had been sawn in order to remove one of the organs. This would have been in accordance with Bruce's deathbed wish in 1329 that upon his death his heart be removed and taken to the Holy Land as his way of making up for not taking part in the Crusades. His heart was buried in Melrose Abbey. Abbot House was the administrative centre of the abbey and it now has a new lease of life as a museum depicting its use over the centuries. Opposite the door of the abbey church is the entrance to the extensive and pleasant Pittencrieff Park. Within the grounds is Pittencrieff House, built in the 17th century. There is a small museum of local history with an art gallery and a costume exhibition here.

SPECIAL TO...

There can be few bridges in the world so distinctive in appearance as the Forth Rail Bridge, which can be seen from many places on this route. This was the world's first major structure to be made entirely of steel and it took eight years, from 1883 to 1890, to erect. It is over 1½ miles (2.5km) long and from mid-winter to mid-summer it expands by 3 feet!

Just by the edge of the park stands the cottage where Andrew Carnegie was born in 1835. In 1848 his family emigrated to the US where he made his massive fortune in the steel industry. He then began to give much of his wealth away, buying Pittencrieff Park for the town and establishing trusts that endowed libraries and other public enterprises. The cottage is now the location of the Andrew Carnegie Birthplace Museum.

Detail of the plaque 'Discovery' at the Carnegie Birthplace Museum

The great fortress of Blackness Castle looking out over the North Sea

[i] 13–15 Maygate (seasonal)

▶ Leave by the **A823** and the **A823M**, then join the **M90** to cross the Forth Road Bridge (toll). Turn right on to the **A904**, then right along the **B903** to Blackness (14 miles/23 km).

6 Blackness, West Lothian
The little village of Blackness, once an important seaport, is dominated by the great fortress of Blackness Castle. This was built to protect the port which was the harbour for the great royal palace at Linlithgow. Construction of the castle started as a fairly small affair in the 15th century, but with later technical improvements in artillery it became necessary to strengthen it to withstand massive sea-borne attacks. After the Union with England in 1707, it was one of the four castles in Scotland allowed to be left fortified.

▶ Return until the **A904** is met. Turn left on to the **A904** and then follow the **A803** to Linlithgow.

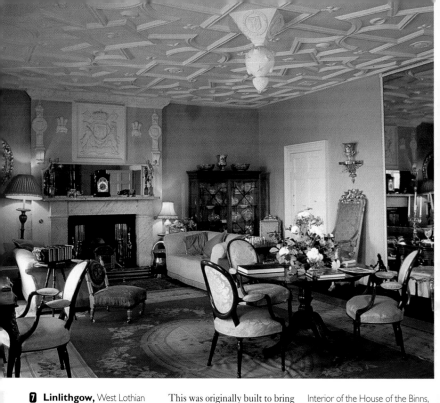

7 **Linlithgow,** West Lothian

The history of the town is intimately interwoven with that of the palace, the birthplace of Mary, Queen of Scots, and one of the country's most important historical buildings. There was some form of royal residence here in the 14th century, but the present palace was not started until the early 16th century. It was certainly a substantial and well-defended building, occupying an attractive site overlooking Linlithgow Loch. Everything seems to have been constructed to a grand scale, especially the enormous fireplaces and the ornate fountain that stands in the quadrangle in the heart of the building.

Linlithgow has a number of other fine buildings and monuments sited near the palace or on the main street and these include the Church of St Michael, the Burgh Halls, the House of the Binns and the Cross Well. The history of the town is told in The Linlithgow Story.

The Union Canal, which joined the Forth and Clyde Canal to the heart of Edinburgh, runs along the town's outskirts.

This was originally built to bring coal from Lanarkshire into the capital. Work on the canal started in 1818 and it opened in 1822, finally closing in 1965. Today there is a canal museum at the Manse Road Basin and cruises are available.

i *Burgh Halls, The Cross (seasonal)*

▶ *Leave by the A706 to Bo'ness.*

8 **Bo'ness,** Falkirk

This long-established industrial town was once the third most important seaport in Scotland until the building of the Forth and Clyde Canal and the establishment of the major port at Grangemouth put it into decline. Bo'ness's past has included such diverse enterprises as potteries, salt pans, iron foundries and coal mines and it is most appropriate that the town's visitor facilities have taken advantage of this rich industrial legacy. It is possible to walk through the tunnels of the Birkhill Clay Mine, accessible via the Bo'ness and Kinneil Railway, which operates steam trains on its 3½-mile (6km) track, that runs along the foreshore.

Interior of the House of the Binns, Linlithgow, the historic home of the Dalyell family

i *Car Park, Seaview Place*

▶ *Leave by the A904 and turn right at the A905. Turn left at the A88 and right at the A9. Continue on this road towards Stirling and turn left at the A872 to reach the NTS Visitor Centre at Bannockburn.*

One of the old trains on Bo'ness's steam railway

9 Bannockburn, Stirling
The Battle of Bannockburn in 1314 was one of the most important events in the fight for Scottish independence. At the time, an English force held Stirling Castle and was being besieged by Robert the Bruce's brother. The English army, led by their king, came north to relieve the castle and a pitched battle took place here. The Scots army, led by Bruce, eventually routed the enemy after they took fright at seeing a 'new' army (in reality, the Scots camp followers) come over the Gillies Hill. The story of the battle and the history of that period is explained in the NTS's Heritage Centre and the impressive memorial to the battle is in the form of a bronze equestrian statue of Bruce erected where his command post is thought to have been positioned.

☐ *NTS Visitor Centre*

▶ *Return along the A872 and turn left at the B8051 to Stirling.*

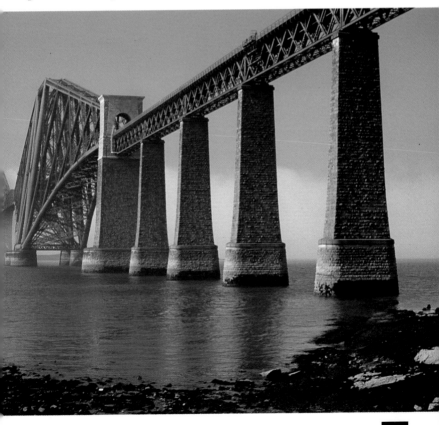

A dramatic view of the Forth Rail Bridge

Raspberry Fields
Forever

1/2 DAYS • 120 MILES • 192KM The land circling the Sidlaw
Hills is an area often overlooked by tourists, yet it has much to
offer in terms of pretty coastal villages and green, gentle countryside. The renowned 'Fair City' of Perth is the chief town of
this important farming region,
and is located in a most
attractive setting beside the
River Tay.

UNI ÆQUUS VIRTUTI

ⓘ *Lower City Mills, West Mill Street, Perth; Caithness Glass Car Park, Inveralmond, by the A9*

▶ *Leave by the A912 and join the A9 (to Inverness). Turn right at the A923 and follow this into Dunkeld (15 miles/24km).*

❶ **Dunkeld,** Perth & Kinross
The history of Dunkeld goes back to Pictish times but the town's importance in Scottish history is as Kenneth MacAlpin's ecclesiastical capital in the 9th century. This eventually led to the construction, in the early 14th century, of the cathedral which stands by the banks of the River Tay. Although much of it is roofless, the choir was restored and within it is the tomb of Alexander Stewart, the notorious 'Wolf of Badenoch'.

In the centre of Dunkeld stands a very ornate fountain and between this and the cathedral are the Little Houses, which were built in the late 17th century. Look out for the NTS's The Ell Shop on whose wall is an original ell measure, a little over a metre long, which was used for measuring cloth. Beside

it The Duchess Anne, formerly a school, is the venue for the cathedral art exhibition each summer.

ⓘ *The Cross*

▶ *Continue on the A923 and follow it for 11 miles (18km) to Blairgowrie.*

Detail from the window above the altar in Dunkeld Cathedral

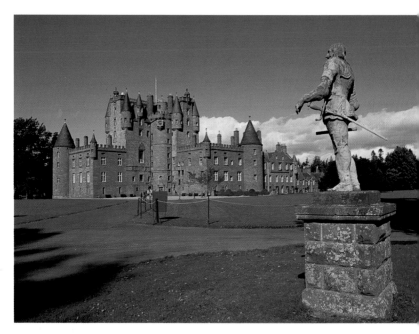

The wonderfully ornate Glamis Castle, childhood home of the late Queen Mother

2 Blairgowrie, Perth & Kinross

Blairgowrie is well situated as a touring centre, lying at the junction of five roads. The district's most remarkable feature is just 5 miles (8km) to the south on the A93: the magnificent Meikleour Beech Hedge. This was originally planted in 1746 and is now some 110 feet (33m) high and 2,000 feet (600m) long. It is trimmed back once every 10 years.

ℹ️ *26 Wellmeadow*

▶ *Leave by the **A926** then turn right at the **B954** to Meigle.*

3 Meigle, Perth & Kinross

For such a small village, the local museum has a remarkable collection of carved stones. More than 30 significant stones have been found in the area and these portray ancient symbols such as Pictish beasts, a Persian god and a horseman. The dates vary, but most of them are from the 8th to 10th centuries.

To add further interest to the local history, the village may have had connections with King Arthur – his consort, Queen Guinevere, is believed to be buried here (a claim also made by Glastonbury).

▶ *Leave by the **A94** to approach Glamis, then take a minor road on the left to reach the village and the castle.*

4 Glamis, Angus

Glamis Castle, the childhood home of the late Queen Mother, and birthplace of the late Princess Margaret, is an excellent example of a large medieval tower house that has, over the centuries, been transformed into a palace. The long

straight driveway leads directly up to its rather small entrance, an approach that seems to emphasise the symmetrical structure of the castle.

In comparison to the castle and its grand style of living, the village of Glamis houses the Angus Folk Museum. This occupies a row of 18th-century cottages and consists of rooms furnished as in bygone days. There are, for example, a kitchen, laundry, schoolhouse and a forge, all with appropriate equipment.

▶ *Continue on the **A94**, then turn left on to the **A90**. Bear right at the **A935** to enter Brechin (17 miles/27km).*

5 Brechin, Angus

The pleasant town of Brechin, with its many red sandstone buildings, lies in the heart of the rich agricultural area of Strathmore. Its most interesting feature is the tall, slim Round Tower, one of only two in Scotland. It dates from the 11th century and stands beside the remains of the 13th-century cathedral.

ⓘ Brechin Castle (seasonal)

▶ Continue on the **A935** and follow it for 5 miles (8km) to the House of Dun. (The driveway is to the left.)

6 House of Dun, Angus
This 18th-century house was designed by William Adam, father of the Adam brothers who designed so many important buildings in Scotland. Restored by the NTS, it now reflects how it would have looked over 250 years ago with its public rooms featuring a wealth of exceptionally ornate baroque plasterwork.

▶ Continue on the **A935**, then turn right at the **A92** for Montrose.

7 Montrose, Angus
Montrose's wide main street lends an air of spaciousness to this seaside town. Its history, going back to the 10th century, owes much to the Montrose Basin, which gave the town a uniquely strategic position on the east coast. It has been an important port for a long time and its economy enjoyed a boost from the North Sea oil industry. Of interest to most visitors is the town's beach, which is backed by sand dunes.

ⓘ Bridge Street (seasonal)

▶ Continue on the **A92** and follow it to Arbroath.

FOR CHILDREN

The seaside resorts have good beaches but one 'remoter' stretch of sand can be found at the village of Lunan. The car park at Lunan Bay's superb beach is reached by turning seawards just as the village is entered.

8 Arbroath, Angus
Arbroath is a busy seaside town which attracts many visitors each summer. It also has an active fishing industry and this is the home of the delicious 'Arbroath smokie', a line-caught haddock that is smoke-cured using oak chips. The town's place in Scottish history was assured by the Declaration of Arbroath, a document drawn up in 1320 to state the independence of Scotland after the Battle of Bannockburn in 1314. The declaration was drawn up in the abbey, originally a priory founded in the 12th century.

ⓘ Market Place

▶ Continue on the **A92**, then turn left at the **A930** to enter Carnoustie.

9 Carnoustie, Angus
Carnoustie's fame as a resort is based on its extensive beach and the golf courses which lie on the sandy links. The championship courses have hosted the British and Scottish Open events.

ⓘ 1B High Street (seasonal)

▶ Continue on the **A930** to Dundee.

10 Dundee, Dundee City
The old saying that the industrial town of Dundee is famous for jute, jam and journalism is less correct these days as the town's prosperity is now based on a much broader spectrum of industries, the jute mills having been converted into luxury flats. Its coastal site has meant that the sea has always been of importance and many wooden ships for the whaling industry were built here. These ships had to withstand cruel polar conditions and this expertise was used in 1901 to build Captain Scott's ship *Discovery*, now berthed alongside the Discovery Point Visitor Centre. In the nearby Victoria Dock is the frigate *Unicorn*, built in 1825. The city's history is told in the McManus Galleries, which hold the local art collection. The galleries also house a natural history collection that includes the skeleton of a whale. The city's connections with the whaling industry are displayed in the 15th-century Broughty Castle Museum, appropriately sited by the Firth of Tay.

ⓘ 21 Castle Street

▶ Leave by the **A85**, then turn left along the **A90** for the return to Perth.

SCENIC ROUTES

Hills are never very far away from much of this route and the views of the Sidlaw Hills and the foothills of the Grampian Mountains are good. On the drive to Dunkeld, it is interesting to note that the road is approaching a distinctive line of hills. These mark the geological boundary called the Highland Boundary Fault and indicate the 'real' start of the Scottish Highlands.

Scott's ship *Discovery*, berthed at Discovery Point

The Kingdom
of Fife

1/2 DAYS • 97 MILES • 156KM   Surrounded by the firths of Forth and Tay, the most important town in the Kingdom of Fife is undoubtedly St Andrews. Famous primarily for being the golfing capital of the world and home to the Royal & Ancient Golf Club, St Andrews is also the location of Britain's third oldest university after Oxford and Cambridge, founded in 1410. The rest of the region is dominated by pretty fishing villages and much land is given over to agriculture.

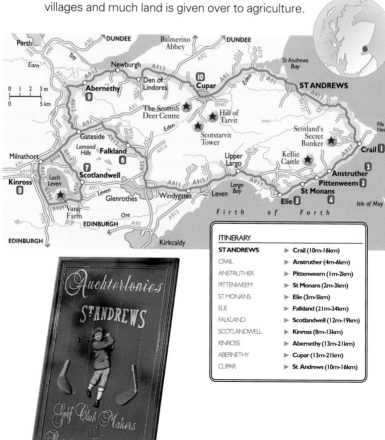

ITINERARY		
ST ANDREWS	►	Crail (10m-16km)
CRAIL	►	Anstruther (4m-6km)
ANSTRUTHER	►	Pittenweem (1m-2km)
PITTENWEEM	►	St Monans (2m-3km)
ST MONANS	►	Elie (3m-5km)
ELIE	►	Falkland (21m-34km)
FALKLAND	►	Scotlandwell (12m-19km)
SCOTLANDWELL	►	Kinross (8m-13km)
KINROSS	►	Abernethy (13m-21km)
ABERNETHY	►	Cupar (13m-21km)
CUPAR	►	St Andrews (10m-16km)

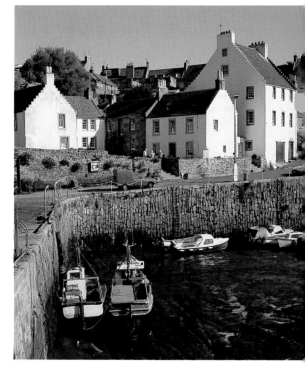

Crow-stepped and pantiled houses cluster round Crail harbour, once the haunt of smugglers

[i] 70 Market Street

❶ Crail, Fife
Crail's small harbour is a delightful place set at the bottom of a steep lane. The Museum and Heritage Centre tells the story of the village. Another attraction is the working pottery, occupying restored medieval buildings.

[i] *Crail Museum and Heritage Centre (seasonal)*

▶ *Follow the **A917** for 4 miles (6km) to Anstruther.*

❷ Anstruther, Fife
The Scottish Fisheries Museum on the seafront tells the story of the fishing industry in this part of the country. In the harbour is one of the museum's great attractions, the fishing boat *The Reaper*. To the north is Scotland's Secret Bunker, where visitors can explore the 100-foot (30m) deep labyrinth created to house government and military bosses in the event of nuclear war.

[i] *Scottish Fisheries Museum, Harbourhead (seasonal)*

▶ *Continue on the **A917** for 1 mile (1.5km) to Pittenweem.*

Laid-up fishing boat being painted

❸ Pittenweem, Fife
There is always lots to see in Pittenweem, the busiest fishing port along this coast, when the boats are coming in with their catches. Herring used to be the major catch here but now the fishermen concentrate on whitefish.

The religious buildings date back many centuries: the parish church's tower was built in the 16th century and there are remains of a 12th-century priory where witches were 'done to death'.

Nearby St Fillan's Cave is said to be the 7th-century sanctuary of St Fillan. It gave Pittenweem its name (Pittenweem is Pictish for The Place of the Cave).

To the north of Pittenweem stands Kellie Castle, dating from 1360, which has very pleasant sheltered gardens.

▶ *Continue on the **A917** for 2 miles (3km) to St Monans.*

❹ St Monans, Fife
St Monans (or St Monance) is a pleasant fishing town, with houses clustered around the local harbour – and its kirk standing almost in the sea.

One rather unusual feature of the town is that it has fewer licensed premises than neighbouring villages, the result of the town being 'dry' between 1900 and 1947. The 18th-century windmill tower is all that remains of a more extensive industrial complex.

▶ *Continue on the **A917** for 3 miles (5km) to Elie.*

The sands stretch away into the distance along this section of the Fife coastal walk between Elie and St Monans

RECOMMENDED WALKS

The path from St Monans to Elie offers an interesting route past St Monans' church and the ruins of two castles, and ends at Elie Ness where there is a fine view of the village. Inland, the walk to the top of East Lomond gives good views over the countryside.

5 Elie, Fife

This appealing resort offers fine sandy beaches and bathing, golf courses and shelter to the yachts that lie in the harbour. The sea has not always been kind to Elie and the houses along the bay have high walls to protect them. There are many fine 17th-century houses in South Street.

▶ Continue on the **A917** to Upper Largo, then join the **A915** to Windygates. Join the **A911** and head towards Glenrothes. Turn right at a roundabout at the junction with the **A92** and head northwards. Turn left when the **A912** is met and follow this to Falkland.

6 Falkland, Fife

The village of Falkland is dominated by the very grand palace, which was originally erected by the Stuarts as a royal hunting seat. It dates from the 16th century and stands on a site that has been fortified from the 13th century. The buildings on the southern side of the main courtyard are in French Renaissance style, and are arguably the best of their kind in Britain. They are in a fine state of preservation and have some excellent furnishings; the painted wooden ceilings are particularly good. Within the grounds is a Royal Tennis Court, built in 1539 for James V, before rackets were invented.

The village itself has numerous fascinating small houses, many of them dating back to the 17th and 18th centuries.

▶ Continue on the **A912** and turn left at the **A91** and left again at the **B919**. Turn left at the **A911** and follow it to Scotlandwell.

SCENIC ROUTE

The Fife Coastal Tourist Route has been devised and signposted by the Scottish Tourist Board (look for the special brown signs). It guides visitors along a scenic journey through pretty ports, historic towns and rolling farmland between the Kincardine and Tay road bridges, taking in views of the Isle of May, the Bass Rock and distant Edinburgh.

7 Scotlandwell, Perth & Kinross

The village is named after the well to which pilgrims travelled during medieval times. Roman soldiers are said to have drunk from it in AD 84. However, the present stone cistern dates back only to the 19th century.

▶ Leave by the **B920** and turn right at the **B9097**. On meeting the **B996**, turn right and follow it to Kinross.

8 Kinross, Perth & Kinross

Kinross, the county town of the former Kinross-shire, stands by the shores of Loch Leven, the largest loch in the Scottish low-lands. Of the two largest islands in the loch, St Serf's Island has the remains of a 9th-century priory.

Castle Island is rather nearer the town and can be reached by a local ferry. On it stands Loch Leven Castle, best known as the prison from which Mary, Queen of Scots made her escape in 1568. The castle dates from the 14th century and the building and its garden used to occupy the whole of the island until in the early 19th century the loch's level was lowered, increasing the size of the island. The castle, a five-storey keep, was occupied for about 250 years but was roof-less by the end of the 17th century. Kinross town is domi-nated by imposing Kinross House.

i Kinross Service Area, Junc 6, M90

▶ *Continue on the B996 and join the A922. After Milnathort, follow the B996 then the A91. Turn left at the A912 and right at the A913 to Abernethy.*

Loch Leven Castle, prison to Mary, Queen of Scots

9 Abernethy, Perth & Kinross
One of the main features of this quiet little village is the 11th-century round tower, very similar to Brechin's. Abernethy may have been an important centre in Pictish times and several symbol stones have been found in the vicinity; one of them is set against the wall of the tower.

▶ *Continue on the A913 and follow it for 13 miles (21km) to Cupar.*

10 Cupar, Fife
It is rather surprising that this little town, and not St Andrews, was the county town of Fife, but this was due to its central position and because it was the seat of the Thanes of Fife.

Cupar must surely have a place in the history of drama as it was here in 1535 that the first public performance of the satire *Ane satire of the Thrie Estaits* took place. This scorned the church, the nobility and the burgesses of the towns. The play has certainly stood the test of time and it is still performed on the Scottish stage.

To the south of Cupar stands the Hill of Tarvit, a mansion

house under the ownership of the NTS. The present building was constructed at the beginning of the 20th century to house a fine collection of antique furniture, much of it French. In contrast to all the finery, the restored Edwardian laundry holds a special fascination for most visitors.

To the west of it is Scotstarvit Tower, a well-preserved five-storey tower house built in the 17th century.

▶ *Leave by the A91 and follow it back to St Andrews.*

FOR CHILDREN

The Scottish Deer Centre at Rankeilour Park includes trailer rides around the park and close encounters with many species of deer.
This is also the home of Raptor World, which offers three flying demonstrations a day, Bird of Prey Experience days and handling sessions which bring visitors close to a variety of owls, hawks and falcons. The park also has indoor and outdoor playgrounds.

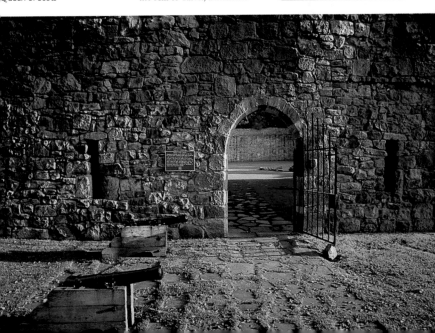

THE NORTHEAST

The Cairngorm Mountains, Britain's highest land mass, dominate the northeast of Scotland in many ways. The great glaciers that flowed down from these granite hills during the Ice Age cut their way through the rock, leaving behind a series of river valleys that radiate out from the mountains and flow down to the sea.

In days gone by, it was easier to travel by sea than land and this encouraged coastal settlements to prosper wherever there was a sheltered harbour and the opportunity to trade with other ports, notably those in countries across the North Sea. Today, this coastline boasts some of Britain's most important fishing harbours. But while the fishing industry is long established, it is the North Sea oil developments that have transformed the Aberdeen area and made that city Scotland's 'oil capital'.

The northeast lies in the hills' rain shadow, making this region much drier than the west coast and helping to produce some of Scotland's most profitable farming land. Agriculture continues to be an important industry and much of the region's population lives in scattered towns and villages set among good agricultural land.

The often turbulent times of the Middle Ages saw the establishment of a class of rich farmers, warriors and traders who built keeps, castles and fortified houses. In time, many of these were destroyed while others were extended and embellished and some later transformed into great country houses. Today, we are left with a rich legacy of castles, large and small, reflecting the changing fortunes of family, clan and nation.

The wide variety of landscapes is reflected in the wildlife found in the region. The hills and the high forests are home to deer and birds of prey while the coast, with its sandstone cliffs providing ledges for nesting birds, has countless millions of seabirds.

Walkers, birdwatchers, families seeking tranquil beaches and visitors simply touring around will all find lots to do in this corner of Scotland. To many foreign visitors, Scotland is famous as the home of whisky and in the northeast a number of internationally famous distilleries are linked together by the 'Malt Whisky Trail', which allows people to learn the secrets of the whisky-making process and inevitably to enjoy a 'wee dram' at the end of a distillery tour.

Traditional Scotsware is sold at MacNaughton's shop at Pitlochry

Farming exhibits from the Falconer Museum, Forres

the small picture-postcard ones like charming Crovie to the big, bustling Peterhead. Each has its own fascination and each reflects the ways in which the sea has been so important to the people of this area. Behind this, the rich countryside, with its landscape of rolling hills, has prosperous farming towns and villages. The long history of settlement in this part of the country is marked by the existence of prehistoric stone circles.

Tour 17

The fact that this tour is the longest one in the region reflects the sheer scale of the Cairngorms. Motorists have to drive round the margins of the hills, but this does allow the visitor many different opportunities to explore the small glens that cut into the sides of these great mountains. There is much variety on the route; the traditional highland resort of Pitlochry, the more modern Aviemore and the small villages that lie to the east. Walkers will find much to keep them busy on this tour as will followers of other outdoor pursuits.

Tour 18

The visitor to this part of the country might be forgiven for getting the impression there's a castle round every corner! But the district has more to offer than fine old buildings; there are peaceful villages, a rugged coastline and rich agricultural countryside to explore.

A splendid border at Crathes Castle Gardens

Tour 14

nverness's strategic position at he meeting point of so many and and sea routes has meant hat the town and its surrounding district have seen the omings and goings of many different people. Picts, Vikings and warring Scots clans have all eft their mark, but the most ignificant historical event, the attle of Culloden in 1746, has eft its mark all over Scotland; in order to understand the history of the Highlands, the battlefields should be visited. This our encompasses a wide variety of scenery, from the glorious sandy beaches of the Moray Firth to the pine forests that lie below the Cairngorms, which attract tourists throughout the year.

Tour 15

The seaside towns and villages of Moray have much to offer the visitor: picturesque harbours, sandy beaches and a wealth of traditional buildings that give the district its own particular charm. Inland, the districts by the peaty waters of the River Spey are home to many of Scotland's most celebrated whisky distilleries.

Tour 16

The coastal part of this route visits a variety of harbours, from

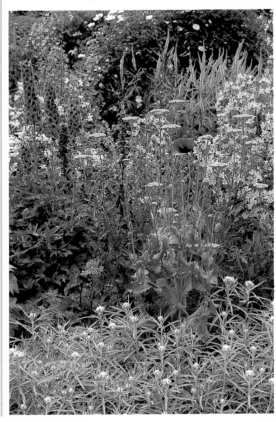

Land of
Macbeth

1/2 DAYS • 106 MILES • 169KM History and magnificent scenery are ever present on this tour. Just outside Inverness lies Culloden, where the defeat of Bonnie Prince Charlie ruined the last hope of a Stuart restoration to the British throne. Mysteries, too, abound on this tour, from brooding Cawdor Castle, of which Shakespeare's Macbeth was Thane, to the dark waters of Loch Ness, perhaps home to Britain's most famous monster.

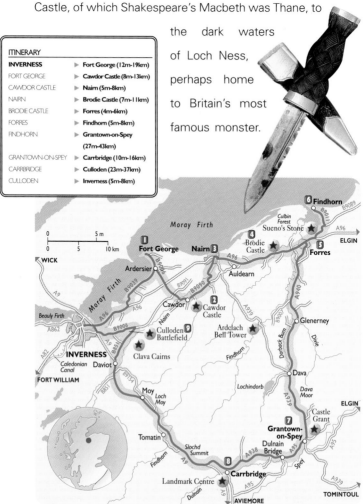

i *Castle Wynd*

▶ *Leave on the **A96**. Turn left at
the **B9039** to reach Ardersier,
then take the **B9006** to Fort
George, a distance of 12
miles (19km).*

1 **Fort George,** Highland
This outstanding piece of military architecture, which is still used by the army, was originally built between 1748 and 1769, after the Battle of Culloden. It was guarded by 2,000 men and it has a series of walls, ramparts and ditches cleverly designed so that an attacking army would come under fire from several positions within the safety of the fort. It controls the seaward approach to Inverness as it is sited on a promontory that juts into the Moray Firth; this is rather fortunate for visitors as it allows good views across the firth to the Black Isle.

The fort is impressively huge, indeed the whole of Edinburgh Castle could fit into the parade ground! Since the fort has never seen military action, very few alterations have been made to its layout and a number of original buildings have been opened to visitors.

The B9006, which leads to the fort, was one of the military roads built by Caulfield in the 18th century when the government was trying to 'tame' this area. It follows the much older Via Regis (King's Road) which came from Aberdeen and crossed the Moray Firth to Chanonry Point at Fortrose.

▶ *Return to Ardersier, then
follow the **B9006** and the
B9090 to Cawdor Castle,
8 miles (13km).*

2 **Cawdor Castle,** Highland
The castle is dominated by the great 14th-century tower. Later additions had far less of a defensive role to play since they were built in less turbulent times. Still, the castle has many of the features that might be expected of a fortified house such as a drawbridge, a moat and a prison that was reached only by a trap door. The proprietors of Cawdor were called the Thanes of Cawdor, a title given by Shakespeare to Macbeth, but there is still much speculation about the real nature of this warrior king.

To the west stands 15th-century Kilravock Castle, a massive tower with walls some 7 feet (2m) thick. The tower has survived through the centuries, despite the laird backing the losing side at Culloden, and the victor, Cumberland, paying it a visit after the battle. Few castles in a similar position survived a visit by the 'Butcher'.

The Woodcock Room at
Cawdor Castle

▶ *Continue on the **B9090** and follow it to Nairn.*

❸ Nairn, Highland
This popular holiday resort, situated where the River Nairn meets the Moray Firth, has a fine beach, good golf course and activities for family holidays. Charlie Chaplin's favourite holiday resort for many years, it is a prosperous town, with large villas and hotels behind the main centre. Nearer the shore, the former fishermen's houses are tightly packed together in Fishertown, where there is a small museum.

To the east, the village of Auldearn was the site of a major battle in 1645 when the Royalist army defeated a force of Covenanters. The battleground can be seen from the top of a 12th-century motte, upon which now sits a 17th-century doocot (dovecot) which has 546 nest holes for pigeons.

[i] *62 King Street (seasonal)*

▶ *Leave by the **A96** and turn left at the entrance to Brodie Castle.*

The golf course at Nairn

FOR HISTORY BUFFS

Highland Ardclach Bell Tower, southeast of Nairn, off the A939, was built in 1655 when the local laird, a Covenanter, was continually being harassed by Royalists. The tower served both as a prison and a watchtower and its bell was used to summon people to the local church.

BACK TO NATURE

Culbin Forest is a large conifer plantation between Nairn and Findhorn, planted in order to stabilise the area of shifting sand. The dunes increased in size during the 17th century and inundated the village of Culbin and its surrounding rich farmland. The forest is now home to varied wildlife, like badgers and capercaillie. Woodland plants include coralroot and twayblade orchids.

❹ Brodie Castle, Moray
Originally, the castle had a Z-plan design, based on a rectangular block with square projecting towers at two opposite corners. This structure, dated 1567, was later added to and has seen many alterations over the centuries. Inside the castle is a good collection of 17th-, 18th- and 19th-century paintings, porcelain and French furniture.

At the eastern entrance to the castle stands the Pictish Rodney's Stone, decorated with a Pictish beast and fish monster.

▶ *Regain the **A96** and continue on it to Forres.*

❺ Forres, Moray
Forres' street pattern gives clues to the town's antiquity, with a main street wide enough to accommodate a market place and narrow 'wynds' linking the medieval streets. High Street is dominated by the Town House of 1838, built on the site of the old Tolbooth, and the market cross which was erected in 1844. The Falconer Museum in Tolbooth Street has displays of

ocal history, natural history and geology.

The town's main antiquity ies just to the east of Forres, as he B9011 leaves the A96. This s Sueno's Stone, a huge cross-lab monument, over 20 feet 6m) high, carved out of a block of sandstone. It may date back to he 9th century and celebrate a victory by the men of Moray over Vikings based in Orkney.

i 116 High Street (seasonal)

▶ *Continue on the A96 then turn left at the B9011 and follow this to Findhorn.*

Findhorn, Moray
This is the third village on this ite to be called Findhorn. The irst was destroyed by the sea and the second was inundated by shifting sand. The people rebuilt the village near the sea and it was once a prominent port, but its harbour is now given

As well as its many treasures, Brodie Castle also has extensive grounds and a playground

over to pleasure craft. The beaches here are extensive, with huge stretches of sand and dunes along the coast on either side of the estuary.

▶ *Return along the B9011 and A96 to Forres. Head south on the A940 and join the A939 for Grantown-on-Spey, 27 miles (43km).*

7 Grantown-on-Spey, Highland
This prosperous village, with its sturdy granite buildings along the main street, is a good touring centre for the district. It began as a planned village and from the start gained a reputation as a

place to which Victorian doctors would send patients who were in need of a change of air. Today it is noted for its salmon-fishing, and walkers; anglers and families frequent the village during the summer, while in winter it accommodates skiers, Aviemore being only a short drive away.

Grantown Museum and Heritage Trust, opened in early 1999, illustrates the story of Grantown with exciting displays.

i 54 High Street (seasonal)

▶ *Leave on the A95 towards Aviemore, and at Dulnain Bridge turn on to the A938 to Carrbridge.*

SPECIAL TO...

The thistle may be the symbol of Scotland, but heather is equally significant – in landscape, song and the hearts of homesick Highlanders. Visit the Speyside Heather Centre to find out all there is to know.

FOR CHILDREN

As well as being endowed with long sandy beaches which will keep children busy for hours on end, Findhorn is a centre for water sports, with sailing, rowing, windsurfing and water skiing available.

RECOMMENDED WALKS

Grantown-on-Spey has many opportunities for walking, either through forests and woodlands or up some of the nearby hills; the Tourist Information Centre should be able to supply some details of suitable walks.

Culbin Forest has many marked walks that lead from the edge of the forest to the seashore where there are long stretches of sandy beach.

8 Carrbridge, Highland

The old bridge at Carrbridge was built in 1717 after two men drowned at the traditional ford-ing place. The bridge has since lost many of its stones and is precariously balanced over the river making it one of the most photogenic bridges in the country.

The village is a popular tour-ing centre, all the more so because of the nearby Landmark Highland Heritage and Adventure Park, an entertaining park which features Clydesdale Horse demonstrations, a steam-powered sawmill, a 70-foot (21m) fire tower, a 3-D show on 'The Great Wood of Caledon', a runaway raft ride and a forest skills area. It is set in a pine forest and has many walks, including a tree-top trail 20 feet (6m) above the ground.

▶ *Continue on the A938 and join the A9, heading towards Inverness. Just after Daviot, turn right on the B851. Turn left at the B9006 and follow it to the NTS Visitor Centre at Culloden Moor.*

9 Culloden, Highland

Many bloody battles have been fought on Scottish soil, but of all the country's battlefields, Culloden is the saddest. Here, in 1746, the last great battle fought on British soil ended forever the Jacobite hopes of regaining the British crown. It was not a battle of Scots against English, nor was it a battle between different parts of Scotland, but it was the final battle of a long civil war. In its bloody aftermath, the face of the Highlands was changed forever. After the government's victory, the might of the British army was used to subjugate Scotland and to destroy many aspects of the Highlanders' way of life.

The battlefield has been laid out to show how the government troops, led by the Duke of Cumberland, faced the army of Charles Edward Stuart (the 'Bonnie Prince Charlie' of song and legend). Displays in the visi-tor centre describe the course of that dreadful battle, and the equally violent events which followed. Various small memori-als on the battlefield indicate where particular clans were buried where they fell, but the principal monument is the Memorial Cairn, erected in 1881. The battle was fought on open moorland and Old Leanach Cottage, which was standing at the time of the battle, still remains. Its reconstructed interior illustrates how Scots people lived at the time of the battle in the mid-18th century.

A little to the east of Culloden, a minor road passes Clava Cairns, some of the most important cairns in the country. The three cairns may have been erected in the Late Stone Age or Early Bronze Age. The two outer ones are called 'passage graves' as a small passageway led through the cairn to a central chamber where bodies or cremated remains were deposited. These cairns have been topped with a massive flat slab and their perimeters were (and still are) marked by a ring of standing stones. Many of these perimeter stones have 'cup marks', small round indentations of unknown origin.

▶ *Daviot Wood, on the A9 by Inverness (seasonal)*

▶ *Continue along the B9006 to the A9. Join the A9 and return to Inverness, 5 miles (8km).*

The much-photographed pack-horse bridge at Carrbridge

The Malt Whisky
Trail

1/2 DAYS • 89 MILES • 144KM   A tour for all members of the
family, taking in as it does the wide, sandy beaches of Moray
and the famed Speyside whisky distilleries of Strathisla,
Glenfiddich and Glen Grant. The town of Elgin is the starting
point for this tour; its many fine buildings, cathedral and ruined
castle make it an ideal base which merits further exploration.
It's still possible to wander down
narrow 'wynds' that link the streets.

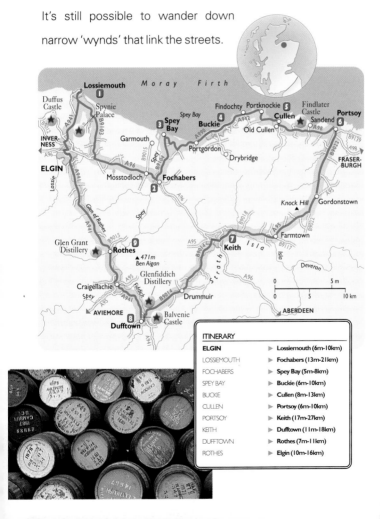

ITINERARY

ELGIN	▶	Lossiemouth (6m-10km)
LOSSIEMOUTH	▶	Fochabers (13m-21km)
FOCHABERS	▶	Spey Bay (5m-8km)
SPEY BAY	▶	Buckie (6m-10km)
BUCKIE	▶	Cullen (8m-13km)
CULLEN	▶	Portsoy (6m-10km)
PORTSOY	▶	Keith (17m-27km)
KEITH	▶	Dufftown (11m-18km)
DUFFTOWN	▶	Rothes (7m-11km)
ROTHES	▶	Elgin (10m-16km)

[i] 17 High Street

Braco's Banking House in Elgin
High Street

FOR HISTORY BUFFS

All around this area there are reminders of the trail of destruction that was left by the notorious Wolf of Badenoch, the outlawed son of Robert II, who terrorised the district in the late 14th century. Elgin's cathedral ruin is a notable example.

▶ Leave Elgin on the **A941** and follow it north to Lossiemouth.

❶ Lossiemouth, Moray
This was developed as a port for landlocked Elgin after its original port of Spynie was cut off from the sea by shifting sand. It later became important during the 19th-century herring boom but today the catches are mainly shellfish and whitefish.

Lossiemouth is now a popular seaside resort, with extensive sandy beaches, a marina and a championship golf course. The Lossiemouth Fisheries and Community Museum features many aspects of local life and also has a display dedicated to Ramsay MacDonald, Britain's first Labour Prime Minister, who was born locally.

Just inland stand the ruins of the 15th-century Palace of Spynie, once the seat of the Bishops of Moray.

Duffus Castle is to the southwest of Lossiemouth in an area of flat, fertile farmland, lying only a few feet above sea

FOR CHILDREN

The coast has many good beaches, which makes this area popular with families. Lossiemouth has two beaches; the east one is suitable for surfing while the west one offers safe bathing. Buckie, Elgin and Keith have swimming pools and pony-trekking is available at Lossiemouth, Drybridge and Garmouth.

level. This was a swamp when the original motte-and-bailey castle was built. A massive tower was added around 1300. Unfortunately the gravel foundations could not support the extra weight and part of the building's walls gave way and slid downhill.

offers good walks and paths leading southward from the village to the very unusual 'earth pillars' which were formed by erosion of the huge quantities of sand and pebble deposits that were laid down here by the Spey.

The factory of Baxters of Speyside is where the well-known tinned soups and other foodstuffs are made and tours round the premises are available. The original Baxters' grocery shop, where the family's soups were first sold in Spey Street, has been reconstructed in the visitor centre and there is also a Victorian kitchen, showing how the family meals were prepared in the 19th century.

The Fochabers Folk Museum in High Street has displays outlining the local history, as well as a costume collection and a display of horse-drawn vehicles.

▶ *Return along the A96, then turn right at the B9104 to Spey Bay, 5 miles (8km).*

❸ Spey Bay, Moray
The River Spey is Scotland's second longest river with a length of 98 miles (158km) and it drains a large area of high ground, including part of the Cairngorms. Huge quantities of ice and water flowed down the river during the Ice Age, accounting for its great width and the massive deposits of sand and gravel. At Spey Bay, where the river meets the sea, the huge volume of peaty water stains the

sea for quite a distance offshore. Longshore drift has encouraged a huge shingle spit to form at the river's mouth and salmon fishers have traditionally netted fish from this point. The Tugnet Ice-House, built in 1830 to store the ice that was used for packing salmon, stands near by. This is Scotland's largest ice-house and it has been restored to take on its new role as a museum that tells the story of the salmon fishery. The Moray Firth Wildlife Centre is also here, and features Moray Firth dolphins among its displays.

The bay is the northern terminus for the Speyside Way, the long-distance footpath that follows part of the river.

BACK TO NATURE

The coastline is home to many feeding birds when the tide is out. Spey Bay can be particularly good for birdwatchers, with terns, waders, oystercatchers and curlews to be sighted; and keep a look-out for seals a little offshore. Cruises to see dolphins in the Moray Firth leave from Inverness.

▶ *Return along the B9104 and turn left at an unclassified road to Portgordon. Follow the roads to Portgordon, then join the A990 and follow it to Buckie.*

Household goods on display at the Folk Museum in Fochabers

▶ *Return along the A941 and turn left at the B9103. Turn left at the A96 and continue to Fochabers.*

❷ Fochabers, Moray
Fochabers was originally situated within the grounds of Gordon Castle (not open) but was demolished at the end of the 18th century to make way for an extension to the castle. When it was being re-established in its present position, the streets were laid out in a grid pattern, and a number of fine Georgian houses remain, especially along the main street. The village's position beside the River Spey led to its growing importance as a river-crossing point, though no bridge crossed the river here until 1804 when the ferry was superseded by Fochabers Old Bridge. The river's east bank

4 **Buckie,** Moray

Buckie stretches for about 3 miles (5km) along the coast and has developed through the amal-gamation of smaller fishing communities. Its main harbour is very busy and the area behind it still has many traditional fisher-men's houses dating back to the 19th century. The town's rich fishing tradition features strongly in the displays in The Buckie Drifter, the town's Maritime Heritage Centre.

The neighbouring village of Portgordon was once a centre for salmon-fishing and near the harbour stands a restored ice-house that was built in 1834.

▶ *Leave by the A942 via Findochty and Portknockie. Turn left at the A98 and follow this to Cullen.*

5 **Cullen,** Moray

The most obvious feature of this pleasant seaside village is the tall and graceful railway viaduct that slices Cullen in two. Trains no longer run on the line but its route is now part of a coastal path. Below the arches, the seaward part of the village has a little harbour with fishermen's houses and a fine stretch of beach. The golf course is jammed in between the shore and the former sea cliffs and on the course's seaward side stand the Three Kings, three tall sea stacks that have managed to withstand the onslaught of the pounding seas. The square has many interesting buildings round it, notably the old Town Hall. The very ornate mercat (market) cross was not originally in the square, but came from Old Cullen, which shared the same fate as the original Fochabers, and was demolished because the local laird felt the village was too close to his house. Cullen Auld Kirk, which is still in Old Cullen, dates from

Stone buildings above Portsoy
harbour, the venue for the annual
Scottish Traditional Small Boats
Festival

the 16th century and contains
some fine stone carvings.

At the western end of Cullen
Bay is the curious Bow Fiddle
Rock, an island with a natural
arch that is probably best seen
from the small village of
Portknockie, which can be
reached via a clifftop path.

To the east of the village
stand the ruins of 15th-century
Findlater Castle. This was
owned by the Ogilvies but abandoned around 1600 in prefer-
ence to the more comfortable
Cullen House.

To the south, Deskford
Church has rich carving.

▶ Continue on the **A98** to
Portsoy.

6 **Portsoy,** Aberdeenshire
Portsoy's sheltered harbour was
once considered to be one of the
safest in this part of Scotland, an
attribute that did much to hasten
the port's growth.

The village's great claim to
fame, however, was its fine vein

of pink and green serpentine
stone, in great demand for its
beauty. Some of it was used in
the Palace of Versailles. This
tradition still lives on and the
harbourside Portsoy Marble
Workshop has good examples of
crafts made locally from Portsoy
Marble, as well as pottery made
on the premises.

▶ Leave by the **A98** and turn
right at the **B9022**. Join the
A95 and follow it to Keith.

7 **Keith,** Moray
Keith's role as an important
centre for the rich neighbouring
farmland reaches its high point
each year at the Agricultural
Show.

The town lies in the broad
valley of Strath Isla, hence the
name of the local Strathisla
Distillery. This is the gateway
to the celebrated 'Malt Whisky
Trail', a route connecting a
number of distilleries that
welcome visitors to their
premises. Strathisla is the
Highlands' oldest working
distillery: production started in

Cullen harbour, with its famous
railway viaduct

Speyside coopers still practising the old craft

▶ Leave on the **A96** (to Inverness), then turn left at the **B9014** which continues into Dufftown.

8 Dufftown, Moray

The centre of the village is dominated by the battlemented Clock Tower that was built in 1839. The clock on the tower came from Banff and played a part in the hanging of the unlucky James MacPherson. This poor fellow was a popular figure who had been robbing the rich and giving the proceeds to the poor, and a petition was raised to obtain a pardon for him. This was successful, but while the pardon was on its way, the local sheriff put the town's clock forward by an hour, making sure that the prisoner was duly dispatched before the reprieve arrived! Dufftown is the home of the Glenfiddich Distillery, which is on the Malt Whisky Trail. Production started here in 1887 and, unusually, the whisky is bottled on the site. At weekends, the Whisky Train departs from the town's railway station to run through several miles of picturesque scenery.

The substantial ruins of Balvenie Castle, ancient stronghold of the Comyns, lie close to the village. This was a massive building surrounding a central courtyard with a curtain wall 7 feet (2m) thick.

1786, though illicit brewing and distilling may have taken place on the site as far back as the 13th century. Malt whisky tastings are a highlight of the tour, but as there are eight distilleries on the trail, make sure you have a teetotaller in the party to do the driving!

SPECIAL TO...

The proximity of so many distilleries makes sampling the local whiskies a popular pastime for many visitors. The local tourist information centres can give details. The whisky is matured in oak barrels and at Craigellachie the Speyside Cooperage produces the barrels using time-honoured skills; there is a visitor centre where you can see the work in progress. The richness of the local fishing grounds means that much delicious fresh seafood should be available locally, and in Cullen why not try the local delicacy, 'Cullen Skink', a soup based on smoked haddock?

---

[i] Clock Tower, The Square (seasonal)

▶ Leave by the **A941** and follow it for 7 miles (11km) to Rothes.

9 Rothes, Moray

On the journey from Dufftown to Rothes the A941 crosses the River Spey near the village of Craigellachie. Just upstream from this crossing stands a graceful iron bridge, built by Thomas Telford between 1812 and 1815 to withstand floods when the river was swollen with spring meltwater from the mountains. Its great test came in 1829 when it survived a rise in water level of 15½ feet (4.5m). This is the country's oldest surviving iron bridge.

Founded in 1766 as a crofting township (a croft may be best described as a Scottish small holding), Rothes developed into an important centre for distilling as no fewer than five distilleries were working here at one time.

The Glen Grant Distillery, which is on the Malt Whisky Trail, was started in 1840 by two brothers and their whisky was one of the first to be bottled as a 'single malt'.

▶ Continue on the **A941** for 10 miles (16km) to return to Elgin.

SCENIC ROUTES

The coastal part of this route is particularly pleasant as there are views of the cliffs, beaches and small settlements with their little harbours. Inland, the route goes through more good arable farming land, though south of Keith sheep farming becomes more important.

The Fishing Trail

Much of Scotland's wealth has depended on the sea, and this tour takes in the major ports of Fraserburgh and Peterhead as well as the picturesque harbours of Crovie and Rosehearty. The tour starts at the town of Banff, whose history as a trading centre has left it with a legacy of fine buildings, including the 18th-century Adam-built Duff House.

2 DAYS • 125 MILES • 201KM

OCEAN LAWN

FRASERBURGH

i   *Collie Lodge (seasonal)*

▶ *Leave by the **A98** and follow it for a mile (2km) to Macduff.*

A decaying sea arch looms up from the shore at Tarlair, near Macduff

❶ Macduff, Aberdeenshire
This is a busy fishing port and many of the townspeople are connected with some aspect of the industry. There is a week-day fishmarket and boats are still built and repaired in the local boatyard.

Doune church has a clock tower of which only three of the four sides have faces. The blank face looks towards neighbouring Banff and was deliberately left like that in response to the hanging of James MacPherson when his last-minute reprieve was on its way. The local people felt so enraged at this miscarriage of justice that they wanted to ensure the people of Banff never knew the correct time again.

▶ *Leave by the **A98** and turn left at the **B9031**. Turn left at the signposted minor road to Crovie.*

❷ Crovie, Aberdeenshire
Crovie is one of the gems of the northeast, a tiny village of about 40 houses. Most of their gable ends face the shore to provide some form of protection from the furious sea that laps so close to them. There is no road beside the houses so the villagers use wheelbarrows to carry heavy objects along the sea wall from the car park to their homes.

▶ *Return to the **B9031** and turn left. Follow this road to Rosehearty, 13 miles (21km).*

❸ Rosehearty, Aberdeenshire
Like so many little ports on this coast, Rosehearty's boom time was during the 19th century, when over 130 boats set out to fish for herring from here. Unfortunately, such heady days are long gone and many of the local fishermen work out of Fraserburgh.

Just outside the village lie the ruins of Pitsligo Castle,

Fraserburgh, one of Scotland's busiest ports

a courtyard castle which developed from a 15th-century keep. The building consisted of only three rooms – a kitchen, a dining room and a communal bedroom with 24 beds in it! To its east is Pittulie Castle, which dates from the 16th century but was abandoned in the 19th century.

FOR CHILDREN

The Northfield Farm Museum, southwest of New Aberdour, features an aviary, llamas, farm machinery and a reconstructed smiddy.
Good beaches suitable for family outings are not as common as in other parts of this region, but St Combs and Cruden Bay are well worth visiting.

▶ *Continue on the **B9031** and turn left at the **A98** on the outskirts of Fraserburgh.*

▉ **Fraserburgh,**
Aberdeenshire
This is one of the busiest fishing ports in the northeast, dealing in whiting, cod, sole, mackerel and herring. The fishmarket is open most days of the week and there is usually something interesting to watch.

The town is built on the promontory of Kinnaird Head (which captured the attention of the Egyptian geographer Ptolemy in the 2nd century AD), and a castle was built here at the end of the 16th century, later converted into a lighthouse. This is now Scotland's Lighthouse Museum, with exhibits from around the country. Close to the castle stands the Wine Tower; this rather odd building, which has trap doors instead of an internal staircase, was erected in the 16th century but the use to which it was put is a mystery. Saltoun Square, in the centre of the town, has the old mercat cross and the Town House, which was built in 1855.

▶ i *Saltoun Square (seasonal)*

▶ *Take the **A90** south to Peterhead (18 miles/29km).*

▉ **Peterhead,**
Aberdeenshire
This was once Scotland's most important whaling centre until it gave way to the herring industry in 1818. Now Europe's busiest whitefish port and the

SPECIAL TO...

This part of Scotland has important outcrops of granite, and many towns and villages on this tour have been built using this distinctive stone. Perhaps the most attractive is Peterhead's, which has large red crystals, quite different from Aberdeen's medium-grained blue-grey rock, or the light grey from Kemnay. Granite is formed when hot molten rock, called magma, cools while still beneath the earth's surface. The colour of the resulting rock depends on the minerals present and the size of the crystals on how slowly the rock cools (the slower the heat loss, the bigger the crystals).

EU's largest fishing port, it also sees a lot of commercial activity connected with supplying the North Sea oil rigs. The Peterhead lifeboat station is open to visitors. The history of the whaling and fishing industries is told in the Arbuthnot Museum and Art Gallery.

▶ *Continue on the **A90**, then turn left at the **A975** to enter Cruden Bay.*

6 Cruden Bay,
Aberdeenshire

This popular summer resort has a long sandy beach and a fine golf course. Visitors may also like to know that the nearby ruins of 17th-century Slains Castle are said to have inspired the novel *Dracula*. The author, Bram Stoker, used to holiday at Cruden Bay and he began writing his famous gothic tale here in 1895.

A little further up the coast, the sea has carved deep clefts into the tall cliffs, the most spectacular feature being the Bullers of Buchan, a natural arch and a blow hole.

▶ *Leave by the minor road that leads to the A90. Turn left at this junction, and follow the A90 to a right turn at the signposted road to Ellon.*

7 Ellon, Aberdeenshire

Ellon was the ancient 'capital' of Buchan, from the time of the Picts up to the defeat of the Norman Comyns, who held the land during the Middle Ages. The village gained importance as a crossing point over the River Ythan and its castle had a strategically important role to play in defending the district. Apart from the ruins of the old castle, the other historical remains are the Moot Hill Monument where there was a motte-and-bailey fort to defend the bridge.

Haddo House, to the northwest of the village, is an imposing mansion built by William

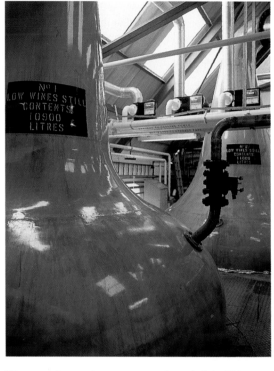

Shiny copper drums at the Glengarrioch Distillery

Adam in 1732, though much of the interior was redecorated around 1880. The house, which is owned by the NTS, has extensive parklands with walks and an adventure playground.

▶ *Leave by the A920 and follow it to Pitmedden House (a little to the northwest of Pitmedden).*

8 Pitmedden Garden,
Aberdeenshire

The gardens at Pitmedden were laid out in the 17th century and the formal garden is made up of elaborate geometric designs filled with brilliantly coloured flowers. The Museum of Farming Life, in the grounds of the estate, has many exhibits of tools and farm machinery from the past. The graveyard in Udny Green, just south of Pitmedden, contains a rather bizarre little building – a circular

mort house, built in 1832 to thwart body snatchers. Coffins were placed in here on a turntable, then removed for burial after a maximum stay of three months, the idea being that they would be quite unsuitable for digging up and sale by then.

▶ *Continue on the A920 and join the A947 to Oldmeldrum.*

9 Oldmeldrum,
Aberdeenshire

The village retains its medieval street pattern, with the large Town Hall dominating the market square. Tucked away on the outskirts of the village is the Glengarrioch Distillery (not open), on a site said to have had a distillery in 1797. The distilling process consumes a great deal of energy and one rather novel feature of this distillery is that its waste heat is used to grow tomatoes in glasshouses.

To the west of the village lies the little settlement of Daviot, just beyond which is the

---

BACK TO NATURE

The Sands of Forvie National Nature Reserve is a vast dune system that has in the past overwhelmed settlements. It is also home to many birds including arctic terns, Sandwich terns, eider ducks and shelducks. Sea ducks are particularly numerous in the winter, along with divers and grebes.

celebrated Loanhead of Daviot stone circle. This imposing circle was constructed about 5,000 years ago and perhaps used in viewing the passage of the moon or in various local rites and customs. The most important part of the circle was the huge recumbent boulder which was put into position so that its uppermost face was horizontal. Ten upright boulders were then placed in a circle to complete the structure. The circle was later used for burials and cremations.

RECOMMENDED WALKS

The hill of Bennachie, standing to the west of Inverurie, gives outstanding views over the surrounding countryside. The remains of an ancient hillfort can be seen near the summit. One popular starting point for the ascent is from the car park on the northeastern side of the hill and on the way there, look out for the Maiden Stone, a 9th-century carved stone that stands by the roadside.

▶ *Leave on the A920 and bear left at the B9170 to Inverurie.*

⑩ Inverurie, Aberdeenshire
This busy little town is the main shopping and administrative centre for the surrounding district. Its wide main street is dominated by the Town Hall, which was built in Grecian style in 1863.

West of the town, minor roads lead to East Aquhorthies stone circle which has a massive recumbent stone and a circle of smaller uprights.

Further north, Archaeolink Prehistory Park is an all-weather attraction illustrating ancient times, including a working Iron-Age farm, landscaped walkways, dramatic film presentations and interactive displays.

The Brandsbutt Stone near Inverurie, which bears ancient Pictish symbols

---

FOR HISTORY BUFFS

Fyvie Castle, northwest of Oldmeldrum, has undergone many changes from its original 13th-century structure but is known as the 'crowning glory of Scots baronial architecture'. The finest feature is the 13-foot (4m) wide stone staircase.

ⓘ *18 High Street*

▶ *Leave by the A96 to Huntly.*

⑪ Huntly, Aberdeenshire
The long straight main road of this neat little town passes under the arch of the Gordon Schools and heads towards the impressive ruins of Huntly Castle, one of the finest castles in this part of the country. A 12th-century Norman motte can still be seen. Construction of the palace was started beside it in the mid-15th century. The most important decorative features are the carved entrance doorway and the fireplaces. Remarkably, for a roofless building of this age, some of the plasterwork still survives – complete with original graffiti!

Huntly Castle's carved entrance with its heraldic adornments

The castle also had its own prison, a dreadful place formed out of a pit cut deep into the foundations.

ⓘ *9A The Square (seasonal)*

▶ *Return eastwards to and continue along the A96, then turn left after a short distance at the A97 to return to Banff.*

Around the
Cairngorms

The rugged granite mountains and forested glens of the Cairngorms National Park are the major features of this tour. Outside of the park, but an ideal highland base, Pitlochry nestles below the hills on the eastern bank of the River Tummel.

2/3 DAYS • 204 MILES • 327KM

ITINERARY

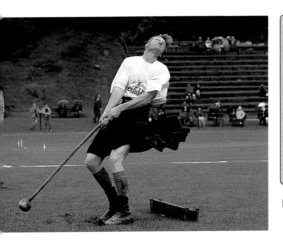

SCENIC ROUTES

The whole of this route offers memorable scenery, but perhaps the most attractive parts are near Blair Atholl, the views of Cairn Gorm and the journey from Donside to Deeside. One very well-known viewpoint just off the route is the Queen's View, which is at the eastern end of Loch Tummel.

▶ *Leave on the B8079, then turn right at the A9 and head towards Inverness. Bear left at the A889 and follow to Dalwhinnie.*

i *22 Atholl Road*

▶ *Leave Pitlochry by the A924, then the B8019 for about 1½ miles (2km) before turning on to the B8079 to the National Trust for Scotland Visitor Centre at Killiecrankie.*

❶ **Killiecrankie,** Perth & Kinross
The wooded gorge of Killiecrankie is a strategic Highland pass. A decisive battle was fought near here in 1689 when a Jacobite army defeated a government force. In the aftermath of the battle, one of the government soldiers, Donald MacBean, escaped from his pursuers by jumping 18 feet (6m) across the River Garry at a point now known as the 'Soldier's Leap'.

FOR HISTORY BUFFS

The two ends of Glen Tilt are met during this tour – at Blair Atholl and at Braemar. This was an historically important route across the Highlands but is now the preserve of walkers. In 1861 Queen Victoria passed through it in her carriage, travelling 69 miles (111km) in one day! Earlier, in the 1840s, the Duke of Atholl attempted to close this right of way; the story is celebrated in *The Ballad of Glen Tilt*.

Hammer-throwing at the Pitlochry Highland Games

i *NTS Visitor Centre (seasonal)*

▶ *Continue along the B8079 for 4 miles (6km) to Blair Atholl.*

❷ **Blair Atholl,** Perth & Kinross
This little village, situated where the Tilt and Garry rivers meet, is dominated by Blair Castle, home of the Dukes of Atholl. The oldest part dates back to 1269 but much of the present structure is relatively 'modern'. At the end of the 18th century the castle was completely renovated; parapets and towers were removed and it was turned into a Georgian mansion. The picturesque towers and crow-stepped gables were later additions when the Scots baronial style came into fashion. The castle has extensive grounds with many fine walks. The Duke of Atholl is the only man in Britain who is permitted to have a private army, a right granted him by Queen Victoria.

❸ **Dalwhinnie,** Highland
At an altitude of 1,188 feet (362m), this is the highest village in the Highlands and was an important stopping place in the days when the main highway passed through here. It has a small distillery which is open to the public.

▶ *Continue on the A889 and turn right at the A86 to Kingussie.*

Britain's only private army on display at Blair Atholl

4 **Kingussie,** Highland

The main attraction here is the Highland Folk Museum and the most fascinating exhibit is the 'black house', built in the manner of the drystone houses that were common on the island of Lewis. Other exhibits focus on Highland agriculture, the life of the tinkers (travelling people) and the furniture used in Highland houses over the last 300 years.

SPECIAL TO...

There are numerous whisky distilleries in the area which offer guided tours round the premises and the chance to sample their particular malt. Shinty (which is similar to hockey) is very popular in the Kingussie/Newtonmore area and an opportunity to see a game should not be missed. For presents, have a look at jewellery incorporating 'cairn-gorms', the smoky semi-precious stones that are found in the area.

Across the River Spey stand the gaunt ruins of Ruthven Barracks, which were built in 1719 but destroyed by the Jacobite army in 1746 to prevent their use by the Hanoverians.

i *Ralia, on the A9 near Newtonmore (seasonal)*

▶ *Leave by the **B9152** and follow it for 6 miles (10km) to Kincraig.*

Highland cattle at Kincraig Highland Wildlife Park. The black variety are rarer than the red

Highland Folk Museum: washing day exhibit

5 **Kincraig,** Highland

The Highland Wildlife Park at Kincraig is home to a collection of animals that once roamed here freely. Reindeer, wild horses, brown bears, wolves, lynx and even bison were at one time native to this part of Scotland. Now they can only be seen from the safety of a car when driving through the park.

The village stands by Loch Insh, which has a water sports centre, while further up the Spey the river widens at Insh

Marshes. This is Scotland's largest inland marsh with a reserve administered by the RSPB (Royal Society for the Protection of Birds). It is particularly good for waders and wildfowl.

FOR CHILDREN

The wildlife park at Kincraig and the reindeer herd at Cairngorm are worth seeing. There are lots of outdoor activities, both land- and water-based, available in the area near Aviemore and the indoor facilities in the town offer useful wet-weather alternatives.

▶ *Continue along the B9152 for 6 miles (10km) to Aviemore.*

6 Aviemore, Highland

Until the 1960s Aviemore was just another small Highland village, but the huge leisure complex that was then established has transformed it into the busiest tourist centre in the Highlands. The new buildings sit uneasily in the Highland

The Cairngorms: view to Loch Morlich and Aviemore

landscape, but they offer many indoor facilities that are not found elsewhere in the area, hence its popularity, especially with winter visitors who come flocking here to ski in the Cairngorms.

Aviemore has a station on the Perth to Inverness railway line and it is also at the southern end of the Strathspey Steam Railway.

i *Grampian Road*

▶ *Take the Cairngorm road out of Aviemore. Follow it through Coylumbridge, past Loch Morlich and up the mountain road to the Coire Cas ski slopes at Cairngorm.*

Strathspey Steam Railway locomotive at Boat of Garten

7 Cairngorm, Highland

The Cairngorm Mountains are formed from a massive dissected plateau of granite with an altitude of around 4,000 feet (1,220m). The chairlift at Coire Cas is operated throughout the year and climbs to a restaurant near the summit of Cairn Gorm, but it should be remembered that even though it is calm and sunny at the chairlift car park, it can be very windy and bitterly cold near the summit. The Cairngorm plateau is covered with frost-shattered boulders which give little shelter to man or beast, but it does support a herd of reindeer which were introduced here in 1952.

The Rothiemurchus estate and the Glen More Forest Park lie between Aviemore and the Cairngorms and there are many attractive low-level walks through the stands of Scots pine and around Loch Morlich, which is a popular water-sports centre.

▶ *Return to Coylumbridge and turn right at the B970. Follow this towards Boat of Garten and turn left at a signposted unclassified road close to the village.*

8 Boat of Garten, Highland
The name derives from a chain-operated ferry across the Spey that was replaced in 1899 by a substantial bridge. This is the northern terminal of the Strathspey Steam Railway, one of the finest tourist attractions in the area, particularly for those nostalgic for the days of steam! With some of the best views of any preserved steam railroad in Britain, the Strathspey Steam Railway line runs along a scenic route to Aviemore.

East of the village stands Abernethy Forest, part of the old Caledonian Forest, where there are many splendid Scots

pines. Beside Loch Garten, which lies within the forest, is an osprey breeding site and many birdwatchers come here each year to witness the progress of the current pair. The ospreys were hunted out of the Highlands altogether at the end of the 19th century, but in the 1950s one nest was discovered in the district. Nowadays, the RSPB maintains a close guard on the nest and visitors can watch the birds from a covered hide. People who spend some time in the district may be fortunate enough to see an osprey fishing in one of the lochs.

BACK TO NATURE

The ospreys at Loch Garten RSPB reserve are the most obvious example of how wild animals are being encouraged to re-populate their old haunts. This is assisted by the careful management of the remains of the old Caledonian Forest in the area to the north of Cairngorm. Visitors should also look for Scottish crossbills and crested tits in the pine forest, and golden-eye ducks and Slavonian grebes on the lochs.

Early morning mist rising above Loch Morlich

▶ *Return along the unclassified road to the B970 and then turn left, and follow this road to Nethy Bridge. Turn right after crossing the River Nethy and follow an unclassified road to the A939. Turn right at this junction to reach Tomintoul.*

9 Tomintoul, Moray
This is another of the Highlands' highest villages and its position means that its weather can be rather unpredictable, with snow not unknown in June!

It has a broad main street and a large central square with the local museum. Although there are only a few shops, one which will be of interest to many visitors is the well-stocked Whisky Castle, which has a vast array of whiskies from many parts of Scotland.

To the north stands the Glenlivet Distillery, which is famous throughout the whisky-drinking world; it has a visitor centre and offers tours.

ⅈ *The Square (seasonal)*

▶ *Continue on the A939 to the skiing area at The Lecht.*

⑩ The Lecht, Moray
Just beyond The Lecht stands the imposing Corgarff Castle. The loop-holed curtain wall surrounding it was added after the 1745 uprising in order that the government might use the castle to police this strong Jacobite centre.

Winter visitors should take care if snow is forecast as the Tomintoul to Cock Bridge section of the A939 is often blocked in the winter.

▶ *Continue on the **A939** then turn left at the **A93** for Ballater.*

⑪ Ballater, Aberdeenshire
Deeside became fashionable after Queen Victoria built a summer retreat at nearby Balmoral Castle, still a favourite holiday home of the royal family. The popularity of 'Royal Deeside' was further increased when the railway line, now closed, was built, but it only ventured as far as Ballater because the Queen did not wish her peace and quiet to be disturbed! A small exhibition about the local railway line is in the tourist information centre.

The town is a good centre from which to explore Deeside, and its solidly built granite houses make it a pleasant place to stroll around. Balmoral Castle was built in 1855 with local granite and is an impressive example of the Scots baronial style. It is the Scottish home of the British royal family and the grounds are open to the public during part of the summer.

ⓘ *Old Royal Station, Station Square*

▶ *Return along the **A93** and continue to Braemar.*

⑫ Braemar, Aberdeenshire
The village is situated in an important position at the junction of three glens and there have been fortifications here from at least 1390 when Kindrochit Castle (now a ruin) was built in what is now the

centre of the village. Outside the village, Braemar Castle is a good example of a Hanoverian fort which was used to police the Highlands.

The Jacobite uprising of 1715 began here and the Invercauld Arms Hotel stands on the site where the standard was raised at the start of the campaign to put a Stuart back on the British throne.

Braemar can be busy at times, but never more so than in September when crowds flock to the local Highland games, the Braemar Gathering. The royal family are regular visitors and among the most popular events are the bagpipe-playing competitions and the tossing of the caber. Sport is not new to the village – in the 11th century King Malcolm Canmore, who needed a messenger, held a race here to find the fastest man.

▶ *Continue on the **A93** past the Glenshee skiing area at Cairnwell and turn right at the **B950**. Turn right again when the road meets the **A924** and follow this road back to Pitlochry.*

Balmoral Castle, reputedly the Queen's favourite residence

The Castle
Trail

Aberdeen, the 'Granite City', is the gateway to Royal Deeside and to the great spread of historic houses known as the Castles of Mar. Aberdeen itself is a fascinating city which has gained a reputation for its flowers, while Old Aberdeen has many buildings dating back to medieval times.

2 DAYS • 143 MILES • 230KM

ITINERARY		
ABERDEEN	▶	**Stonehaven** (15m-24km)
STONEHAVEN	▶	**Fettercairn** (17m-27km)
FETTERCAIRN	▶	**Drum Castle** (26m-42km)
DRUM CASTLE	▶	**Crathes Castle** (6m-10km)
CRATHES CASTLE	▶	**Banchory** (3m-5km)
BANCHORY	▶	**Kincardine O'Neil** (7m-11km)
KINCARDINE O'NEIL	▶	**Burn o'Vat** (12m-20km)
BURN O'VAT	▶	**Kildrummy Castle** (20m-32.5km)
KILDRUMMY CASTLE	▶	**Alford** (9m-14.5km)
ALFORD	▶	**Monymusk** (9m-14km)
MONYMUSK	▶	**Castle Fraser** (4m-6km)
CASTLE FRASER	▶	**Aberdeen** (15m-24km)

[i] *Provost Ross's House, Shiprow*

▶ *Leave by the **A90** and turn left at the minor road that leads to Stonehaven, 15 miles (24km).*

❶ Stonehaven, Aberdeenshire
As well as being a port with a long-established harbour, Stonehaven also has the beaches and other facilities that attract many visitors. The oldest part of the town has a 16th-century Tolbooth which is now used as a museum with special emphasis on local history and the fishing industry. Above the town, the war memorial stands on a hilltop which offers fine views of the coast and the countryside.

The Scots are well renowned for their celebrations at Hogmanay and Stonehaven celebrates the close of the old year with its Fireball Festival. The 'ceremony' may stem from ancient pagan rites, and as the

Town House bells strike midnight, the participants march up High Street twirling burning balls of rags and twigs round their heads.

To the south of the town is Dunnottar Castle, a 14th-century building on a site fortified since the 5th century. The castle stands on a dramatically positioned headland and from 1651 to 1652 it was able to withstand eight months of siege by Cromwell's army before having to surrender. It was also the place where Scotland's royal regalia was hidden from Cromwell.

Dramatic Dunnottar Castle overlooking the sea

Exhibit at the Aberdeen Maritime Museum

[i] *66 Allardice Street (seasonal)*

▶ Take the **A90** south. After 7 miles (11 km) turn right at the **B966** to Fettercairn.

❷ Fettercairn,
Aberdeenshire

The older houses in this little village are built from a red sandstone, much warmer-looking than the rather austere grey of the granites so common around the Aberdeen area. The mercat cross stands in the village square and dates back to 1670. In comparison to this traditional piece of local architecture, a large and very ostentatious Gothic arch celebrates a visit by Queen Victoria in 1861.

Fettercairn Distillery stands on the village outskirts and tours round it are available. The original building was established in 1820. To the north you will find the estate of Fasque, which is open to the public. This was the home of William Gladstone, four times Prime Minister. Many of the rooms have changed little since the house was built in the 1820s and there is a wealth of Victorian artefacts, especially in the kitchens.

▶ Leave by the **B974** on the Cairn o' Mount road and head towards Banchory. Just before the town, turn right at a minor road (to Kirkton of Durris) and follow this along the southern bank of the

Fasque House in Fettercairn; one-time home to Prime Minister William Gladstone

River Dee. Turn left at the **A957** to reach Crathes. Turn right at the **A93** and then left at an unclassified road to Drum Castle.

❸ Drum Castle,
Aberdeenshire

The old Tower of Drum was built in the 13th century with walls 12 feet (4m) thick. Beside it the relatively 'modern' 17th-century house has particularly interesting domestic rooms. The buildings stand in the Old Wood of Drum, a remnant of the ancient Caledonian Forest, and many large oaks, pines and wild cherry trees still flourish here, while a walled garden houses a collection of historic roses. Nearby Garlogie Mill Power

The splendid gardens surrounding Crathes Castle

House Museum features a unique beam engine and associated displays.

▶ *Return to the A93 and turn right. Turn right at the entrance to Crathes Castle.*

❹ Crathes Castle,
Aberdeenshire
This L-shaped tower house was built in the 16th century and contains notable interior decoration. The painted ceilings are exceptionally fine – these date from the late 16th century and very early 17th century and feature ancient and mythical heroes such as Hector, Alexander the Great and King Arthur. The gardens are within yew hedges that are about 300 years old, and contain some excellent examples of topiary.

SCENIC ROUTES

As the B974 makes its way over the hills to Banchory, it passes the Cairn o' Mount, a massive roadside cairn that has been added to over the centuries by generations of travellers. The road crosses over a fine heather moor and there is a very wide panoramic sweep from the cairn over the moors and the low-lying land known as the Howe of the Mearns towards the sea.

The vibrantly painted ceiling at Crathes Castle

▶ *Continue on the A93 for 3 miles (5km) to Banchory.*

❺ Banchory, Aberdeenshire
Situated at the confluence of the River Dee and the Water of Feugh, Banchory is a pleasant little Highland town and is a good base from which to explore the area. There is a local history museum in Bridge Street, which includes displays on the prolific composer of traditional Scottish tunes, Scott Skinner. The town also hosts an annual festival of Scottish music each May.

Close to the village, the Bridge of Feugh spans a little gorge and has become a very popular place from which to watch salmon leaping their way upstream.

This is good farming country and numerous old farm buildings survive.

ℹ️ *Bridge Street*

▶ *Continue on the A93 to Kincardine O'Neil.*

❻ Kincardine O'Neil,
Aberdeenshire
This small village gained early importance for its position at the Deeside side of the Cairn o' Mount route, and a ferry crossed the river here, later

superseded by a bridge in the 13th century. This is one of Deeside's oldest villages and it has a very fine ruined church, built in 1233 and associated with a hospice for travellers.

FOR HISTORY BUFFS

To the north of Kincardine O'Neil lies the village of Lumphanan, where Macbeth is said to have been killed, and to its southwest stands the Peel Ring of Lumphanan, one of the region's earliest earthworks. It dates from the 13th century and the buildings that were stationed on the mound were protected by a wide ditch.

▶ *Continue on the A93 and turn right at the B9119. Turn left at the car park for the Burn o'Vat.*

7 Burn o'Vat, Aberdeenshire
The area around the Vat has been laid out with paths to guide visitors round the many examples showing how the landscape was formed during the Ice Age, about 12,000 to 15,000 years ago. Huge rivers and streams carried vast quantities of rock debris down from the ice-covered mountains and as they did so carved out gullies and gorges and dumped the debris on the low-lying land to the east. The Burn o' Vat itself is a huge bottle-shaped pot-hole that was worn out of the solid rock by the rushing water. It is some 65 feet (20m) in diameter, and its base is filled with sand and gravel.

Lochs Davan and Kinord lie to the east. These are 'kettle holes', formed where huge stranded blocks of ice eventually melted. There are a number of pleasant walks round Loch Kinord and on the northern shore of the loch is the Kinord cross-slab, a 9th-century granite Celtic cross.

The district known as Cromar, which lies to the north and east of the Vat, has numerous monuments that indicate its occupation by ancient peoples over a long time. One unusual structure is the Culsh Earth House, which was found at Culsh Farm, on the B9119, after Tarland. This was probably a storehouse built over 2,000 years ago.

▶ *Continue on the B9119 heading northeast. Turn left at the A97 in order to reach Kildrummy Castle.*

8 Kildrummy Castle, Aberdeenshire
Before reaching Kildrummy, Glenbuchat Castle is passed at a bend in the River Don. This 16th-century castle was built above the ravine of

Artefact found during excavations at Kildrummy Castle

The 18th-century Bridge of Feugh spanning the River Feugh, from which visitors can watch salmon leaping below the Water of Buchan by John Gordon, and above the door of the southwest tower he had carved the rather philosophical inscription 'nothing on arth remains bot faime'.

The great medieval castle of Kildrummy lies on raised ground near the River Don. This was once one of the north's most important castles and, although now in ruins, many of its surrounding walls still stand. It survived numerous sieges but in 1306, when Robert the Bruce's brother was defending it against English attack, he was betrayed by a smith named Osbarn. Legend has it the gold he was promised for his treachery was poured down his throat, molten!

▶ *Continue on the A97, then turn right on to the A944, which leads to Alford.*

9 Alford, Aberdeenshire
This is the home of the Grampian Transport Museum, where visitors can enjoy such diverse exhibits as horse-drawn vehicles, vintage cars, a road roller and even a huge snow plough. One very unusual vehicle is the steam-driven car called the 'Craigievar Express', built by the local postman at

Exhibit from the Grampian Transport Museum, Alford

Craigievar in 1895. It has three wheels and he used it to carry the post on his round.

The village was the terminus of a railway line from Aberdeen and the former station of the Great Northern Scottish Railway now houses a museum. A narrow-gauge railway runs to Haughton House Country Park and Murray Park. Alford's former cattle market has been preserved and now houses a Heritage Centre.

ⓘ *Railway Museum, Station Yard (seasonal)*

▶ *Continue on the A944 and turn left at the B993. Turn left at a minor road to enter Monymusk, 9 miles (14km).*

10 Monymusk, Aberdeenshire
This quiet little village, sited just off the main road, has a splendid Norman church dating back to the 12th century when an Augustinian priory was also built. The village is laid out very neatly in the fashion of a planned 'estate village', with a little grassy area in its centre.

A former toll house stands at the junction of the B993 and the road into the village.

▶ *Return to the B993 and turn left. Turn right at a minor road to Craigearn, then right again to Castle Fraser.*

11 Castle Fraser, Aberdeenshire
The castle, topped with the usual turrets and towers of the Scots baronial style, originated as a rectangular tower in the mid-15th century. Later additions and alterations transformed it into a handsome mansion house. The Round Tower gives an excellent view of the rest of the building and in particular all the different designs of small towers that decorate the upper part of the building. The pleasant gardens are well worth visiting.

▶ *Turn left after leaving the castle grounds and follow the unclassified road to the B977 where a right turn is taken. Turn left at the A944 to return to Aberdeen.*

RECOMMENDED WALKS

There are many popular walks in this area and most tourist information centres have leaflets with information on them, including forest walks, in their area. Places of particular interest include Burn o'Vat, Haughton House Country Park and the West Gordon Way (which passes near Alford).

THE HIGHLANDS & ISLANDS

Nowhere else in Britain can match the Scottish Highlands and Islands for sheer splendour. The grand mountains, heather-clad hillsides and indented coastline (complete with some of Britain's best beaches) make this classic touring country.

The west coast, with its long broken coastline, provides the most dramatic scenery. Communities are few and far between in some districts, leaving the land to the sheep, the cattle and the midges. The east coast and the Great Glen are more populated and offer better facilities.

This historic region abounds with tales and legends of saints and Picts, of Viking invaders and endlessly warring native clans. It is a long history, much of it bloodied with battles, and it has left the countryside rich in antiquities, and burial chambers, standing stones, brochs, forts and castles which can be seen wherever people found land to settle. However, in the last 200 years, the proportion of Scots living in the Highlands and Islands has more than halved. Many people have been forced off the land, as during the infamous Highland Clearances, which spanned the mid-18th to the late 19th centuries, when landowners chose to evict their tenants, destroy their homes, and turn the land over to more profitably exploitable tenants – sheep. Many joined the population drift to the Central Belt of Scotland, where work was to be found. But many Highland communities are now finding that their population is rising again, as more 'incomers' discover the high quality of life.

The view towards the Isles of Rum and Eigg from Arisaig

Visitors will find that certain events in Scottish history crop up again and again as they tour round the region. The Highland Clearances, the feuding between the clans, the Jacobite Uprising of 1745, the boom and slump of the herring industry: these and other landmarks in Scotland's history shaped the country and have been well recorded in many monuments, large and small.

Above all, it is the people that make up the country and those that live and work in the Highlands and Islands are having to adapt to great changes. Many rely on the land for a living, but new skills are being learned, new trades taken up and new visitors welcomed to the delights of this part of Scotland.

Tour 19

West of the Highland 'gateway' of Fort William, great fingers of land stick out into the sea. These peninsulas have scattered crofting communities that are linked by narrow twisting roads offering new views round every corner. Road conditions dictate that progress will not be fast, but then that is no drawback when travelling through one of the least visited parts of the mainland, where each bay and glen is worthy of exploration.

Tour 20

The length of this tour reflects the paucity of major cross-country routes in the Highlands and the extent to which the sea lochs bite into the west coast. This is the Highlands at its best, with giant mountains providing the backdrop to some unforgettable beaches. Inland, the Great Glen carves a wide gash in the fabric of the land and this route has been followed over the millennia by settlers, hunters, missionaries, soldiers – and even sailors!

Tour 21

Two cross-country routes link the eastern village of Bonar Bridge with more dramatic west coast scenery. Europe has few wildernesses left, but as visitors approach the uninhabited moor and mountain area of Inverpolly, they can get some feeling of just how starkly beautiful (and inhospitable!) the Highland

landscape can be. However, the rich harvest from the sea provides many communities with a good livelihood and helps maintain the Highland crofting traditions.

Tour 22

Much of this long tour around the top of Scotland follows the narrow, populated coastal fringe. There seems to be almost no limit to the number of beautiful sandy beaches to be found here, and many of them will be deserted. Caithness, set in a much gentler landscape than Sutherland, has something of a timeless quality about it, especially in the farming areas, and it is rich in prehistoric antiquities that continue to puzzle archaeologists to this day.

Passenger boat leaving Iona for Staffa

Tour 23

In many ways, Easter Ross and the Black Isle are very different from the rest of the region. This is particularly good farming country, with large prosperous farms and bustling towns. The blend of gentler Highland landscape with the facilities of seaside resorts makes this district popular with families and those seeking a relaxed tour through pleasant countryside.

Tour 24

Skye, the 'Misty Isle', draws to its shores visitors eager to see the rugged grandeur of the Cuillin Hills and to experience a place where time passes more slowly than on the mainland. The island is so steeped in tradition and history, and has such splendid scenery that it lures visitors back time and again.

Tour 25

With its interior composed largely of mountain, moorland and bog, Mull's coastline roads link villages, harbours, farms and castles. The sea is never far away, and with a coastline some 300 miles (480km) long the views towards the sea are as fine as they are varied.

Kittiwakes on Handa's cliffs

The Road To
The Isles

Fort William is often referred to as the Gateway to the Highlands, and although not essentially a tourist resort, it does have a wealth of services and shops for books, tartans, tweeds and outdoor wear. Just outside the town lies Ben Nevis, at 4,406 feet (1,344m), Britain's highest mountain.

2/3 DAYS • 195 MILES • 315KM

ITINERARY

FORT WILLIAM	▶ **Banavie** (4m-6km)
BANAVIE	▶ **Glenfinnan** (16m-26km)
GLENFINNAN	▶ **Loch nan Uamh** (14m-23km)
LOCH NAN UAMH	▶ **Arisaig** (6m-10km)
ARISAIG	▶ **Morar** (6m-10km)
MORAR	▶ **Mallaig** (3m-5km)
MALLAIG	▶ **Kinlochmoidart** (31m-50km)
KINLOCHMOIDART	▶ **Acharacle** (7m-11km)
ACHARACLE	▶ **Glenbeg** (12m-19km)
GLENBEG	▶ **Kilchoan** (11m-18km)
KILCHOAN	▶ **Strontian** (29m-47km)
STRONTIAN	▶ **Lochaline** (18m-29km)
LOCHALINE	▶ **Ardgour** (30m-48km)
ARDGOUR	▶ **Fort William** (8m-13km)

The Road To The Isles

i Cameron Centre, Cameron Square

Neptune's Staircase: a series of eight locks on the Caledonian Canal

▶ *Leave by the **A82** (to Inverness), then turn left at the **A830** (to Mallaig). Turn right at the **B8004** to the Caledonian Canal's locks at Banavie, 4 miles (6km).*

❶ Banavie, Highland
Northeast of Fort William, on the way to Banavie, are the impressive ruins of 13th-century Inverlochy Castle, on the banks of the River Lochy. It has massive round towers at the corners and walls 10 feet (3m) thick.

The Caledonian Canal runs through the Great Glen from Corpach (just southwest of Banavie) to Inverness, a total distance of 60 miles (97km). It was built between 1803 and 1822 by Thomas Telford so that boats could avoid the treacherous waters round Cape Wrath; the political decision to build the canal was hastened by the government's fear of Napoleon's naval strength. Although some commercial boats still use this beautifully sited waterway, most of the craft on it are motor cruisers or yachts. Neptune's Staircase, the most spectacular part of the canal, is at Banavie. This is a series of eight locks that raise boats a total height of 64 feet (20m) in a distance of only 1,500 feet (460m).

A short walk along the towpath leads to the basin and sea lock at Corpach, with its neat 'pepper pot' lighthouse. From this point there is an excellent view of Loch Linnhe, the surrounding hills and Ben Nevis.

Near by is the Treasures of the Earth, a stunning array of sparkling crystal and gemstones in simulated cave scenes.

▶ *Return to the **A830**. Turn right and follow the road to Glenfinnan.*

❷ Glenfinnan, Highland
On the fateful afternoon of 19 August, 1745, Charles Edward Stuart raised the Stuart standard here and rallied more than a thousand armed supporters to the Jacobite cause. His father was proclaimed King James VIII of Scotland and III of England and Ireland and this historic act

Steam train crossing the Glenfinnan viaduct

started the tragic chain of events known in Scots history as the 'Forty-Five'. The army, though initially successful in moving far into England, was eventually defeated at Culloden, near Inverness, on 16 April, 1746, a defeat that did much to change the history of Scotland. The NTS Visitor Centre has a good display explaining the events surrounding the arrival of the prince and the raising of the standard. The nearby tall and slender monument at the head of Loch Shiel is Scotland's most famous memorial to the Jacobite cause.

The Fort William to Mallaig road runs parallel to the railway line for much of the way. The line's most spectacular structure is the Glenfinnan Viaduct with its 21 arches; the local railway station has a little museum depicting the history of the line.

i NTS Visitor Centre (seasonal)

▶ *Follow the **A830** for 14 miles (23km) to Loch nan Uamh.*

❸ **Loch nan Uamh,** Highland

After the battle of Culloden, Bonnie Prince Charlie made his way back to this area and, on 20 September, 1746, he sailed away from this loch on a ship bound for France. The spot from which he sailed is marked by the Prince's Cairn. He had a price of £30,000 on his head but no one betrayed his presence while on the run from government troops, so loyal were local people to the Jacobite cause.

▶ *Continue on the **A830** to Arisaig.*

❹ **Arisaig,** Highland

This little seaside village has many sandy beaches near by which makes it popular with families in summer. Arisaig has a fine view of the islands of Rum and Eigg and boats sail from the small harbour to these and other local islands.

▶ *Continue on the **A830** to Morar.*

The Prince's Cairn at Loch nan Uamh

❺ **Morar,** Highland

Loch Morar, with a depth of 1,017 feet (310m), is Britain's deepest inland water and the home of Morag, a 'monster' reputed to be related to Loch Ness's Nessie. The loch is a

---

FOR CHILDREN

Of the many fine beaches along this coast, particular mention should be made of the ones at Morar, north of Arisaig, and at Kentra Bay. There are not many wet-weather facilities in the area, but Fort William has the Lochaber Leisure Centre, which has a swimming pool and facilities for many sports including outdoor activities such as tennis.
There are also dry-ski slopes at the skiing area at Aonach Mor, just off the A82, east of Fort William.

A landed catch of mixed shellfish

FOR HISTORY BUFFS

As the A861 descends to Acharacle, it passes a minor road (left) to Dalelia and this leads to a walk to the shores of Loch Shiel. This is the narrowest part of the loch and is almost completely blocked by Eilean Fhianain (St Finnan's Island), where St Finnan, a disciple of St Columba, built a chapel. The ruins survive, and legend has it that a curse has been placed on anyone daring to remove the bell Finnan brought from Ireland. The churchyard was the burial place of the chiefs of Clanranald. This was also the spot from which Charles Edward Stuart started his journey up Loch Shiel to Glenfinnan, where he raised the Stuart standard in 1745.

for a wide expanse of pure white silica sand.

▶ *Continue on the A830 to Mallaig.*

6 Mallaig, Highland

Before the arrival of the railway, Mallaig was a small crofting community with a few thatched houses. Today it is the home port of a substantial fishing fleet, host to the Marine World Aquarium down by the harbour, and a heritage centre by the station, as well as being the mainland terminal for many boats operating ferry services to the islands.

Day excursions from the harbour are also available in season and these give visitors the opportunity to visit Skye or Muck, Eigg, Rum and Canna.

The peninsula of Knoydart is another fascinating place accessible only by boat. Surrounded on three sides by sea and on the fourth by mountains, it is one of Scotland's few wilderness areas; it retains its character because it cannot be reached by road. This is wonderful walking country, where real peace and quiet can be enjoyed.

The West Highland Railway from Fort William was opened in 1894 in order to transport the west coast herring catches to the southern markets as quickly as possible, and although the fish-carrying role

Fishing boats in Mallaig's pretty harbour

remarkable example of the effect of glaciers during the Ice Age. The ice here was 4,000 feet (1,220m) thick and gouged out the loch's basin to a depth of more than 1,000 feet (300m) below sea level.

After tumbling over the Falls of Morar, the River Morar flows over the Sands of Morar, notable of the line has diminished, it is still of vital economic and social importance to the area. It is also very popular with summer visitors, especially when steam trains are used, and it has been described as one of the world's most scenic railway journeys.

SCENIC ROUTES

The 'Road to the Isles' is the name given to the attractive route from Fort William to Mallaig, which passes through an ever-changing landscape of hills, forest and lochs. Another outstanding journey is the one along Loch Linnhe, giving good views of Ben Nevis and the hills of Glen Coe.

▶ *Return along the A830 to Lochailort. Turn right at the A861 and follow to Kinlochmoidart.*

7 **Kinlochmoidart,** Highland

To the right of the road stand the Seven Men of Moidart, seven beech trees planted early in the 19th century in tribute to the seven men who landed here with Bonnie Prince Charlie in 1745. The area around Loch Moidart is beautifully wooded with a large natural oak and birch forest; holly, cherry and ash are also common. Today these trees are protected, but in previous centuries they were used for charcoal burning or for making lime. An old lime kiln stands opposite the car-park at the Seven Men of Moidart. After climbing out of Kinlochmoidart, look out for a group of four cairns by the roadside. These are on an old 'coffin route' and mark where coffins were laid to give their bearers a rest while carrying their burden over the trackless hills to the local churchyard.

▶ *Continue on the A861 for 7 miles (11km) to Acharacle.*

8 **Acharacle,** Highland

This small village, which makes a pleasant base from which to explore the surrounding area, is approached by crossing the Old Shiel Bridge.

To the west lies Kentra Bay with its fine sandy beaches, and Castle Tioram, a 14th-century castle standing on a tidal island in Loch Moidart. Though an empty ruin, it was not destroyed in battle, but put to the torch by its owner, the chief of Clanranald, during the 1715 Jacobite uprising. He did this to prevent it falling into the hands of his enemies.

▶ *Continue on the A861 to Salen, then turn right at the B8007 and follow it to Glenbeg.*

9 **Glenbeg,** Highland

One mile (1.5km) southeast of the village is the RSPB

The remains of tragic Castle Tioram

Glenborrodale site, with its stunning landscape and wildlife. Further along the road is the little bay of Camas nan Geall beneath the steep slopes of Ben Hiant. In the field at the back of the bay can be found an 18th-century burial site and a Bronze-Age standing stone which has a number of carvings on it; the remains of a small settlement can also be seen here.

▶ *Continue on the B8007 for 11 miles (18km) to Kilchoan.*

10 **Kilchoan,** Highland

This little settlement of scattered houses makes a good base for exploring the western end of the Ardnamurchan peninsula; it also has a summer season ferry service to Tobermory on the island of Mull. Close to the settlement stands 13th-century Mingary Castle (not open). This was originally the seat of the MacIains and later the Campbells of Ardnamurchan, who held it for the king during the Jacobite rising in 1745.

Beyond Kilchoan is Ardnamurchan Point, the most westerly point on the British mainland. The view from here encompasses the Inner Hebrides and the islands of Barra and South Uist. Its light-house was built in the 1840s by Alan Stevenson, one of the three Stevenson brothers who followed their father in design-ing lighthouses. The building is constructed of pink granite from the Ross of Mull and the design was influenced by Egyptian architecture.

[i] *Pier Road (seasonal)*

▶ *Return to Salen along the* **B8007**, *then turn right at the* **A861** *to Strontian.*

11 **Strontian,** Highland
The modern portion of this village lies near the main road while the older part is to be found on the western side of the Strontian River. From 1722 to 1904, this was the site of mines extracting lead, zinc and silver, but the most lasting contribu-tion the village gave to science was through the discov-ery here in 1764 of the mineral strontianite. The examination of this mineral led to the discovery of the metal element strontium, used in fireworks. Its radioisotope, Strontium 90, is used in nuclear power sources. The former mining area is now a source of barytes, which is used in drillers' 'mud' as a lubricat-ing agent for the

drilling mechanism on North Sea oil rigs.

Ariundle Oakwood Nature Reserve lies to the north of the Strontian River and has a collection of fine oaks and Scots pines. A pleasant nature trail can be followed through the reserve.

[i] *Strontian (seasonal)*

▶ *Continue on the* **A861**, *then turn right at the* **A884**. *Follow this to Loch Aline and then continue to the village of Lochaline.*

12 **Lochaline,** Highland
Peaceful Loch Aline, which slices into the broad peninsula of Morvern, seems a rather incongruous place to have a modern mine, but close to the village is a source of very pure silica sand which is used in the production of high quality glassware. Behind the village, in the grave-yard of Keil Church, stands a tall 15th-century Celtic cross, known as the Morvern Cross. Lochaline has a ferry service to Fishnish on Mull. At the head of the loch stand Kinlochaline Castle (not open) and Ardtornish House, which has extensive gardens, well worth visiting. To the south of the mansion stands 14th-

century Ardtornish Castle, an imposing building on the coast that still acts as an important landmark to sailors travelling down through the Sound of Mull.

▶ *Return on the* **A884** *to the junction (right) with the* **B8043**. *Cars should follow this unclassified road until the* **A861** *is met and then turn right and follow this road to Ardgour. Vehicles pulling cara-vans should avoid the* **B8043** *and instead continue on the* **A884** *to its junction with the* **A861**; *then turn right to Ardgour.*

13 **Ardgour,** Highland
The small village of Ardgour has developed at this important crossing over Loch Linnhe. The old jetty here was built by Thomas Telford in 1815, at about the same time as the lighthouse, which still acts as a prominent landmark.

▶ *Take the Corran ferry across Loch Linnhe at the Corran Narrows. At the other side turn left at the* **A82** *and return to Fort William, 8 miles (13km).*

The distinctive landmark of Ardgour lighthouse and Corran ferry on Loch Linnhe

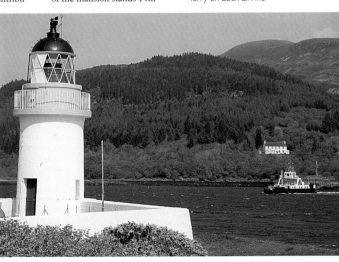

The Western
Highlands

The fort at Fort Augustus, built by General Wade in 1730, was named after William Augustus, Duke of Cumberland, who brutally suppressed the Highlanders after the Battle of Culloden in 1746. In 1867 the fort became a Benedictine school; today it is a heritage centre, and Fort Augustus is a popular base for cruisers on the Caledonian Canal.

3 DAYS • 301 MILES • 484 KM

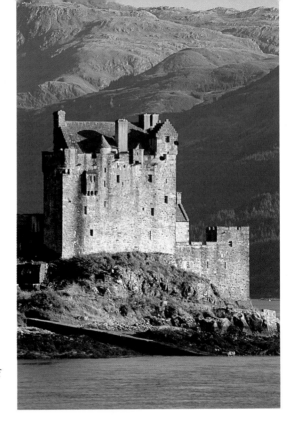

Eilean Donan Castle, resurrected from the rubble in 1912

i Car Park (seasonal)

▶ *Head southwards on the A82 for 7 miles (11km) to Invergarry.*

❶ Invergarry, Highland
This rather sleepy-looking village was the home of an important clan, the MacDonnells of Glengarry. To the south, within the grounds of a hotel, lie the ruins of Invergarry Castle; three castles have stood here, the last one having been burnt in 1746 by Cumberland because Charles Edward Stuart stayed here before and after the battle of Culloden. Just to the north of Invergarry stands the roadside Well of Seven Heads, a gruesome reminder of the slaying of seven MacDonnell brothers who had murdered their dead brother's two sons. The full story of this gory event is recorded on a monument inscribed in Gaelic, English, Latin and French.

▶ *Leave by the A87 (to Kyle of Lochalsh) and follow this for 36 miles (58km) to Shiel Bridge.*

❷ Shiel Bridge, Highland
The imposing entry to Shiel Bridge is by the magnificent Glen Shiel, with the group of mountains known as the Five Sisters of Kintail to the north. The mountains are seen to great advantage at Mam Ratagan, just a little to the west of Invershiel on the Glenelg road. Like many communities in this region, Shiel Bridge is a collection of houses at an important junction, in this case at the head of Loch Duich. Along the northern shore of the loch stands Eilean Donan Castle, which dates back to 1220. Shelled by a British frigate in 1719 during an abortive Jacobite rising, it lay in ruins until rebuilding started in 1912. It is now one of the Highlands' most popular and beautiful castles and is said to be the most photographed castle in Scotland.

There is an unmanned NTS centre at Strath Croe, to the northeast of Shiel Bridge, with useful wildlife displays explaining the natural history of this wild and beautiful area. A very rough cross-country path from Strath Croe leads to the Falls of Glomach where the water of the Allt a' Ghlomaich tumbles 750 feet (230m).

▶ *Continue on the A87 to Kyle of Lochalsh.*

❸ Kyle of Lochalsh,
Highland
This bustling industrial village is the terminus of the railway line from Inverness. The controversial bridge that replaced the Skye ferries is reached by the A87. The western part of this peninsula lies within the NTS's Balmacara estate; 1 mile (1.5km) beyond the village of Reraig, Lochalsh House Woodland Garden is on the left. This boasts a fine collection of mature trees, and is developing more exotic species of plants such as bamboo trees.

i Car Park (seasonal)

▶ *Leave by the unclassified road that leads northwards to Plockton.*

FOR HISTORY BUFFS

To the west of Shiel Bridge lies Glenelg. The route to it has long been of strategic importance, hence the 18th-century military road and the (ruined) Bernera Barracks. It was used by Samuel Johnson and James Boswell in 1773 and is now followed by many summer visitors heading for the Kyle Rhea ferry to Skye. South of the village are two brochs, Dun Telve and Dun Trodden, built as defensive structures about 2,000 years ago, when they were over 40 feet (13m) high and had stairs and galleries built into their walls.

4 Plockton, Highland

With palm trees growing by the shore of Loch Carron, Plockton exudes the kind of peace and quiet that has attracted generations of painters; indeed, many would regard it as one of the northwest coast's loveliest villages. The sheltered position also provides a much-needed haven for yachts sailing along the west coast.

▶ *Return along the approach road to Plockton and turn left to head eastwards towards Stromeferry, following the shore of Loch Carron. Turn left when the* **A890** *is met. Follow to just beyond Strathcarron railway station then turn left on to the* **A896** *to Lochcarron.*

5 Lochcarron, Highland

Lochcarron is essentially a long string of houses (and a few hotels) along the shore of the sea loch. To its south is Strome Castle, once a stronghold of the MacDonnells of Glengarry, but destroyed by the MacKenzies in 1602. It commands a fine view of Skye. Just west of the village is Loch Kishorn, a deep and sheltered loch where enormous oil rigs were once built.

☐ *Main Street (seasonal)*

▶ *Continue on the* **A896** *but turn left at the head of Loch Kishorn to Applecross. This road is definitely not for caravans, but the* **A896** *from Loch Kishorn to Shieldaig and the minor road from Shieldaig to Applecross are suitable.*

6 Applecross, Highland

Applecross was one of the country's most isolated communities until the coastal road from Shieldaig was built in the 1970s. The traditional route, over the 2,053-foot (626m) pass of Bealach na Ba (Pass of the Cattle), one of the highest roads in Britain, was a formidable obstacle to many vehicles and it is often closed by snow in winter.

RECOMMENDED WALKS

A low-level walk runs behind Liathach, with a detour to the corrie north of Ben Eighe, Coire Mhic Fhearchair, which has three buttresses towering over a lochan (small loch). Take care, as this is very exposed country and 'casual' walkers should not attempt it.

An Irish monk, Maelrubha, landed at Applecross in the AD 670s and founded a monastery which was later destroyed by Vikings. The local church has an ancient cross slab 9 feet (3m) high, with a Celtic cross inscribed. This and others inside the church may date back to Maelrubha's time. An old chapel stands in the graveyard and two rounded stones in front of it mark the resting place of Maelrubha.

▶ *Head north on the unclassified road out of Applecross to Shieldaig. Turn left at the* **A896**, *then bear left to enter Shieldaig.*

7 Shieldaig, Highland

This charming village consists of a row of whitewashed houses standing along the loch's shore. Once famous for its herring fishing (its name is Norse for herring bay), it now relies more on tourism to maintain its livelihood.

Opposite the harbour lies the small wooded Shieldaig Island. From around Shieldaig there are wonderful views of

---

SPECIAL TO...

Many west coast fishing boats catch prawns and lobsters and local hotels often have wonderfully fresh seafood dishes on their menus. The shellfish, including delicious scallops, are particularly good.

---

some of the Highlands' best scenery. The mountains from Loch Kishorn northwards to Loch Maree are composed of red Torridonian sandstone, some 750 millions years old. However, around Shieldaig the rocks are a highly altered variety called gneiss which has been eroded to provide a low, smooth, platform above which the giant Torridon Mountains soar.

Sitting on the top of the world, looking north to Torridon village

▶ *Continue on the **A896** for 8 miles (13km) to Torridon.*

8 Torridon, Highland
The houses huddled together in the village are dwarfed by the mass of 3,360-foot (1,024m) Liathach, a mountain to be attempted only by experienced mountainwalkers as its ridge is very narrow and exposed. Composed of Torridonian sandstone, its name means the Grey

One, as four of its seven tops are formed from grey-white quartzite rock.

An NTS countryside centre is situated just by the main road and this has displays and audiovisual presentations on the local geology and wildlife. Near by, there is a small Deer Museum; many breeds of deer may be spotted near here and can even be found wandering around the village itself.

i *NTS Centre (seasonal)*

▶ *Follow the **A896** for 11 miles (18km) to Kinlochewe.*

9 Kinlochewe, Highland
This village stands at the head of Loch Maree, which was once called Loch Ewe, hence the name of the village. To its west

lies the Beinn Eighe National Nature Reserve and the reserve's Aultroy Visitor Centre is just along the A832 from the village. Further on is an interesting nature trail which climbs to a fine view over the loch towards Slioch, the 3,217-foot (980m) high mountain that dominates the surrounding district. Loch Maree is one of the country's finest lochs and is steeped in history. The tiny Isle Maree was once a sacred place of the Druids, who are said to have introduced oak trees, significant religious symbols in the Celtic culture. In the 7th century, St Maelrubha came and set up his cell here and, for similar reasons, planted holly trees. In later centuries, paganism was practised here and rites involving the sacrifice of a bull occurred on the island as late as the 17th century.

The Loch Maree Hotel has a large boulder outside it on which is a Gaelic inscription celebrating a visit by Queen Victoria.

▶ *Leave Kinlochewe on the **A832** for 20 miles (32km) to Gairloch.*

10 Gairloch, Highland
This widely scattered crofting and fishing community is the district's main centre and it has developed into a popular place for holidays as it combines fine scenery with long stretches of sandy beach. Fishing is important here and the harbour is well worth visiting when the boats come in. The fishing industry, crofting and other aspects of local life form important displays at the local Gairloch

Exotic and more common plants at Inverewe Gardens

Heritage Museum, which was developed from a farmstead with a cobbled courtyard.

[i] *Auchtercairn (seasonal)*

▶ *Continue on the A832 to Inverewe Gardens, just beyond the village of Poolewe.*

[11] Inverewe Gardens,
Highland

In 1862 Osgood MacKenzie started a long labour of love when he began transforming an area of barren ground here into one of Britain's most remarkable gardens. Conifers were planted to form shelter belts, wet land was drained, soil was carried in on men's backs, and in 60 years the local people had created a garden that gives great pleasure to over 100,000 visitors each year. Inverewe lies at the same latitude as Siberia, but here, bathed by the warm Gulf Stream, it boasts palms, magnolias, rhododendrons and many other beautiful plants.

On a summer's day Loch Ewe is a peaceful place, a far cry from the days of World War II when it was a convoy station for ships bound for Russia or Iceland. Aultbea (a little further along the road) was the depot's HQ and remains of gun emplacements have been kept as reminders of the district's role in those dangerous days. Look out for information boards near Aultbea's pier.

[i] *NTS Centre (seasonal)*

▶ *Continue on the A832 to the A835. Turn left and continue for less than a mile (1.5km).*

[12] Corrieshalloch Gorge,
Highland

Much of the Highland landscape was sculpted by the movement of ice during the last Ice Age. Often the ice smoothed the land, but at Corrieshalloch Gorge its meltwater flowing down the River Broom gouged out this spectacular rugged gorge about one mile (1.5km) long. A narrow bridge crosses the chasm with the water plunging over the Falls of Measach some 150 feet (45m) below – this is not the place for vertigo sufferers! The bridge was built by Sir John Fowler, joint designer of the Forth Rail Bridge, but this is hardly on the same scale and there is a limit to the number of people permitted on the bridge at one time.

The busy fishing port of Ullapool lies further down Loch Broom. It was founded in 1788 by the British Fisheries Society to take advantage of the huge shoals of herring found in the nearby seas. It is an important ferry terminal for Stornoway; cruises to the Summer Isles are also available from the harbour.

▶ *Head southeast on the A835 towards Inverness. Turn left at Contin on to the A834 to Strathpeffer.*

[13] Strathpeffer, Highland

Strathpeffer prospered as a spa in the 19th century after springs (four sulphur and one chalybeate) were developed. The Victorian hotels and large villas date from the spa's heyday and today the hotels still do a brisk trade, catering mainly for bus tours. The spa water can be sampled in a small building by the Square but beware – its taste is even more pungent than its smell! Local handicrafts can be bought at the small shops now occupying the old railway station buildings.

At the northern end of the village is the Eagle Stone, a Pictish stone also said to celebrate a victory of the Munros over the MacDonalds. To the east, the prominent hill of Knockfarrel affords fine views over the district.

[i] *The Square (seasonal)*

▶ *Return along the A834 to the A835 and turn left. Turn right at the A832 and at Muir of Ord take the A862 southwards to Beauly.*

[14] Beauly, Highland

Mary, Queen of Scots is supposed to have come here in 1564 and taken a liking to the place; tradition has it she described it as a '*beau lieu*' (beautiful place), hence its name. However, it is more likely Beauly derives from the name given to the 13th-century priory around which the town was built. Beauly Priory was founded in 1230 and the present ruins date from the 13th to the 16th centuries. In 1572 Lord Ruthven obtained royal permission to strip the lead off the roof and by 1633 the building was in a ruinous condition. The town's 'modern' planned layout (built around 1840) features a wide market square and a grid street pattern.

There are many castles in the area. To the southeast is Moniack Castle, which makes wine from local produce; to the south is Beaufort Castle (not open), built about 1880 in Scots baronial style; and near the road to Cannich is Erchless Castle (not open), described in the 19th century as 'modernised, yet still a stately old pile'.

▶ *Leave on the A862 (to Inverness) and turn right at the A831 and continue to Cannich.*

15 Cannich, Highland

Cannich stands at the head of Strathglass, a glen not normally on tourist routes. The lower part of the glen has an impressive narrow gorge (at An Druim) and there are a number of hydro-electric power stations here.

To the west of Cannich lie some very beautiful glens – Glen Affric, Glen Cannich and Glen Strathfarrar. These make for good walks as the scenery can be spectacularly wild in places: Scots pines are being regenerated and there are chances of seeing red deer. Corrimony Cairn is found just off the Cannich to Drumnadrochit road. This is about 4,000 years old and has a central grave chamber which can be reached by crawling through the passageway. Standing stones ring the cairn and the large capstone lying on top of it has small circular indentations called 'cup marks' on it. Further along this narrow road, the standing stone known as Mony's Stone can be found, as well as the walled rectangular graveyard of Clach Churadain (St Curadan's Cemetery).

▶ Continue on the **A831** for 12 miles (19km) to Drumnadrochit.

Loch Ness's most famous resident

16 Drumnadrochit, Highland

Huge numbers of visitors come here hoping to see the Loch Ness monster. The loch is only 2 miles (3km) wide at this point but about 750 feet (230m) deep and many 'sightings' have been reported. In the AD 600s, St Adamnan told how Columba drove back a monster when it was about to attack a swimmer. Frequent scientific expeditions have failed to prove that a monster exists; however, even sceptical visitors should keep a loaded camera handy! Two Loch Ness Centres (the 'official Loch Ness 2000' and the 'original') in Drumnadrochit have exhibits connected with Nessie, including possible photographs of the beast herself.

Just outside the village stands Urquhart Castle. The site may have been fortified in the Dark Ages but the present structure dates back to the 13th century. Its commanding position in the Great Glen gave it immense military importance and part of it was blown up in the late 17th century to prevent it falling into the hands of Jacobites. Further south, the road passes a cairn erected to John Cobb, who died on the

Brooding Urquhart Castle

loch in 1952 while attempting to set a new world speed record; he achieved the remarkable speed of 206mph (331kph) before the accident.

The village of Foyers can be seen on the opposite shore of the loch. In 1896, Britain's first major commercial hydroelectric power station was built here to provide energy for an aluminium works. These buildings can still be seen though the factory has long since closed. Today, a large pump-storage scheme produces electricity using the water of Loch Mhor, which is on the moorland above the village.

▶ Head south on the **A82** and return to Fort Augustus.

SCENIC ROUTES

As a detour, the narrow and twisty road from Torridon to Lower Diabaig is highly recommended as there are splendid views of Loch Torridon. In addition, the small picturesque lochside settlements of Inveralligin and Lower Diabaig are worth seeing.

The Wild

West

This tour really does reveal
the wide, wild expanse of the
Highlands landscape. It begins
at Bonar Bridge, named after the
first bridge to be built over the Kyle
of Sutherland at this point, designed by
Thomas Telford but later destroyed by a
flood. The village at Ardgay lies on the
other side of the bridge.

2 DAYS • 172 MILES • 277KM

ITINERARY		
BONAR BRIDGE	►	**Knockan Cliff**
		(36m–58km)
KNOCKAN CLIFF	►	Inchnadamph
		(11m–18km)
INCHNADAMPH	►	Lochinver (13m–21km)
LOCHINVER	►	Kylesku (27m–43km)
KYLESKU	►	Scourie (12m–19km)
SCOURIE	►	Kinlochbervie
		(16m–26km)
KINLOCHBERVIE	►	Lairg (46m–74km)
LAIRG	►	Bonar Bridge (11m–18km)

Inverpolly National Nature Reserve, as viewed from Cul Mor

FOR HISTORY BUFFS

To the west of Bonar Bridge, a narrow road leads through Strathcarron to Croick Church. This was designed by Thomas Telford in 1827 for what was then a well-populated district. However, in 1845, during the infamous Highland Clearances, the landowner tried to evict the people. Three attempts were made to throw the 18 families out of their homes and eventually they were forced to gather at this church with only a few possessions. They stayed there for a week, sheltering under blankets, and recorded their plight by scratching messages on the church's window panes.

▶ Leave by the **A836** and turn left at the **A837**. Continue on this road as far as Ledmore Junction, then turn left on to the **A835** to the Nature Trail at Knockan Cliff.

FOR CHILDREN

As an unusual treat, why not spend a night in a castle? Carbisdale Castle is now used to house a youth hostel, complete with statues, paintings and beautiful wood-work, and will delight many children.

❶ Knockan Cliff, Highland
The geological trail at Knockan Cliff provides a wonderful view of the district's unique land-scape. Tall and isolated sand-stone mountains rise steeply from the boggy moorland which is based on the very old rock known as Lewisian gneiss. This wilderness is part of the Inverpolly National Nature Reserve, which preserves this strange and fascinating land-scape and the indigenous flora and fauna. The walks are spec-tacular, but only for prepared and experienced walkers. At

one point on the trail, you can stand beside the world-famous Moine Thrust where a huge slab of land (running from Loch Eriboll on the north coast all the way to the island of Islay) moved many miles westward, resulting in the geologically older rock coming to rest on the younger rock.

Much of Inverpolly is covered with wet heath, its main plants being heather, cottongrass and deergrass. The myriad boggy areas and little pools give shelter to bog myrtle and unusual plants such as the carnivorous sundew. Deer roam the land, spending summer in the high corries, but moving down to sheltered places during the winter. Otters, wild cats, pine martens and badgers can also be seen in the district. In good weather, this is the

The ruins of Ardvreck Castle on the shores of Loch Assynt

Highlands at its best; in bad weather, you won't see anything!

▶ *Return along the* **A835** *to Ledmore Junction. Turn left at the* **A837** *and follow this to Inchnadamph, 11 miles (18km).*

2 **Inchnadamph,** Highland
A hotel and a few houses stand near the road at the Inchnadamph Nature Reserve in an area popular with anglers. This is limestone country and the Allt nan Uamh caves near the valley of the River Traligill were used by late Stone Age people. Some of the earliest traces of people living in Scotland have been found here, presumably attracted by the better soil and the 'ready-made' houses. Near the roadside houses, a cairn stands as a memorial to the two geologists, Benjamin Peach and John

Horne, who unravelled the mysteries of the local landscape. Beyond the settlement lies Loch Assynt, its dark pine-clad islands in stark contrast to the grassy hillsides. By its shore stands the ruin of Ardvreck Castle. In 1650 the Marquis of Montrose (well known for his exploits against the Covenanters, religious dissenters) fled here. Neil Macleod imprisoned him and dispatched him to Edinburgh to be barbarously hanged, drawn and quartered. Although Macleod expected a bounty of £20,000 for Montrose, he was paid in oatmeal – 56,000 pounds (25,000kg) of it!

Calda House, which stands near the castle, was built in 1695 but was burned to the ground in somewhat mysterious circumstances in 1737.

▶ *Continue on the* **A837** *for 13 miles (21km) to Lochinver.*

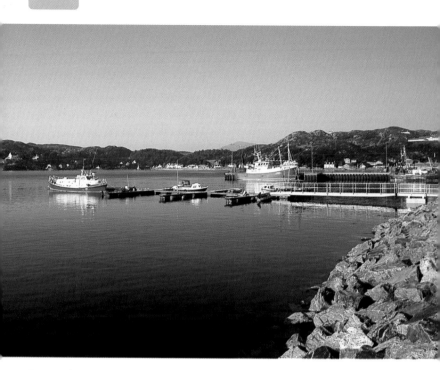

8 Lochinver, Highland

This is Assynt's main village and an important fishing port specialising in whitefish and shellfish. The life and history of the area is told in the village's Assynt Visitor Centre.

During the summer it is popular with visitors, walkers and fishermen. A local place of interest is the Highland Stoneware factory, which produces many types of high-quality hand-painted pottery.

From north of Lochinver, there are magnificent views of Suilven, at 2,399 feet (731m), one of Britain's most spectacularly shaped mountains. From this direction it rises as a huge dome of reddish-brown sandstone above the platform of the much lighter-coloured gneiss. The Vikings called it Sul Fhal, the Pillar Mountain, but the Gaelic name is Caisteal Liath, the Grey Castle. It is regarded by many Scots as one of the

The tranquil harbour of Lochinver

country's most attractive hills; however, it is not one of the district's most-climbed hills as the moorland walk-in – although enjoyable – is quite long.

> *i* *Kirk Lane (seasonal)*

> ▶ *Leave by the **A837** and turn left at the **B869**. Continue on this road to the **A894**, then*

FOR CHILDREN

The area north of Lochinver has some wonderful sandy beaches, many of which can be relatively quiet even at the height of summer. Some of the best-known ones are at Achmelvich, Clachtoll and Clashnessie, all of which have sheltered bays and are very clean.

Crated local fish ready for export

RECOMMENDED WALKS

To the south of Lochinver, a path follows the River Kirkaig to the Falls of Kirkaig; further on, at Fionn Loch, there is a very good view of Suilven.

*turn left to reach the bridge at Kylesku. The **B869** is a narrow twisting road with many steep hills and it is unsuitable for caravans. An alternative route for caravans is the **A837** from Lochinver to Skiag Bridge and then left at the **A894**.*

4 Kylesku, Highland

The Kylesku Bridge, a graceful concrete construction that has won many accolades, crosses Loch a' Cháirn Bhàin with a view towards the pointed peak of Quinag, which dominates the southern shore. To the east, the loch splits into two arms and boat trips are available on Loch Glencoul to visit seals and herons and to get a view of the remote waterfall Eas-Coul-

SCENIC ROUTES

There are many beautiful stretches of road on this tour, and one such part is the route from Lochinver to Kylesku. Photographers may take days to travel this route as there are so many places where the views of the sea are quite outstanding. One particular detour north of Lochinver that is worth exploring is to follow the narrow roads to the Rhu Stoer lighthouse (built in 1870) or to Culkein. At the northern end of the Stoer peninsula is the Old Man of Stoer, a tall sandstone sea stack that stands just offshore.

Aulin. This is Britain's highest waterfall at over 650 feet (200m) high.

The car park on the northern side of the bridge offers excellent views of Quinag, the huge mountain that lies between Kylesku and Loch Assynt. It has seven peaks, the highest being 2,653 feet (809m). Like many of the neighbouring

hills, it has a base of gneiss, but for the most part is sandstone; a few of the peaks have quartzite caps. Its name comes from the Gaelic Cuinneag, meaning a churn or pail.

▶ *Continue on the **A894** for 12 miles (19km) to Scourie.*

5 Scourie, Highland

This crofting community nestles comfortably in a sheltered hollow. It is a popular centre from which to tour the district and many walkers, fishermen and other visitors find this charming base. Despite its northerly position, palm trees grow in the garden of Scourie Lodge. The local landscape has earned the description 'knob and lochan' (a lochan is a small loch) as the undulating gneiss landscape is studded with little hillocks and countless pools. Where peat bogs have developed, these are used as a source of fuel and many of the villagers spend time during the early summer cutting the peats and

The Kylesku Bridge spanning Loch a' Cháirn Bhàin

Crofters' cottages in Scourie, where a more traditional way of life still persists

stacking them to dry before taking them home for the winter.

To the north is Loch Laxford, a haven for seabirds and seals. Summer cruises on the loch are available from Fanagmore.

▶ Continue on the **A894** to Laxford Bridge and turn left at the **A838**. Turn left at the **B801** which ends at Kinlochbervie, a distance of 16 miles (26km).

6 Kinlochbervie, Highland
In the 1960s this crofting village began its transformation into one of Scotland's most important modern harbours. Nowadays many boats, a large proportion of them originally from the more traditional fishing ports of the east coast of Scotland, land substantial catches of cod, haddock, whiting and many other varieties here.

The minor road beyond Kinlochbervie leads to the little community of Sheigra, passing glorious coastal scenery at crofting townships such as Oldshoremore (where there is also a superb beach). The 13th-century manuscript of the *Haakon Saga* records the fact that King Haakon anchored at Oldshoremore in 1263 when he commenced his invasion of Scotland.

The view to the east is dominated by the impressive hills of Ben Stack, Arkle and Foinaven.

▶ Return along the **B801** and the **A838** to Laxford Bridge and turn to the left. Continue along the **A838**, then turn right at the **A836** to reach Lairg.

7 Lairg, Highland
Lairg was established beside the River Shin in one of the few areas of decent arable land in Sutherland. This district was once quite well populated, but after the Clearances many of the displaced people emigrated to America or the British colonies. The Ferrycroft Countryside Centre features the history and archaeology of the area. Further down the river are the Falls of Shin with a visitor centre. This is a good salmon river and fish must climb the falls in order to return to their spawning grounds upstream. In days of old, poachers used to come to the falls so that they could spear or shoot the fish as they attempted to leap the falls.

[i] *Ferrycroft Countryside Centre (seasonal)*

A tapestry depicting the notorious Highland Clearances of the 18th century

▶ Leave by the **A836** and follow it back to Bonar Bridge.

Northern
Highlights

This tour traces the most northerly point of Scotland, visiting
many wide, sandy – and largely empty – beaches. Dornoch is
its starting point, with a fine bay and championship golf course.
Its attractiveness is enhanced by its sandstone buildings and a
spacious centre dominated by the cathedral.

2/3 DAYS • 269 MILES • 433KM

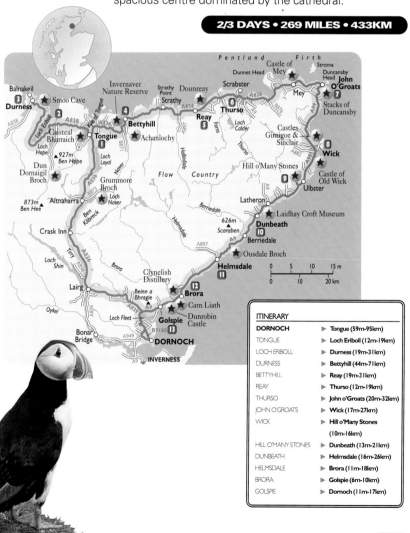

ITINERARY		
DORNOCH	▶	**Tongue** (59m-95km)
TONGUE	▶	**Loch Eriboll** (12m-19km)
LOCH ERIBOLL	▶	**Durness** (19m-31km)
DURNESS	▶	**Bettyhill** (44m-71km)
BETTYHILL	▶	**Reay** (19m-31km)
REAY	▶	**Thurso** (12m-19km)
THURSO	▶	**John o'Groats** (20m-32km)
JOHN O'GROATS	▶	**Wick** (17m-27km)
WICK	▶	**Hill o'Many Stones** (10m-16km)
HILL O'MANY STONES	▶	**Dunbeath** (13m-21km)
DUNBEATH	▶	**Helmsdale** (16m-26km)
HELMSDALE	▶	**Brora** (11m-18km)
BRORA	▶	**Golspie** (6m-10km)
GOLSPIE	▶	**Dornoch** (11m-17km)

i **The Square**

▶ Leave by the **A949** and turn right when the **A9** is met. Turn left at the **A839** and follow it to Lairg. Leave Lairg by the **A836** and follow it to Tongue.

1 Tongue, Highland

Tongue occupies a marvellous position overlooking the wide sandy estuary of the Kyle of Tongue. To the west of the village stands the ruin of Castle Varrich, or Caisteal Bharraich, a 14th-century stronghold of the MacKays on a site that may have been used by an 11th-century Norse king. Nearby Tongue House (not open) used to be the home of the chiefs of the MacKay clan.

▶ Leave by the **A838** and follow it for 12 miles (19km) to Loch Eriboll.

2 Loch Eriboll, Highland

This is one of the north coast's deepest and most sheltered sea lochs and it was used during World War II by convoys of ships waiting to sail across the North Atlantic. The sailors knew this rather desolate place as 'Loch 'Orrible'!

On the eastern side of the loch, a spit runs out to the rocky promontory of Ard Neackie on which are the very substantial remains of four lime kilns which were constructed around 1870.

▶ Continue on the **A838** for 19 miles (31km) to Durness.

3 Durness, Highland

A popular stopping point for visitors, not only for the local scenery, but also for the huge expanses of sandy beaches at the village and at neighbouring Balnakeil.

The wide, sandy estuary of the Kyle of Tongue

Durness is situated in a limestone area and is best known for Smoo Cave. The main cavern is huge – about 200 feet (60m) long and 110 feet (35m) wide – and is easy to enter. Beyond this, a second cave has a 'swallow hole' in its roof and a stream, the Allt Smoo, tumbles 80 feet (25m) into it. A third cave can only be entered by boat. To the west of the village lies beautiful Balnakeil Bay which has a wide sweep of sand backed by tall grass-covered dunes. The site of the ruined church near by may date back to the 8th century when St Maelrubha of Applecross was in this district. The southern wall of the church contains the tomb of the murdered Donald MacLeod,

BACK TO NATURE

While the attention of most visitors will be focused on the coast, the landward scenery should not be ignored as the peat bogs from Loch Loyal eastward are regarded as being of world importance. This is the Flow Country, a wilderness relatively undisturbed by humans for 6,000 or more years. It is home to such rarities as the freshwater pearl mussel, insectivorous plants such as the sundew and to birds – including 70 per cent of Europe's breeding population of greenshanks. Golden eagles, short-eared owls and peregrines all treat this as their hunting and breeding ground. Unfortunately, this beautiful and very desolate region is threatened by intensive forestry, often planted for tax advantages rather than from a wish to grow a worthwhile crop, and a great debate is still continuing on how to preserve this fine example of Scotland's natural heritage for future generations.

BACK TO NATURE

The variety of good habitats, the plentiful supply of fish and the low human population have encouraged huge numbers of seabirds to nest along the coast. Particular places of interest include Faraid Head (near Durness) for puffins; Duncansby Head for many different types of cliff-nesting seabirds; Dunnet Bay for sea duck, divers and gulls in winter; and Golspie for sea duck and in particular eider. Loch Fleet is home to many birds, especially waders, so keen birdwatchers may wish to make a detour off the A9 and follow the southern shore of the loch before returning to Dornoch.

reckoned to be responsible for 18 deaths. It is said that he was so worried that his remains would be dug up after burial by families seeking revenge, he offered a local landowner a huge sum of money to reserve this tomb where he thought his bones might be safe. In many ways, the Balnakeil Craft Village is a memorial to days gone by. It was planned by the Ministry of Defence as an 'early warning station' but by the time it was built the technology was obsolete so the buildings were abandoned. They were subsequently taken up by craftsmen and women and their families who together have built up one of the Highlands' most fascinating communities. Crafts such as marquetry, knitting, pottery and woodturning are represented here and each of the craft shops has a display where the high-quality goods can be viewed.

Cape Wrath is reached by ferry and bus from the Kyle of Durness. The headland at Cape Wrath, the northwestern tip of mainland Britain, rises 360 feet (110m) from the sea and is topped by a lighthouse built by the grandfather of Robert Louis Stevenson, in 1828. Between the cape and the kyle is a vast expanse of peat bog known as the Parph and this comes to an abrupt end at the coast which has the highest cliffs on the mainland, the biggest being Clo Mor, which is over 600 feet (180m) high.

A potter at work at Balnakeil Craft Village

i *Durine, Durness (seasonal)*

▶ *Return along the A838 to Tongue, then follow the A836 along the coast to Bettyhill.*

4 Bettyhill, Highland
Bettyhill was founded by people displaced during the Clearances and the name derives from Elizabeth, Countess of Sutherland, wife of the duke who was responsible for many of the region's evictions. The local Strathnaver Museum is housed in a church built in 1774 and in the churchyard stands the Farr Stone, a good example of early Christian Celtic sculpture. The museum has features on the local

Dramatic Smoo Cave near Durness

clearances as Strathnaver was one of the centres of the evictions. To the south of Bettyhill stand the remains of the clearance village of Achanlochy, where seven families were thrown out of their homes.

The village stands close to the River Naver and looks over sandy Torrisdale Bay, on the southern side of which is the Invernaver Nature Reserve. Its flora is of an unusual mix as blown shell-sand has mixed with the otherwise acid soil and supports a wide variety of plants, including dwarf juniper, thrift, alpine bistort and creeping willow.

ℹ️ *Clachan, Bettyhill (seasonal)*

▶ *Continue on the **A836** to Reay.*

❺ **Reay,** Highland
The original Reay was buried in sand in the early 18th century, but the village was rebuilt and the local church dates from 1839 when the new community was being re-established. Reay has given its name to the 'Reay Country', the great inland tract of deer 'forest', though it should be noted that when the word

'forest' is used to describe a hunting ground, it does not necessarily imply that there are many trees there!

Today, Reay is best known for the hemispherical dome of the nearby nuclear reactor at Dounreay. In 1955 construction of the Dounreay Fast Reactor was begun in order to produce electricity. In 1974 the Prototype Fast Reactor began operating. Neither of these plants now produce electricity, but the site houses the UKAEA Exhibition Centre.

▶ *Continue on the **A836** for 12 miles (19km) to Thurso.*

❻ **Thurso,** Highland
Thurso began life as a fishing settlement and the fishermen's houses can be seen above the harbour. However, it developed rapidly in the early 19th century when huge quantities of Caithness 'flags' were exported. These are the flat slabs of local sandstone that were in demand for pavements in the greatly expanding towns and cities of Britain and other countries. The flags are so common that even local fences are made of them.

Thurso expanded dramati-

The ruins of Old St Peter's Kirk in Thurso

cally as a result of the building of the reactors at Dounreay. However, it still has a number of substantial sandstone buildings and these help to retain its homely character. The ruined 17th-century Thurso Castle (fenced off) overlooks the harbour and beyond it is Harold's Tower, erected over the grave of Earl Harold, the 12th-century ruler who presided over parts of Caithness, Orkney and Shetland.

The Thurso Heritage Museum contains a wide variety of interesting artefacts, including the Ulbster Stone (a Pictish sculptured stone), and also an important collection of rocks and fossils collected by Robert Dick in the 19th century.

Northwest of Thurso, on the A836, is the village of Mey. The Castle of Mey was the summer residence of the late Queen Mother.

ℹ️ *Riverside (seasonal)*

▶ *Continue on the **A836** for 20 miles (32km) to John o' Groats.*

7 John o' Groats, Highland
This is often thought to be mainland Britain's most northerly point, but in fact Dunnet Head (to the west) holds that distinction. However, it is the country's most northerly village and therefore either the start or finish of the ever popular John o' Groats to Land's End long-distance walks. The village was named after Jan de Groot, a Dutchman who started a ferry service from here to Orkney in the 16th century.

Near by, Duncansby Head, the northeastern tip of the mainland, has cliffs 210 feet (64m) high and a lighthouse. With care, the cliff tops can be followed to view the pinnacles called the Stacks of Duncansby and other sea stacks and cliffs that the sea has carved out of the sandstone.

further north, the 15th-century Castle Girnigoe and 17th-century Castle Sinclair remain, though reduced to spectacular clifftop ruins.

Wick is still an important and busy place, with a fine harbour that was originally built for the once-prosperous herring industry. An earlier harbour was built at Pulteneytown by Thomas Telford in 1806 to encourage evicted crofters to take up fishing. Wick's Heritage Centre, on Bank Row, is in the heart of a district of old buildings associated with the fishing industry, and has displays on the history of the town and the herring industry. On High Street stands Wick's old parish church, with the ruined 13th-century chapel of St Fergus in its grounds.

The Last House in John o' Groats, erroneously thought to be Britain's most northerly point

ℹ *County Road (seasonal)*

▶ *Leave by the **A99** to Wick.*

8 Wick, Highland
Wick has been an important anchorage at least since the days of the Vikings; its name means 'bay'. Three castles testify to its strategic importance. The 12th-century castle of Old Wick stands to the south of the town;

ℹ *Whitechapel Road, off High Street*

▶ *Remain on the **A99**. Turn right at a signposted unclassified road to the Hill o' Many Stones.*

9 Hill o' Many Stones, Highland
This intriguing fan-shaped array of 22 rows of stones dates back to the early Bronze Age, and is a type of monument unique to northern Sutherland (though they are similar to ones found in Brittany). Their purpose is still an unresolved mystery though it has been said that this could be some sort of ancient computer used to predict the movement of heavenly bodies.

FOR HISTORY BUFFS

Pictish brochs can be found in many places on this tour. The most substantial ones near the route are Cairn Laith (south of Brae) and Ousdale Broch (north of Helmsdale). Good ones further off the route are Dun Dornaigil (south of Loch Hope) and Grummore Broch (north of Loch Naver).

▶ *Continue on the **A99** and **A9** for 13 miles (21km) to Dunbeath.*

10 Dunbeath, Highland
Dunbeath was the home of Highland writer Neil Gunn, whose books include *The Silver Darlings*. The local Heritage Centre (housed in the school that Gunn attended) has displays on the lives of crofters and the history of the district. Laidhay Croft Museum, just north of the village, occupies a traditional longhouse and barn steading worked up until 1968. Parts of this thatched building may date back to the late 18th century though most of it is mid-19th-century.

RECOMMENDED WALK

From the Dunbeath Heritage Centre head towards the viewpoint overlooking the harbour and village, then proceed to cross the old bridge. Turn left after the bridge onto a footpath which leads past the old meal mill and continues to the remains of a broch. Nearby is Ballachly, where Neil Gunn's ancestors farmed.

▶ *Continue on the **A9** for 16 miles (26km) to Helmsdale.*

❶ Helmsdale, Highland

Set on the River Helmsdale, at the seaward end of the attractive Strath of Kildonan, this was where some of the most infamous acts of the Clearances were carried out by Patrick Sellars on behalf of the Countess of Sutherland. The story of these sad days is admirably told in Helmsdale's Timespan Heritage Centre. This award-winning exhibition also has an exhibition on the Kildonan 'gold rush' of 1868–9. Although gold was never found in economically viable quantities, some people still go panning in the river and find small flakes of the metal.

▶ *Continue on the A9 to Brora.*

❷ Brora, Highland

Brora has the unusual distinction of having had a small coal mine based on a seam 'only' 125 million years old and, of course, a great distance from the country's main coalfields in the Midland Valley.

Today, one of its most notable industries is the Clynelish Distillery, Sutherland's only malt whisky distillery; tours are available.

▶ *Continue on the A9 to Golspie.*

❸ Golspie, Highland

This small resort lies beneath the wooded slope of Beinn a' Bhragaidh, near whose summit is perched a statue of the first Duke of Sutherland, who was known as the 'Leviathan of Wealth'. Between the years 1810 and 1820 he was responsible for the eviction of some 15,000 tenants from their homes, in order to use the land for lucrative sheep farming. The scars of these times are still visible all over Sutherland. Ruined croft buildings stand and decay where families were forcibly moved from their land.

A rather unusual shop in the village is the Orcadian Stone Company, which sells examples

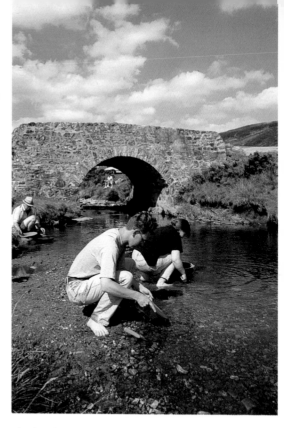

of rocks, minerals and fossils. It also has a fine exhibition of these natural treasures.

The Dukes of Sutherland built nearby Dunrobin Castle on a site that has been fortified for many centuries. The present castle dates mainly from the 13th century but much of it was built between 1835 and 1850. Queen Victoria described it as a 'mixture of an old Scotch castle and a French château' and it does have a certain fairy-tale look about it. The gardens are extensive and contain a museum with interesting Pictish stones, an ice-house (for storing perishable food) and an 18th-century doocot.

South of Golspie, the main road crosses the head of Loch Fleet, over a huge earthen embankment known as The Mound. This was constructed in 1816 by Thomas Telford, partly to support the new road heading northwards, but also to reclaim the upper reaches of the loch. Today, this section is colonised by alder and willow and has been classed as a

Above: Panning for gold in the Kildonan Burn, Helmsdale
Right: The fairy-tale Dunrobin Castle, one of Queen Victoria's favourite places

National Nature Reserve. The River Fleet runs through a sluice at the end of the embankment and at certain times of the year salmon may be seen there waiting for the gate to open so they can continue their journey.

▶ *Continue on the A9, then turn left at the B9168 in order to return to Dornoch, 11 miles (17km).*

SCENIC ROUTES

The superb coastal scenery, both cliffs and beaches, make this tour very attractive, especially along the north coast and near the high headlands in the northeast. The Strath of Kildonan is a fine drive for those wanting a detour.

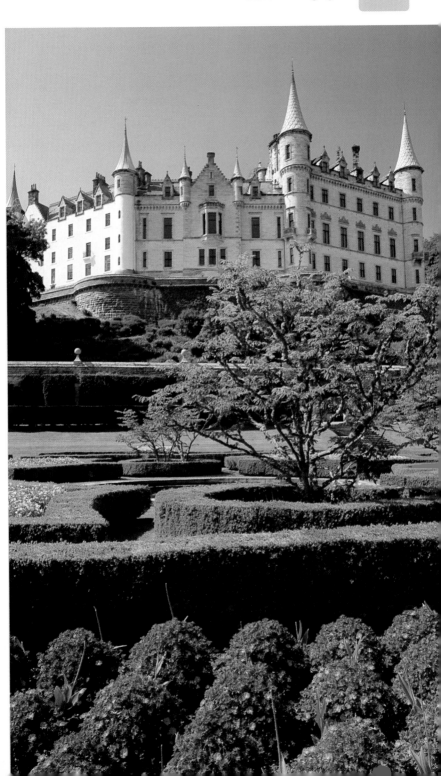

Easter Ross &
the Black Isle

Away from the dramatic Highlands scenery of previous chapters, this tour takes in gentler countryside and coastal roads. The tour begins in Dingwall, a town which has enjoyed a chequered history, having been a Viking settlement and later a market town with the status of a royal burgh.

2 DAYS • 107 MILES • 173KM

ITINERARY		
DINGWALL	▶	Evanton (6m-10km)
EVANTON	▶	Tain (21m-34km)
TAIN	▶	Portmahomack (10m-16km)
PORTMAHOMACK	▶	Fearn Abbey (7m-11km)
FEARN ABBEY	▶	Cromarty (37m-60km)
CROMARTY	▶	Rosemarkie (9m-14km)
ROSEMARKIE	▶	Fortrose (1m-2km)
FORTROSE	▶	Dingwall (16m-26km)

> Leave by the **A862**. Join the **A9** heading northwards, then turn left at the **B817** to Evanton.

SCENIC ROUTES

The sea views are particularly striking especially when driving past the firths' narrowest parts. One of the best known views is found on the Struie road; as this road descends there is a viewpoint on the right overlooking the Kyle of Sutherland.

1 Evanton, Highland

From the road, a curious monument will be seen on the summit of Cnoc Fyrish, the hill just beyond Evanton. This is a folly built in 1782 by General Sir Hector Munro to help alleviate local unemployment. The general had served in India and this monument is a replica of an Indian gate. Down by the Foulis Ferry, an 18th-century rent house is now at the heart of the Storehouse of Foulis attraction. Its features include imaginative history and wildlife exhibitions and an audio-visual theatre, and outside there is a display of traditional fishing vessels and a shoreline walk.

> Continue on the **B817** and turn left at the **B9176** (the Struie road). Turn right at the **A836** and join the **A9** for Tain. Bear left after 2 miles (3km) to enter Tain.

2 Tain, Highland

Tain's name comes from the Norse word 'thing', meaning a parliament, as a Viking colony was established in this district. Later, the town's patron, St Duthus, was born here (in AD 1000) and he established a chapel just outside the town. He died in Ireland, but his remains were brought back and interred in the 14th-century St Duthus' Church. The town subsequently became a place of pilgrimage and James IV often

RECOMMENDED WALKS

The walk at Evanton to see the Black Rock Gorge is worthwhile, as is the nerve-racking walk over the narrow bridge at the gorge. Walks to lighthouses or looking points are usually interesting: try Tarbat Ness (a circular walk from Portmahomack via the coastal path that goes past Ballone Castle) or the look-out at the top of the Sutors of Cromarty.

travelled here, thus increasing its prestige and importance.

Tain's history was blotted, however, when it became an administrative centre for the Clearances. It was here that orders for the appropriation of the crofters' land were made. The deeds were carried out from the Tolbooth that still stands in the High Street, and it was within this building that crofters

Stained-glass window at St Duthus' Church, Tain

were imprisoned if they refused to obey the eviction notices. The Tolbooth is Tain's finest building; it was built between 1706 and 1733 with fine conical roofs on top of the turrets, and replaced an earlier tolbooth of 1631.

At Castle Brae, the Tain Through Time exhibition describes the history of the town; the centre also includes St Duthus' Church.

The Glenmorangie Distillery, renowned for its single malt whisky, lies on the outskirts of town.

Publicans' copper measures, Tain Museum

145

The fishing village of
Portmahomack

FOR HISTORY BUFFS

The great Pictish cross slab,
known as Clach a'Charridh,
stands above the seaside village
of Shandwick, near Balintore. It
occupies its original position,
and the face looking out to sea
is engraved with a cross, angels
and a beast. The other side has
fivel panels, one of which
shows a Pictish beast.

▶ Continue on the **B9165** and
turn left at the **A9**. Cross the
Cromarty Firth, then turn left
at the **B9163** to Cromarty.

▶ Leave by the minor road to
Portmahomack. Turn left at
the **B9165** to enter the
village.

3 Portmahomack, Highland

This pleasant lobster-fishing
village sits in a broad bay with
views across the Dornoch Firth.
Just by the main street, an
ornate Victorian cast-iron fountain celebrates the introduction
of 'gravitation water' to the
village in 1887 (water had previ-
ously come up from a well).
Another unusual structure is the
tower of the local church, which
is domed.

Beyond the village, a minor
road leads to a lighthouse at
Tarbat Ness. To the east of
Portmahomack stand the ruins
of Ballone Castle, which can be
reached from either the village
or the lighthouse.

▶ Return along the **B9165** for 7
miles (11km) to Fearn Abbey.

4 Fearn Abbey, Highland

The original abbey was founded
in the 13th century and is unfortunately best known for the
collapse of its roof in 1742, which
killed 42 people. This had been
prophesied by the Brahan Seer,
Coinneach Odhar. The 16th-

BACK TO NATURE

Both the Dornoch and the
Cromarty Firth are good for
birdwatching, particularly for
waders when the tide is out.
Since the district projects
some distance into the North
Sea it is the first landfall for
many migratory birds and
Tarbat Ness is often a tempo-
rary resting place for visiting
birds on their migratory
routes. The best times of year
are April, May, August and
October, particularly when the
winds are from the east.

century clairvoyant had the gift
of the 'second sight' and during
his life he gave many warnings
of unhappy events that were to
happen. Many of these came
true and his penultimate
prophecy, telling of the infidelity
of the Countess of Seaforth's
husband, led to him being
burned alive in a barrel of tar.
His last prophecy, made just
before he died, foretold of the
extinction of the Seaforth family.
That took place in the early 19th
century. Brahan, where he came
from, is an estate to the southwest of Dingwall.

5 Cromarty, Highland

Cromarty stands at the entrance
to the Cromarty Firth, a passage
dominated by the headlands of
the Sutors of Cromarty and the
North Sutor on the opposite
shore. This is an important
anchorage and was used during
both world wars. Today, the
firth has an oil rig fabrication
site and these massive rigs
dominate the sheltered waters.

The village was once important as it was on the main route
north from Inverness which ran
along the coast and used a series
of ferries across the various
stretches of water. The village
declined after the fishing failed
and after it was decided that the
railway route was to go on the
other side of the firth. The most
outstanding building from more
prosperous times is the Town
House, built in the 18th
century. This contains the
courthouse and has been
opened as a visitor centre.

Cromarty's most notable
inhabitant was Hugh Miller,
whose cottage has been
preserved by the National Trust
for Scotland. Miller was a stonemason by trade but he never
lost his childhood curiosity for
collecting fossils and interesting
rocks. He helped to popularise
geology as he avoided the
jargon of the professionals and

FOR CHILDREN

There are many fine beaches along the coast, including those at Cromarty, Fortrose, Portmahomack and Tain. As wet-weather alternatives, there are swimming pools in Alness, Dingwall and Tain. In addition, Alness has a sports hall and both Dingwall and Invergordon have sports centres.

the exhibits in the local museum in Groam House, which has special displays on the Picts and the Brahan Seer. The Fairy Glen, reputedly the home of a witch, runs inland from the village and there are two waterfalls further up this nicely wooded valley.

▶ *Continue on the A832 for 1 mile (2km) to Fortrose.*

7 Fortrose, Highland
Fortrose's main attraction is its medieval cathedral, which has an octagonal clock tower and a detached Chapter House. The local bishopric was originally at Rosemarkie, but it moved to Fortrose in the early years of the 13th century and work on the new cathedral was started at that time,

although it was not completed until the 15th century. A treasure trove of over 1,000 medieval coins was discovered buried in the green in 1880.

The harbour is well sheltered but is now mainly used by pleasure craft. From the village, a narrow neck of land stretches out into the Moray Firth to Chanonry Point where there is a lighthouse. It was here that the Brahan Seer was burned to death, and a monument has been set up to celebrate this rather remarkable man.

▶ *Continue on the A832 to the Tore roundabout. Join the A835 and turn right at the A862 to return to Dingwall.*

Fortrose cathedral: detail

he wrote a widely read series of articles entitled *The Old Red Sandstone*, published in 1841. However, Miller had strong religious ideas that contradicted his scientific findings and his writings were furiously attacked by the religious bigots of the day. His thatched cottage, built in the early 18th century, contains mementoes of his life. Within the house is an example of the fossil fish named after him, *Pterichthys milleri*, and outside stands a sundial that he carved himself.

▶ *Leave by the A832 and follow it to Rosemarkie.*

6 Rosemarkie, Highland
With red sandstone houses and a red sandy beach to match, attractive Rosemarkie sits at the mouth of the Moray Firth opposite Fort George. St Moluag founded a monastic school here in the 6th century and a Pictish stone in the local churchyard is said to mark the saint's resting place. Other carved stones are among

The remains of Fortrose's medieval cathedral

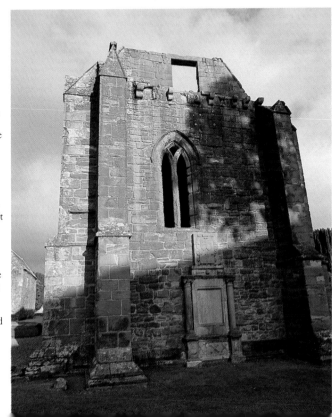

Over the Sea
to Skye

Skye is the most scenically spectacular island of the whole of the British Isles, with glorious mountain landscapes. The gateway to Skye, Kyleakin, is guarded by the ruin of Castle Moil, a small Norse keep. The village is crowded during the summer months as this is the terminus of the railway line from Inverness.

2/3 DAYS • 244 MILES • 392KM

► *Leave by the **A850** and follow it for 8 miles (13km) to Broadford.*

1 Broadford, Highland
This widely scattered crofting community lies beneath the Red Hills, a group of rounded granite mountains. This is a good base for the south of the island.

ⓘ *Car Park (seasonal)*

► *Continue on the **A87** to the Sligachan Hotel at the head of Loch Sligachan.*

2 Loch Sligachan, Highland
This is an idyllic base for any visitor, and especially for those who come to walk in the Cuillin Hills. The campsite by the shore must surely have one of the finest locations of any site in Britain – opposite towering 2,536-foot (773m) Glamaig, and with a view across the Inner Sound towards the mainland. A stroll from the road leads to an old bridge over the River Sligachan from which the Cuillin Hills can be seen to greater advantage.

The Cuillin Hills, reflected in the waters of Loch Sligachan

► *Continue on the **A87** for 9 miles (14km) to Portree.*

3 Portree, Highland
This is the island's capital and although the islanders them-selves might think of it as a busy place, the pace of life follows the generally relaxed Highland pattern. This is certainly a most picturesquely positioned town, with its well-sheltered harbour nestling at the foot of wooded hills.

The town's name, Port an Righ, or 'king's port', celebrates the visit here in 1540 by James V in his attempt to persuade local chiefs that they should swear allegiance to him. He brought 12 ships with him to help them make up their minds!

ⓘ *Bayfield House, Bayfield Road*

► *Leave by the **A855** and continue for 7 miles (11km) to The Storr (after Loch Leathan).*

FOR HISTORY BUFFS

South of Portree, the B883 road leads to the settlement of Braes, where a monument celebrates the battles between local crofters and the police in 1882. The locals had asked their Laird, Lord MacDonald, for extra land on which to graze their animals. He refused, even though the crofters were prepared to pay, and they decided to withhold their rents. Court orders were then taken out against them but the orders were seized and torn up when the sheriff's officers tried to deliver them. In a further confrontation, the local police were helped by 50 policemen from Glasgow (and backed up by naval ships stand-ing by with troops aboard should the 'trouble' spread). These events caused a public outcry about the way in which landowners treated crofters and this led to legislation being passed which guaranteed fair rents and security of tenure.

4 The Storr, Highland

As the road heads northwards it runs beneath a steep escarpment, the highest point of which is The Storr, 2,363 feet (719m) high. To the right of this can be seen the tall pinnacle called the Old Man of Storr which is 160 feet (49m) tall. This is the site of Britain's most spectacular example of landslipping; the jumble of boulders, screes and pinnacles indicates where chunks of the mountain have slipped as the weak underlying clays and limestones collapsed under the weight of the overlying lavas.

SCENIC ROUTES

In good weather the whole of this tour passes through scenery which is truly memorable. Perhaps the most dramatic parts are north of Portree when the Old Man of Storr is seen with Loch Fada in the foreground, and also going down Glen Brittle and seeing the massive northern corries of the Cuillin Hills.

▶ Continue on the **A855** for 12 miles (19km) to the Quiraing.

5 Quiraing, Highland

To the northwest of the crofting community of Staffin, another escarpment indicates the site of a massive landslip. This is known as the Quiraing and is best approached on foot from the Staffin to Uig road. Nature has produced some strange shapes here, and some of the features have been given names like the Table, the Prison and the Needle.

▶ Continue on the **A855** for 13 miles (21km) to Kilmuir.

6 Kilmuir, Highland

This scattered crofting community is home to the Skye Museum of Island Life, which has a number of attractive thatched cottages that have been restored to show how people lived in these small houses a century ago. Near by, a tall monument in the local graveyard marks the grave of Flora MacDonald. She has a very special place in Scottish history as the woman who helped Bonnie Prince Charlie escape after Culloden. He had fled to South Uist but found the island crawling with hundreds of government soldiers, all of them keen to capture a man with a price of £30,000 on his head. Flora disguised the Prince as her maidservant Betty Burke and smuggled him over to Skye, from where he was able to reach the mainland and make his escape to safety in France.

To the north of Kilmuir stand the ruins of Duntulm Castle, built in the early 17th century by the MacDonalds. The building stands on a crag, protected by cliffs and steep slopes on the three seaward sides and a dry ditch on the landward side.

▶ Continue on the **A855** to Uig.

The Old Man of Storr on the Isle of Skye

Flora MacDonald's grave at Kilmuir

7 Uig, Highland

This little port is the terminus for the ferries that serve Lochmaddy on North Uist and Tarbert on Harris, so the harbourside can be busy around sailing times. A little tower overlooks the harbour and though it looks rather old, it is in fact a Victorian folly dating back to the 19th century.

i *Ferry Terminal (seasonal)*

▶ *Leave by the **A87** and turn right at the **A850**. Follow this to Dunvegan Castle.*

8 Dunvegan Castle, Highland

The home of the chiefs of Clan MacLeod was built as a keep in the 14th century with its only entrance through the sea gate. Within the castle is the famous 'fairy flag', said to have been given to a MacLeod chief by his fairy wife. The flag is of Eastern origin and according to the legend it will protect the clan if waved at moments of great danger. Also on display is the drinking horn of chieftain Sir

---

BACK TO NATURE

Common seals and great grey Atlantic seals are found in Loch Dunvegan and boat trips to the seal colonies are available from Dunvegan. Golden eagles and white-tailed sea eagles may also be seen in the locality. The latter are the subject of a re-introduction programme in Scotland. In spring, the flower-rich meadows can be a colourful sight and alpine species are sometimes found growing beside the road in upland areas.

Rory Mor: this can hold the equivalent of two bottles of wine, and it is claimed that he could drain it in one draught!

On the other side of Loch Dunvegan stand the two flat-topped hills called MacLeod's Tables. Their name recalls a chieftain bragging to a Lowlander of the size of his dining table; to prove his boast

View of the ferry loading at Uig

RECOMMENDED WALKS

Skye offers countless opportunities for walking – provided the weather is kind! One straightforward walk starts at Claigan, which is north of Dunvegan. This follows the shore and leads to a little 'coral' beach. The Old Man of Storr can be reached from a roadside path but the path is steep and there is a lot of loose scree in places. The landscape here is unique and the view is a fine reward indeed.

The Cuillin Hills should certainly not be attempted by walkers with little hillwalking experience, but there are low-level walks that are easier. The best advice is to buy one of the local walking guides which are widely available.

---

he entertained his guest on one of the summits.

i *2 Lochside, Dunvegan (seasonal)*

> *Leave by the A863, then turn right at the B884 to Colbost.*

9 Colbost, Highland

The little Croft Museum here has a thatched cottage and a display of 19th-century furniture and farming implements. If you have never smelled a peat fire burning then here is your chance!

FOR CHILDREN

The moors and lower hills of Skye provide good terrain for pony-trekking and there are facilities at Struan (south of Dunvegan on the A832), Penifiler (south of Portree) and Uig. However, it must be remembered that Skye's weather can be very mixed.

> *Return along the B884 and turn right at the A863. Turn right at the B8009 and follow this to Carbost.*

10 Carbost, Highland

This is the site of the Isle of Skye's only distillery, the Talisker Distillery. The peat fires used to dry the grain gives the whisky its distinctive smokey flavour.

> *Return along the B8009 and turn right at the minor road that takes you down Glen Brittle.*

11 Glen Brittle, Highland

Many of the Cuillin Hills' lower slopes are covered with loose scree, while the upper parts are bare rock with little or no vegetation – the preserve of experienced hillwalkers. For walkers trying to capture all the 'Munros' (Scottish hills with a peak over 3,000 feet/914m high), their most difficult obstacle is usually the Inaccessible Pinnacle on Sgurr Dearg, which involves climbing a pinnacle at the top of the mountain. Definitely not for casual walkers, who would be best advised to stick to easier walks in the area.

The foot of the glen is often busy with walkers and climbers who are here to scale the hills. Looking up and around, there are marvellous views of the jagged hills with their long steep scree slopes.

> *Return to the B8009 and turn right. Turn right at the A863 and continue to Sligachan, then turn right at the A87. Follow this to Broadford, then turn right at the B8083 in order to reach Torrin.*

The Cuillin Hills seen above Loch Scavaig, near Elgol

12 Torrin, Highland

Torrin is best known for its fine view of the 3,043-foot (927m) mountain Blà Bheinn (or Blaven) and its precipitous rocky ridge known as Clach Glas. The latter entices the experienced climber. A couple of quarries near by are sources of the white Skye marble.

> *Continue on the B8083 and follow it to Elgol.*

13 Elgol, Highland

Elgol, overlooking Loch Scavaig, has a small jetty from which there is one of the best views of the Cuillin Hills. From here it is possible to appreciate the shape of the complex, with a ring of hills surrounding Loch Coruisk. Boat trips to Loch Coruisk are available from Elgol. Looking in the other direction, the breathtaking view over the sea encompasses the islands of Soay, Rum, Canna and Eigg.

> *Return along the B8083 as far as Broadford, then turn right at the A87. Turn right again at the A851 to Isleornsay.*

14 Isleornsay, Highland
The village lies a little off the main road. At the road end is a headland on which there is an inn, a pier and a view towards the tidal island of Ornsay. The wilderness of Knoydart stands opposite, on the other side of the Sound of Sleat. Further south lies Knock Bay and above this is a rocky mound on which stands Knock Castle. Its ivy-covered ruins are sometimes called Castle Camus. It was built in medieval times by the MacDonalds of Sleat and its best known occupant was a lady known as Mary of the Castle.

▶ Continue on the **A851** for 8 miles (13km) to Armadale.

15 Armadale, Highland
Armadale can be a busy little place at times as it has a car ferry connection with Mallaig, but it is really a very picturesque spot in a sheltered bay. Close to the village stands the Clan Donald Visitor Centre. This is in the grounds of the now partly ruined Armadale Castle, which was built in 1815 and has interesting displays on the history of the MacDonalds. There are also gardens and woodland trails in the grounds. This part of Skye, known as Sleat, is sometimes called the 'Garden of Skye' because of its luxuriant coastal vegetation. Dr Johnson visited Armadale in 1773 and was duly impressed by what he saw of the fine gardens here, commenting that the planting of the gardens 'proved that the present nakedness of the Hebrides is not wholly the fault of Nature'. An alternative route back to Isleornsay (instead of taking the A851) is via Tarskavaig on the western side of Sleat. This route gives really superb views over to Soay and Rum. There are also fine unspoiled beaches at Tarskavaig Bay and Ord.

▶ Return along the **A851** towards Broadford. Turn right at the **A87** to return to Kyleakin.

Isolated church and graveyard on the road to Elgol

Spanish Gold &
Celtic Crosses

Mull is an island of great beauty and emptiness. Its capital, Tobermory, can be a busy place in the summer, with Main Street thronged with cars, caravans and visitors, while its bay is usually full of pleasure boats. In 1588 a galleon of the Spanish Armada sank in the bay, and rumours of sunken gold still abound.

1/2 DAYS • 143 MILES • 231KM

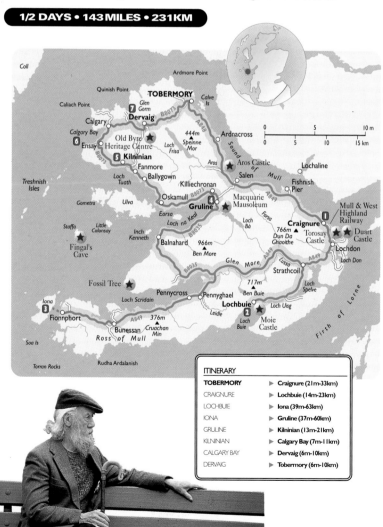

ITINERARY		
TOBERMORY	▶	Craignure (21m-33km)
CRAIGNURE	▶	Lochbuie (14m-23km)
LOCHBUIE	▶	Iona (39m-63km)
IONA	▶	Gruline (37m-60km)
GRULINE	▶	Kilninian (13m-21km)
KILNINIAN	▶	Calgary Bay (7m-11km)
CALGARY BAY	▶	Dervaig (6m-10km)
DERVAIG	▶	Tobermory (6m-10km)

Spanish Gold & Celtic Crosses

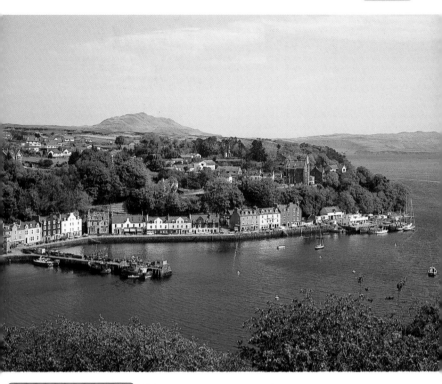

Torosay Castle gardens: statue details

ⓘ *The Pier, Main Street (seasonal)*

▶ *Leave by the A848 to Salen, then continue along the coast on the A849 to Craignure.*

❶ Craignure, Argyll & Bute
This is the island's main ferry terminal and the first place in Mull that most visitors will see. Torosay Castle stands close to Craignure and visitors can reach it by driving further down the road, strolling along a forest walk from Craignure or taking a trip on the miniature railway. The castle is not a fortified structure, but a Victorian mansion built in 1856; it has extensive gardens designed by Sir Robert Lorimer and a 'statue garden' with 19 Italian figures. A little further down the coast stands the strong-

View of the colourful harbour front, Tobermory

hold of Duart Castle. This was originally built in the 13th century by the MacDougalls but later passed into the hands of the Macleans. Much of the present structure comprises their 14th-century additions.

▶ *Follow the A849 to Strathcoil, then turn left at the unclassified road to Lochbuie.*

❷ Lochbuie, Argyll & Bute
The minor road down to Lochbuie is narrow and winding and passes through a well-wooded glen and a landscape that is quite different from the open moorlands so common in much of Mull. At the shore, the wide bay is ringed by hills and to the east stands the fenced-off ruined tower of Moy Castle, which featured in the 1940s film *I Know Where I'm Going*. The castle has a special dungeon off the dining room. It is a pit filled

The ruined abbey on the Isle
of Iona

with water to a depth of 9 feet
(3m) with a stone sticking up in
the middle of the pool; this is
where the poor prisoner sat – in
total darkness! The fertile land
at the head of the loch earned
the estate the name the 'Garden
of Mull'. Behind Lochbuie
House stands a reminder of a
very early settlement, a stone
circle with nine uprights and
three outlying monoliths.

▶ Return to the **A849** and turn
   left. Follow this road to
   Fionnphort and take the ferry
   over to Iona. Cars should be
   left at Fionnphort.

3 Iona, Argyll & Bute
The small island of Iona is a
magnet for summer visitors, and
is a place of great historic and
spiritual significance. Part of
Scotland's history is re-created in
its abbey, now painstakingly
reconstructed using traditional
materials. The historic importance of Iona stems from the
arrival here in AD 563 of the Irish
missionary Columba, who established a monastery. The island
became a religious centre and its
influence spread throughout
Scotland and into England, but
it suffered at the hands of the
Viking raiders in the 8th century.
A Benedictine abbey was
founded around the start of the
13th century and the oldest part
of the abbey dates from that
time. Until the time of the
Reformation, there were over
300 crosses standing near the
abbey but many were broken
during those turbulent times and
only a few massive examples
now remain as beautifully carved
memorials to the skills of the
early craftsmen.

Apart from the abbey, there
are a number of other buildings
worth looking at, including the
ruined Augustinian nunnery and
St Oran's Chapel. The chapel is
the oldest building on Iona. The
story behind its name involves
its troubled construction. The
walls kept collapsing and to
placate the evil spirit that was
felt to be causing this problem, it
was decided that a human sacrifice was needed to be placed
under the foundations – Oran
was the volunteer. The chapel is
in the Reilig Oran – the graveyard of kings – where many of
Scotland's early kings and
queens, and a number of Irish,
Norwegian and possibly French
kings are buried.

▶ Return to Fionnphort and
   follow the **A849** eastwards.
   Turn left at the **B8035** to
   reach Gruline.

4 Gruline, Argyll & Bute
At Gruline, a narrow road (right)
leads to the mausoleum of
Major-General Lachlan
Macquarie. Born locally, he
followed a career in the British
army before becoming
Governor-General of New
South Wales in Australia, a post
he held from 1810 to 1820. In
recognition of this connection,
the building is maintained on
behalf of the National Trust of
Australia.

**Spanish Gold & ** Celtic Crosses

▶ *Continue on the **B8073** for 7 miles (11km) to Calgary Bay.*

BACK TO NATURE

Much of Mull has been built up by basalt lavaflows from long-lost volcanoes and the island has some unique volcanic features that are worth seeing. The uninhabited peninsula on the northern side of Loch Scridain is aptly named 'The Wilderness' and on its southern shore is the world-famous McCulloch's Fossil Tree, a large conifer that was engulfed by lava. It can only be approached at low tide and then after a long walk, so careful preparation is needed for a visit.

▶ *Continue on the **B8035**, then turn left on to the **B8073** to reach Kilninian, 13 miles (21km).*

5 Kilninian, Argyll & Bute
There has been a little church here overlooking the sea since at least 1561 but the present structure was built in 1755. At the back of the church there are a number of large carved grave slabs from the early 16th century. Dun Aisgain is found a little further along the road, standing on a rocky knoll overlooking the sea. This defensive site still has some of its 6-foot (2m) thick walls intact, and has traces of the internal mural gallery that was built within it. The Dun is best approached from Burg.

SCENIC ROUTES

Most of the coastal roads give fine views over the sea, especially the sections by Loch na Keal and Loch Tuath where there are excellent views of the offshore islands, the largest of which is Ulva, where the parents of Scots missionary David Livingstone came from.

---

6 Calgary Bay, Argyll & Bute
This wide bay with its sandy beach is a popular stopping place for visitors. Few people live here now, but on the northern side of the bay there are deserted townships and an old pier. The builders of the pier took full advantage of the local geology when they used a prominent volcanic dike as one of the walls. The existence of this prominent vertical sheet of rock could have led to the name of the bay, as Calgary may have come from the Gaelic word Calagharaidh, meaning 'the haven by the wall'. The town of Calgary in Alberta, Canada, was named after the bay.

▶ *Continue on the **B8073** for 6 miles (10km) to Dervaig.*

7 Dervaig, Argyll & Bute
Dervaig is a very pleasant little community that was established as a 'planned village' in 1799. The village and its environs have been designated a conservation area and this is a good base from which to explore the north of the island, Calgary and

---

FOR CHILDREN

There are a number of good beaches round the coast, notably at Calgary Bay, which is ideal for bathing, and Lochbuie. The narrow-gauge railway at Torosay Castle is always appealing to children (and adults). This is the country's only island railway and was originally built in 1984 to encourage reluctant walkers to go from Craignure Pier to Torosay Castle; however, it has become an attraction in its own right. It has four engines, two of them steam-powered.

Tobermory. The most obvious village landmark is the church's round tower, reminiscent of Irish churches. The building is relatively modern, having been constructed as recently as 1905. Two other local places of interest are the Mull Little Theatre and, a little further out of the village, the Old Byre Heritage Centre, which depicts island life.

▶ *Continue on the **B8073** and return to Tobermory.*

The Isle of Mull's local steam railway

PRACTICAL INFORMATION

ACCIDENTS
In the event of an accident, the vehicle should be moved off the carriageway wherever possible. If the vehicle is fitted with hazard warning lights, they should be used. If available, a red triangle should be put on the road at least 165 feet (50m) before the obstruction, on the same side of the road.

If damage or injury is caused to any other person or vehicle you must stop, give your own and the vehicle owner's name and address and the registration number of the vehicle to anyone having reasonable grounds for requiring them. If you do not give your name and address at the time of the accident, report the accident to the police as soon as reasonably practicable, and in any case within 24 hours.

BREAKDOWNS
Visitors who bring their cars to Scotland and are members of a recognised automobile club in their own country may benefit from the services that are provided free of charge by the AA. Car rental companies normally provide cover with one or other of the major motoring organisations in Britain. On motorways there are emergency telephones at the side of the hard shoulder at one-mile (1.6km) intervals.

In the event of a breakdown, the vehicle should be moved off the carriageway wherever possible. If the vehicle is fitted with hazard warning lights, they should be used. If you have one in the car, a red warning triangle should be placed on the road at least 165 feet (50m) before the obstruction and on the same side of the road.

CARAVANS
Brakes
Check that the caravan braking mechanism is correctly

MOTORING IN SCOTLAND

adjusted. If it is fitted with a breakaway safety mechanism, the cable between the car and caravan must be firmly anchored so that the trailer brakes act immediately if the two part company.

Caravan and luggage trailers
Take a list of contents, especially if any valuable or unusual equipment is being carried, as this may be required on arrival in Britain. A towed vehicle should be readily identifiable by a plate in an accessible position showing the name of the make of the vehicle and the production and serial number.

Lights
Make sure that all the lights are working – rear lights, stop lights, numberplate lights, rear fog guard lamps and flashers (check that the flasher rate is correct: 60–120 times a minute).

Tyres
Both tyres on the caravan should be of the same size and type. Inspect them carefully: if you think they are likely to be more than three-quarters worn before you get back, replace them before you set off. If you notice uneven wear, scuffed treads, or damaged walls, you should get expert advice on whether the tyres are suitable for further use.

Find out the recommended tyre pressures from the caravan manufacturer.

CAR HIRE AND FLY/DRIVE
Drivers must hold, and have held for one year, a valid national licence or an International Driving Permit. The minimum age for hiring a car ranges from 18 to 25, depending on the model of car. With some companies, there is

a maximum age limit of 70. You can arrange to pick up your car in one town and return it in another. If you are hiring a car, you can often get a good deal with a fly/drive package deal from the airline.

The larger car hire companies have desks at airports and branches in major towns. These may not be the cheapest; telephone around for the best deal.

CHILDREN
The following restrictions apply to children travelling in private motor vehicles:

Children under 3 years: front seat – appropriate child restraint must be worn; rear seats – appropriate child restraint must be worn if available.

Children aged 3 to 11 and under 5 feet (1.5m) tall: front seat – appropriate child restraint must be worn if available; if not, adult seat belt must be worn. Rear seat – appropriate child restraint must be worn if available; if not, adult seat belt must be worn if available.

Children aged 12 or 13 or younger child 5 feet (1.5m) or more in height – front and rear seats – adult seat belt must be worn if available.
Note: under no circumstances should a rear-facing restraint be used in a seat with an airbag.

CRASH (SAFETY) HELMETS
Visiting motorcyclists and their passengers must wear crash or safety helmets.

DOCUMENTS
You must have a valid driver's licence or an International Driving Permit. Holders of permits written in a foreign language are advised to obtain an official translation from an embassy or recognised automobile association. Non-EC nationals must have Green Card insurance.

DRINKING AND DRIVING

The laws regarding drinking and driving are strict and the penalties severe. If you drink, don't drive.

DRIVING CONDITIONS

Traffic drives on the left and goes clockwise at roundabouts (traffic circles). Speed-limit and destination signs use miles (one kilometre is roughly 5/8 of a mile). Motorways link most major cities; service areas are indicated well in advance. Roads in some areas of Scotland are very narrow. See also **ROADS**.

FUEL

Vehicle fuels widely available are petrol and diesel, while LPG (Liquid Petroleum Gas) can be found at only 1,300 outlets in the UK. Most of the petrol sold in the UK is Premium Grade unleaded with an octane rating of 95. This is suitable for use in all cars made after 1992. Super Unleaded (more expensive) has an octane rating of 97. This may provide improved performance in modern cars with electronic ignition and fuel injection systems. Petrol stations are usually self-service and are mostly around towns and on motorways and major roads. Most motorway service stations and some on busy roads and in large towns open 24 hours, or at least late into the night. Most accept credit cards. Fuel costs vary; generally the further north you go the more expensive it becomes. Lowest prices are at supermarket filling stations.

INSURANCE

Fully comprehensive insurance, which covers you for some of the expenses incurred after a breakdown or an accident, is advisable.

LIGHTS

You must ensure that your front and rear side lights and rear registration plate lights are lit at night. You must use headlights when visibility is seriously reduced and at night on all unlit roads and those where the street lights are more than 600 feet (185m) apart.

ROADS

Roads in Scotland are generally good. In the Highlands and Islands of Scotland, however, and in some country areas the roads are often narrow. On single track roads pull into the passing places only if they are on your left; stop level with those on your right: the oncoming traffic will make the detour. Never hold up faster traffic approaching from behind; stop at suitable places to allow drivers to overtake. Try to travel outside the main rush hours of 8–9.30am and 4.30–6pm when visiting the larger cities and towns.

ROUTE DIRECTIONS

Throughout the book the following abbreviations are used for Scottish roads:
A – main roads
B – local roads
unclassified roads – minor roads (unnumbered).

SEAT BELTS

Seat belts are compulsory for drivers and front seat passenger. Passengers travelling in the rear of the vehicle must wear a seat belt if fitted.

SPEED LIMITS

Speed limits for cars are 70mph (112kph) on motorways and dual carriageways; 60mph (96kph) on other roads; 30mph (48kph) in built-up areas unless otherwise indicated.

TOLLS

Tolls are levied on certain bridges and tunnels.

WARNING TRIANGLE/ HAZARD LIGHTS

If the vehicle is fitted with hazard warning lights, they should be used in the event of a breakdown or accident. If available, a red triangle should be placed on the road at least 165 feet (50m) before the obstruction and on the same side of the road.

ACCOMMODATION AND RESTAURANTS

Listed below is a selection of hotels (🏨) and restaurants (🍴) which can be found along the routes of each tour. The price brackets given below are intended as a guide only; check details before visiting.

Accommodation Prices

Hotel prices are divided into three price brackets:
Expensive £££ – over £100
Moderate ££ – £60–£100
Budget £ – under £60
These are the rates for a double room for one night, and the price will usually include breakfast.

Restaurant Prices

Meal prices are divided into three price brackets:
Expensive £££ – over £31
Moderate ££ – £15–£30
Budget £ – under £15

AA Hotel Booking Service

A free, fast and easy way to find a place to stay for your short break or holiday.
Tel: 0870 5050505 (lines open every day, 24 hours a day)
Email: accommodation@ aabookings.com or book online at www.theaa.com/hotels

TOUR 1
AYR South Ayrshire
🏨 **Carrick Lodge ££**
46 Carrick Road (tel: 01292 262846; fax: 01292 611101).
🏨 **Savoy Park ££**
16 Racecourse Road (tel: 01292 266112; fax: 01292 611488).
🍴 **Fouters Bistro ££**
2a Academy Street (tel: 01292 261391). *Scottish cuisine. Open weekdays.*

TURNBERRY South Ayrshire
🏨 **Malin Court £££**
On A719 (tel: 01655 331457; fax: 01655 331072).
🍴 **Turnberry Hotel £££**
(tel: 01655 331000). *Scottish/ French cuisine.*

LARGS North Ayrshire
🏨 **Stonehaven £**
8 Netherpark Crescent
(tel: 01475 673319).
🏨 **Willow Bank ££**
96 Greenock Road (tel/fax:
01475 672311).

TOUR 2
NEWTON STEWART
Dumfries & Galloway
🏨 **Bruce ££**
88 Queen Street (tel/fax: 01671
402294).
🏨 **Creebridge House ££**
Off A75 (tel: 01671 402121; fax:
01671 403258).
🍽️ **Kirroughtree House £££**
Minnigaff (tel: 01671 402141).
*Classical French with Scottish
influences. Open all year daily.*

PORTPATRICK Dumfries &
Galloway
🏨 **Fernhill ££**
Off A77 (tel: 01776 810220; fax:
01776 810596).

STRANRAER Dumfries &
Galloway
🏨 **North West Castle ££**
Seafront (tel: 01776 704413;
fax: 01776 702646).

TOUR 3
DUMFRIES Dumfries &
Galloway
🏨 **Cairndale ££**
English Street (tel: 01387
254111; fax: 01387 250555).
🏨 **Travelodge £**
Annan Road, Collin (tel/fax:
01387 750658).

CASTLE DOUGLAS
Dumfries & Galloway
🏨 **Imperial £**
35 Kings Road (tel: 01556
502086; fax: 01556 503009).
🏨 **Urr Valley Country
House £**
Ernespie Road (tel: 01556
502188; fax: 01556 504055).
🍽️ **Plumed Horse £–££**
Main Street, Crossmichael (tel:
01556 67033). *French cuisine.
Closed Mon.*

GATEHOUSE OF FLEET
Dumfries & Galloway
🏨 **Cally Palace £££**
1 mile (1.6km) out of town

(tel: 01557 814341; fax: 01557
814522). Closed 3 Jan–3 Feb.
🏨 **Murray Arms ££**
Off A75 near clock tower
(tel: 01557 814207; fax: 01557
814370).

TOUR 4
LANARK South
Lanarkshire
🏨 **Cartland Bridge ££**
Glasgow Road (tel: 01555
664426; fax: 01555 663773).

BIGGAR South Lanarkshire
🏨 **Shieldhill £££**
Shieldhill Road, Quothquan
(tel: 01899 220035; fax: 01899
221092).
🍽️ **Toftcombs Country
House ££**
Peebles Road (tel: 01899
220142). *Modern British fare.*

SANQUHAR Dumfries &
Galloway
🏨 **Blackaddie House ££**
Blackaddie Road (tel: 01659
50270; fax: 01659 50900).

STRATHAVEN South
Lanarkshire
🏨 **Springvale Hotel £**
18 Lethame Road (tel: 01357
521131).
🏨 **Strathaven ££**
Hamilton Road (tel: 01357
521778; fax: 01357 520789).

HAMILTON South
Lanarkshire
🏨 **Holiday Inn Express £**
Strathclyde Country Park, off
M74 (tel: 01698 858585; fax:
01698 852375).

TOUR 5
MOFFAT Dumfries &
Galloway
🏨 **Beechwood Country
House ££**
Harthope Place (tel: 01683
220210; fax: 01683 220889).
Closed 2 Jan–14 Feb.
🏨 **The Star £**
44 High Street (tel: 01683
220156; fax: 01683 221524).
🍽️ **Well View £££**
Ballplay Road (tel: 01683
220184). *Daily changing taster
menu. Closed Sat lunch; reserva-
tions required.*

PEEBLES Scottish Borders
🏨 **Peebles Hydro £££**
On A702 (tel: 01721 720602;
fax: 01721 722999).
🏨 **Tontine Hotel ££**
High Street (tel: 01721 720892;
fax: 01721 729732). *Scottish
cuisine. Open all year daily.*
🍽️ **Cringletie House £££**
2 miles (3.2km) north on A703
(tel: 01721 725750). *Seafood;
seasonal game. Open all year
daily.*

GALASHIELS Scottish
Borders
🏨 **Woodlands House ££**
Windyknowe Road (tel: 01896
754722; fax: 01896 754892).
Closed 25–26 Dec.

TOUR 6
MELROSE Scottish Borders
🏨🍽️ **Burt's ££**
The Square (tel: 01896 822285;
fax: 01896 822870). *Border
lamb; game. Closed 24–26 Dec.*

HAWICK Scottish Borders
🏨 **Elm House £**
North Bridge Street (tel: 01450
372866).

TOUR 7
EDINBURGH City of
Edinburgh
🏨 **Braid Hills £££**
134 Braid Road, Braid Hills
(tel: 0131 447 8888; fax: 0131
452 8477).
🏨 **Bruntsfield £££**
69–74 Bruntsfield Place (tel:
0131 229 1393; fax: 0131 229
5634).
🏨 **Ibis ££**
Hunter Square (tel: 0131 240
7000; fax: 0131 240 7007).
🍽️ **Bonars ££**
56 St Mary's Street (tel: 0131
556 5888). *Stylish setting; adven-
turous cooking.*

DUNBAR East Lothian
🏨 **Bayswell ££**
Bayswell Park (tel/fax: 01368
862225).

KELSO Scottish Borders
🏨 **Ednam House £££**
Bridge Street (tel: 01573
224168; fax: 01573 226319).
Closed 25 Dec–10 Jan.

⌂ **White Swan £–££**
Abbey Row (tel: 01573
225800).

LAUDER Scottish Borders
⌂ **Lauderdale ££**
1 Edinburgh Road (tel: 01578
722231; fax: 01578 718642).

TOUR 8
OBAN Argyll & Bute
⌂ **Alexandra ££**
Corran Esplanade (tel: 01631
562381; fax: 01631 564497).
⌂ **Columba ££**
North Pier (tel: 01631 562183;
fax: 01631 564683).
⍾ **Manor House Hotel ££**
Gallanach Road (tel: 01631
562087). *Scottish fish and game.
Open all year daily.*

CLACHAN-SEIL Argyll &
Bute
⌂ **Willowburn £££**
Island of Seil, half mile (1km)
from Atlantic Bridge (tel:
01852 300276; fax: 01852
300597). *Closed Jan–Feb.*

LOCHGILPHEAD Argyll
& Bute
⌂ **The Stag ££**
Argyll Street (tel: 01546
602496; fax: 01546 603549).

GLENCOE Highland
⌂ **Glencoe ££**
On A82 in Glencoe village
(tel: 01855 811245; fax: 01855
811687).

TOUR 9
PAISLEY Renfrewshire
⌂ **Dean Park ££**
91 Glasgow Road (tel: 0141 886
3771; fax: 0141 885 0681).

DUMBARTON West
Dunbartonshire
⌂ **Dumbuck ££**
Glasgow Road (tel: 01389
734336; fax: 01389 742270).

HELENSBURGH Argyll
& Bute
⍾ **Rosslea Hall Country
House ££**
Ferry Road, Rhu (tel: 01436
439955). *Fine cuisine. Open
daily; restaurant open for dinner
only; bar lunches available.*

DUNOON Argyll & Bute
⌂ **Enmore £££**
Marine Parade, Kirn (tel: 01369
702230; fax: 01369 702148).
Closed 2–12 Jan.

⌂ **Lyall Cliff £**
141 Alexandre Parade, East
Bay (tel/fax: 01369 702041).
Closed Nov–26 Dec.

TOUR 10
GLASGOW City of Glasgow
⌂ **Ewington £££**
Balmoral Terrace, 132 Queens
Drive, Queens Park (tel: 0141
423 1152; fax: 0141 422 2030).
⌂ **Malmaison £££**
278 West George Street (tel:
0141 572 1000).
⍾ **Gamba ££**
225a West George Street (tel:
0141 572 0899). *Scottish seafood
a speciality. Closed Sun.*
⍾ **Puppet Theatre ££**
11 Ruthven Lane (tel: 0141 339
8444). *Scottish/Mediterranean
cuisine. Closed Mon.*

ABERFELDY Perthshire &
Kinross
⌂ **The Weem ££**
On B846 northwest (tel: 01887
820381; fax: 01887 8297020).

LOCHEARNHEAD Stirling
⌂ **Lochearnhead £**
(tel: 01567 830229; fax: 01567
830364). *Closed Dec–Mar.*

TOUR 11
STIRLING Stirling
⌂ **Terraces ££**
4 Melville Terrace (tel: 01786
472268; fax: 01786 450314).
⍾ **River House ££**
Castle Business Park,
Craigforth (tel: 01786 465577).
*Mediterranean-style cuisine. Open
all year daily.*

DUNFERMLINE Fife
⌂ **Keavil House ££**
Crossford (tel: 01383 736258;
fax: 01383 621600).

TOUR 12
PERTH Perthshire & Kinross
⌂ **Woodlea £**
23 York Place (tel: 01738
621744; fax: 01738 621744). *No
credit cards.*

⍾ **Let's Eat ££**
77–79 Kinnoull Street (tel:
01738 643377). *Modern Scottish
cuisine. Closed Sun and Mon; also
two weeks Jan and two weeks Jul.*

GLAMIS Angus
⌂ **Castleton House ££**
Castleton of Essie (tel: 01307
840340; fax: 01307 840506).

MONTROSE Angus
⌂ **Links ££**
Mid Links (tel: 01674 671000;
fax: 01674 672698).

DUNDEE Dundee City
⌂ **Shaftesbury ££**
1 Hyndford Street (tel: 01382
669216; fax: 01382 641598).

TOUR 13
ST ANDREWS Fife
⌂ **Russell ££**
26 The Scores (tel: 01334
473447; fax: 01334 478279).
⌂ **St Andrews Golf £££**
40 The Scores (tel: 01334
472611; fax: 01334 472188).
⍾ **Parkland Hotel ££**
Double Dykes Road (tel:
01334 473620). *Scottish regional
cuisine.*

ELIE Fife
⌂ **Golf ££**
Bank Street (tel: 01333 330209;
fax: 01333 330381).

KINROSS Perthshire and
Kinross
⌂ **Windlestrae £££**
Windlestrae (tel: 01577 863217;
fax: 01577 864733).

CUPAR Fife
⌂ **Eden House £££**
2 Pitscottie Road (tel: 01334
652510; fax: 01334 652277).

TOUR 14
INVERNESS Highland
⌂ **Lochardil House ££**
Stratherrick Road (tel: 01463
235995; fax: 01463 713394).
⍾ **Bunchrew House
Hotel ££**
Bunchrew (tel: 01463 234917).
*Modern Scottish cuisine. May be
closed for functions – call for
information.*

NAIRN Highland
🏨 **Alton Burn £**
Alton Burn Road (tel: 01667
452051; fax: 01667 456697).
🏨 **Boath House ££**
Auldearn (tel: 01667 454896;
fax: 01667 455469).
🍴 **Newton Hotel ££**
Inverness Road (tel: 01667
453144). *Modern Scottish cuisine.
Open all year daily; reservations
advised.*

FORRES Moray
🏨 **Ramnee ££**
Victoria Road (tel: 01309
672410; fax: 01309 673392).

GRANTOWN-ON-SPEY
Highland
🏨 **Coppice £**
Grant Road (tel/fax: 01479
872688).
🏨 **Culdearn House £££**
Woodlands Terrace (tel: 01479
872106; fax: 01479 873641).
Closed 30 Oct–28 Feb.

TOUR 15
ELGIN Moray
🏨 **Laichmoray ££**
Maisondieu Road (tel: 01343
540045; fax: 01343 540055).
🍴 **Mansion House Hotel ££**
The Haugh (tel: 01343
548811). *Innovative cooking.
Open all year daily.*

CULLEN Moray
🏨 **Cullen Bay ££**
On A98 west of village
(tel: 01542 840432; fax: 01542
840900).

ROTHES Moray
🏨 **Rothes Glen £££**
On A941 (tel: 01340 831254;
fax: 01340 831566).

TOUR 16
BANFF Aberdeenshire
🏨 **Banff Springs ££**
Golden Knowes Road
(tel: 01261 812881).

PETERHEAD Aberdeenshire
🏨 **Palace ££**
Prince Street (tel: 01779
474821; fax: 01779 476119).
🏨 **Waterside Inn ££**
Fraserburgh Road (tel: 01779
471121; fax: 01779 470670).

INVERURIE Aberdeenshire
🏨 **Strathburn ££**
Burghmuir Drive (tel: 01467
624422; fax: 01467 625133).
🍴 **Thainstone House £££**
(tel: 01467 621643). *Local beef,
game and seafood. Open all year
daily.*

HUNTLY Aberdeenshire
🏨 **Castle ££**
Near castle ruins (tel: 01466
792696; fax: 01466 792641).

TOUR 17
PITLOCHRY Perthshire and
Kinross
🏨 **Acarsaid ££**
8 Atholl Road (tel: 01796
472389). *Closed 4 Jan–10 Mar.*

KINGUSSIE Highland
🏨 **The Scot House ££**
Newtonmore Road (tel: 01540
661351; fax: 01540 661111).
Closed 6–31 Jan.
🍴 **The Cross £££**
Ardbroilach Road (tel: 01540
661166). *Good local produce –
scallops, salmon etc. Dinner only.
Closed Tue.*

AVIEMORE Highland
🏨 **Aviemore Highlands ££**
Aviemore Mountain Resort
(tel: 01479 810771).

BRAEMAR Aberdeenshire
🏨 **Braemar Lodge £**
Glenshee Road (tel/fax: 013397
41627).

TOUR 18
ABERDEEN Aberdeen City
🏨 **Allan Guest House £**
56 Polmuir Road, Ferryhill
(tel/fax: 01224 584484).
🏨 **Craighaar £££**
Waterton Road, Bankhead
(tel: 01224 712275; fax: 01224
716362). *Closed 26 Dec, 1–2 Jan.*
🍴 **Patio Hotel ££**
Beach Boulevard (tel: 01224
633339). *International and
Scottish fare. Open all year
daily.*

STONEHAVEN
Aberdeenshire
🏨 **County ££**
Arduthie Road (tel: 01569
764386; fax: 01569 762214).

BANCHORY Aberdeenshire
🏨 **Burnett Arms ££**
25 High Street (tel: 01330
824944; fax: 01330 825553).
🍴 **Tor-na-Coille Hotel ££**
(tel: 01330 822242). *Scottish
cuisine. Lunch and dinner daily.*

TOUR 19
FORT WILLIAM Highland
🏨 **Imperial ££**
Fraser's Square (tel: 01397
702040; fax: 01397 706277).
🍴 **No 4 Cameron Square ££**
4 Cameron Square (tel: 01397
704222). *Modern British cuisine.
Closed Sun lunch.*

ARISAIG Highland
🏨 **Arisaig ££**
On A830 opposite harbour
(tel: 01687 450210; fax: 01687
450310). *Closed 24–26 Dec.*

MALLAIG Highland
🏨 **Marine £**
Beside railway terminal
(tel: 01687 462217; fax: 01687
462821). *Closed 25 Dec–1 Jan.*

TOUR 20
INVERGARRY Highland
🏨 🍴 **Forest Lodge £**
South Laggan (tel: 01809
501219; fax: 01809 501476).
*Contemporary Scottish dishes.
Closed Nov–Apr.*
🏨 **Glengarry Castle £££**
On the A82 beside Loch
Oich (tel: 01809 501254; fax:
01809 501207). *Closed Nov–mid-
Mar.*

KYLE OF LOCHALSH
Highland
🏨 **Kyle Hotel ££**
Main Street (tel: 01599 534204;
fax: 01599 534932).
🏨 **Lochalsh £££**
Ferry Road (tel: 01599 534202;
fax: 01599 534881).

PLOCKTON Highland
🍴 **Haven Hotel £**
Innes Street (tel: 01599
544334). *Robust Scottish fare.
Closed 20 Dec–1 Feb.*

GAIRLOCH Highland
🏨 **Creag Mor £££**
Charleston (tel: 01445 712068;
fax: 01445 712044).

🏛 **Millcroft Hotel £**
Strath (tel: 01445 712376;
fax: 01445 712091).
🏛 **Myrtle Bank ££**
Low Road (tel: 01445 712004;
fax: 01445 712214).

STRATHPEFFER Highland
🏛 **Brunstane Lodge £**
Golf Road (tel: 01997 421261).
Closed 1–2 Jan.

BEAULY Highland
🏛 **Priory ££**
The Square (tel: 01463 782309;
fax: 01463 782531).

DRUMNADROCHIT
Highland
🏛 **Polmaily House £££**
On Cannich road (tel: 01456
450343; fax: 01456 450813).
Closed 31 Oct–30 Dec.

TOUR 21
LOCHINVER Highland
🏛 ¶¶ **Inver Lodge £££**
Off A835 from village (tel:
01571 844496; fax: 01571
844395). *Contemporary slant to
Scottish produce. Closed Nov–Apr.*
🏛 **Polcraig Guest House £**
(tel/fax: 01571 844429).

SCOURIE Highland
🏛 **Eddrachilles ££**
Badcall Bay (tel: 01971 502080;
fax: 01971 502477). *Closed
Nov–Feb.*

KINLOCHBERVIE Highland
🏛 **Kinlochbervie ££**
(tel: 01971 521275; fax: 01971
521438). *Closed 23 Dec–4 Jan.*
🏛 **Old School Hotel £**
Inshegra (tel/fax: 01971
521383).

LAIRG Highland
🏛 **Overscaig £**
Loch Shin, on A838 (tel: 01549
431203).

TOUR 22
DORNOCH Highland
🏛 **Burghfield House ££**
(tel: 01862 810212; fax: 01862
810404).
🏛 **Dornoch Castle ££**
Castle Street (tel: 01862
810216; fax: 01862 810981).
Closed Nov–Mar.

¶¶ **Eagle Hotel £**
Castle Street (tel: 01862
810008). *Closed 25 Dec, 1 Jan.*

TONGUE Highland
🏛 ¶¶ **Ben Loyal £**
Village centre (tel: 01847
611216; fax: 01847 611336).
*Modern Scottish cooking. Closed
Nov–Feb.*

THURSO Highland
🏛 **Park ££**
On A882 near town centre (tel:
01847 893251). *Closed 1–3 Jan.*
🏛 **Station Hotel ££**
Princes Street (tel: 01847
892003).

MEY Highland
🏛 **Castle Arms £**
On A836 (tel: 01847 851244;
fax: 01847 851244).

WICK Highland
🏛 **Mackay's ££**
Union Street (tel: 01955
602323; fax: 01955 605930).
Closed 1–2 Jan.

TOUR 23
DINGWALL Highland
🏛 ¶¶ **Kinkell House ££**
Easter Kinkell, Conon Bridge
(tel: 01349 861270; fax: 01349
865902). *Local lamb, fish and
pork. Open all year.*

TAIN Highland
🏛 **GolfView Guest House £**
13 Knockbreck Road
(tel: 01862 892856; fax: 01862
892172).
🏛 **Mansfield House ££**
Scotsburn Road (tel: 01862
892052; fax: 01862 892260).

PORTMAHOMACK
Highland
🏛 **Caledonian £**
Main Street (tel: 01862 871345;
fax: 01862 871757).

TOUR 24
PORTREE Highland
🏛 **Almondbank £**
Viewfield Road (tel: 01478
612696; fax: 01478 613114).
🏛 **Cuillin Hills £££**
Off A855 north of Portree (tel:
01478 612003; fax: 01478
613092).

🏛 **Rosedale ££**
Harbourside (tel: 01478
613131; fax: 01478 612531).
Closed mid-Nov–mid-Mar.

UIG Highland
🏛 **Ferry Inn £**
On Portree road near ferry
terminal (tel: 01470 544242).
Closed 25 Dec & 1 Jan.

DUNVEGAN Highland
🏛 **Atholl House £**
(tel: 01470 521219; fax: 01470
521481). *Closed end Dec–Feb.*
🏛 **Roskhill House £–££**
Roskhill, 3 miles (5km) south
(tel: 01470 521317; fax: 01470
521827).

HARLOSH Highland
🏛 **Harlosh House ££**
On A863 south of Dunvegan
(tel: 01470 521367).

ISLEORNSAY Highland
🏛 **Kinloch Lodge £££**
(tel: 01471 833214 & 833333;
fax: 01471 833277). *Closed 22
Dec–31 Jan.*
¶¶ **Hotel Eilean Iarmain £££**
Isle of Skye (tel: 01471
833332). *Modern and traditional
Scottish cuisine. Dinner daily
7.30–8.45 (reservation required);
bar lunches.*

TOUR 25
TOBERMORY Argyll & Bute
🏛 **Western Isles ££**
(tel: 01688 302012; fax: 01688
302297). *Closed 17–28 Dec.*
¶¶ **Tobermory Hotel £–££**
53 Main Street (tel: 01688
302091). *Excellent cuisine using
fresh local produce. Closed
Christmas.*

PENNYGHAEL Argyll & Bute
🏛 **Pennyghael ££**
Main road (tel: 01681 704288).

BUNESSAN Argyll & Bute
🏛 **Argyll Arms £££**
On the waterfront (tel: 01681
700240).

DERVAIG Argyll & Bute
🏛 **Druimard Country
House £££**
(tel/fax: 01688 400345). *Closed
Nov–Mar.*

Practical information

ⓘ Tourist Information Office
⑫ Number on tour

TOUR INFORMATION

The addresses, telephone numbers and opening times of the attractions mentioned in the tours, together with the telephone numbers of the Tourist Information Offices, are listed below.

TOUR I

For all telephone enquiries call 01292 678100. Personal callers can visit the following centres:

ⓘ 22 Sandgate, Ayr.

ⓘ New Street, Irvine.

ⓘ Main Street, Largs (seasonal).

ⓘ 282 Stuart Street, Millport (seasonal).

❶ Alloway
Burns National Heritage Park
Murdoch's Lone. Tel: 01292 443700.
Open daily Apr–Oct 9.30–5.30, Nov–Mar 10–5 (Sun noon–4).
Burns Cottage
Tel: (Burns National Heritage Park) 01292 443700.
Open daily Apr–Oct 9.30–5.30, Nov–Mar 10–5 (Sun noon–4).

❸ Culzean Castle
4 miles (6km) west of Maybole, off A77.
Tel: 01655 884455.
Open Apr (or Good Fri if earlier)–Oct daily 10.30–5.30; country park daily 9.30–sunset.

❺ Kirkoswald
Souter Johnnie's Cottage
Main Road. Tel: 01655 760603.
Open Apr–Sep Fri–Tue 11.30–5.

❻ Maybole
Crossraguel Abbey
2 miles (3km) south on the A77. Tel: 01655 883113.
Open Mon–Sat 9.30–4.30 (last entry 4), Sun 2–4.30.

❼ Mauchline
Burns House Museum
Castle Street. Tel: 01290 550045.
Open Apr–Oct Tue–Sat 10–5.

❽ Kilmarnock
Dean Castle and Country Park
Dean Road. Tel: 01563 522702.
Open all year daily: country park dawn to dusk; castle 12–5; visitor centre 11–5 (to 4pm in winter).

❾ Irvine
Scottish Maritime Museum
Harbour Street. Tel: 01294 278283.
Open Apr–Oct daily 10–5.
Glasgow Vennel Museum and Burns Heckling Shop
4 & 10 Glasgow Vennel.
Tel: 01294 275059.
Open all year Mon–Sat 10–4.
Cunninghame House
Friars Croft. Tel: 01294 324100.
Open all year, Mon–Thu 9–4.45, Fri 9–4.30 (may close for lunch, check before visiting).
Burns Club and Museum
28 Eglinton Street.
Tel: 01294 274511.
Open Easter–Sep Mon–Wed, Fri–Sat 2.30–4.30; Oct–Mar Sat 2.30–4.30.

❿ Largs
Skelmorlie Aisle
Tel: 01475 687081.
Open (pick up key from the museum) Jun–Aug Mon–Sat 2–5.
Vikingar
Greenock Road. Tel: 01475 689777.
Open daily Apr–Sep 10.30–5.30; Oct & Mar 10.30–3.30; Nov–Feb Sat–Sun 10.30–3.30.

For Children
Galleon Centre
99 Titchfield Street, Kilmarnock. Tel: 01563 524014.
Open daily 7am–11pm (to 6pm Sat).
Loudon Castle Theme Park
Galston. Tel: 01563 822296.
Open Apr–Aug daily 10–5;

Sep–Oct weekends only 10–5 (later at peak times).

For Children
Magnum Centre
Harbourside, Irvine.
Tel: 01294 278381.
Open daily, from 9am Fri–Mon, 10am Tue–Thu; closes 10pm weekdays, 6pm weekends.

TOUR 2

ⓘ Dashwood Square, Newton Stewart (seasonal). Tel: 01671 402431.

ⓘ The Whithorn Trust, Whithorn (seasonal). Tel: 01988 500508.

ⓘ 30 Harbour Street, Stranraer. Tel: 01776 702595.

ⓘ Bridge Street, Girvan (seasonal). Tel: 01465 715500.

❶ Wigtown
Bladnoch Distillery
Half mile (1km) south on A746. Tel: 01988 402605.
Open Easter–Oct Mon–Fri tours 10–4.30, shop 9–5.30; Nov–mid Dec Mon–Fri tours 11–3.30.

❷ Whithorn
Whithorn Story Visitor Centre
45–7 George Street.
Tel: 01988 500508.
Open Apr–Oct daily 10.30–5.

❸ Isle of Whithorn
St Ninian's Chapel
Open at all times.

❺ Glenluce
Glenluce Abbey
2 miles (3km) northwest off the A75. Tel: 01581 300541.
Open Apr–Sep daily 9.30–6.30; Oct–Mar Sat 9.30–4.30, Sun 2–4.30.

❻ Port Logan
Logan Fish Pond Marine Life Centre
Tel: 01776 860300.
Open daily Feb–Sep 10–5; Oct–early Nov 10–4.
Logan Botanic Garden
off B7065. Tel: 01776 860231.
Open daily Mar–Oct 10–5/6.

❼ Portpatrick
Dunskey Castle
South of Portpatrick along the clifftop footpath.
Accessible at all times.

❽ Stranraer
Stranraer Museum
George Street. Tel: 01776 705088.
Open all year, Mon–Sat 10–5 (closed for lunch between 1 and 2pm on Sat).
Castle of St John
Tel: 01776 705088.
Open Apr–mid-Sep, Mon–Sat 10–1, 2–5.

❾ Girvan
McKechnie Institute
Dalrymple Street.
Tel: 01465 713643.
Open all year, Tue–Sat 10–4.

❿ Glen Trool Visitor Centre
Off A714 at Bargrennan.
Tel: 01671 402420.
Open daily, late Mar–late Sep 10.30–5; late Sep–Oct 10.30–4.30.

For Children
Monreith Animal World
On A747, 6 miles (10km) west of Whithorn.
Tel: 01988 700217.
Open Mar–Oct daily 10–5.30.

For History Buffs
Castle Kennedy Gardens
3 miles (5km) east of Stranraer on A75.
Tel: 01776 702024.
Open Apr–Sep daily 10–5.

Back to Nature
Wood of Cree Nature Reserve
4 miles (6km) north of Newton Stewart.
Tel: 01671 402861.
Open at all times.

TOUR 3

ⓘ Whitesands, Dumfries.
Tel: 01387 253862

ⓘ Markethill Car Park, Castle Douglas (seasonal).
Tel: 01556 502611

ⓘ NTS Threave Gardens, Castle Douglas (seasonal).
Tel: 01556 502575

i Harbour Square, Kirkcudbright (seasonal). Tel: 01557 330494

i Car Park, Gatehouse of Fleet (seasonal). Tel: 01557 814212

❶ New Abbey
Sweetheart Abbey
Tel: 01387 850397.
Open Apr–Sep daily 9.30–6.30; Oct–Mar Mon–Wed & Sat 9.30–4.30, Thu 9.30–12.30, Sun 2–4.30.
Shambellie House and Museum of Costume
Tel: 01387 850375.
Open Apr–Oct daily 11–5.
New Abbey Corn Mill
Tel: 01387 850260.
Open Apr–Sep daily 9.30–6.30; Oct–Mar 9.30–4.30 (closed Thu afternoon, all day Fri & Sun morning).

❸ Castle Douglas
Threave Garden
1 mile (1.6km) west off A75. Tel: 01556 502575.
Open daily 9.30–sunset.
Threave Castle
3 miles (5km) west on the A75. Tel: 07711 223101.
Open Apr–Sep daily 9.30–6.30.

❹ Kirkcudbright
Tolbooth Art Centre
Tel: 01557 331556.
Open Mon–Sat 11–4; also Sun 2–5 Jun–Sep.
MacLellan's Castle
Tel: 01557 331856.
Open Apr–Sep daily 9.30–6.30
Stewartry Museum
St Mary Street. Tel: 01557 331643.
Open Mon–Sat 11–4; Jun–Sep also Sun 2–5; Nov–Feb Sat 11–4.
Broughton House
12 High Street. Tel: 01557 330437.
Open Apr–Oct daily 1–5.30.
Tongland Hydroelectric Power Station
2 miles (3km) north on A711. Tel: 01557 330114.
Open May–Sep Mon–Sat; also Sun during Aug.

❺ Gatehouse of Fleet
Cardoness Castle
1 mile (1.6km) southwest

on the A75. Tel: 01557 814427.
Open daily in summer; weekends only rest of the year.

❻ Cairnholy
Carsluith.
Open at all times.

❼ Creetown
Gem Rock Museum
Chain Road. Tel: 01671 820357.
Open Easter–Sep daily 9.30–5.30; Jan–Feb weekends only 10–4.
Exhibition Centre
91 St John's Street.
Tel: 01671 820343.
Open Apr–Sep daily 11–4 (check for Wed & Sat)
Carsluith Castle
3½ miles (5.6km) south on A75.
Open daily 9.30–6.30 (4.30 Oct–Mar).

❽ Clatteringshaws Loch
Clatteringshaws Visitor Centre
6 miles (10km) west of New Galloway. Tel: 01644 420285.
Open daily late Mar–late Sep 10.30–5; late Sep–Oct 10.30–4.30.

Back to Nature
Wildfowl and Wetlands Trust Caerlaverock
Eastpark Farm, Caerlaverock. Tel: 01387 770200.
Open all year daily 10–5.

For History Buffs
Caerlaverock Castle
Glencaple. Tel: 01387 770244.
Open Mon–Sat 9.30–6.30, Sun 2–6.30 (closes 4.30pm Oct–Mar).

For Children
Kirkcudbright Wildlife Park
Lochfergus Plantation, 1 mile (1.6km) east on B727. Tel: 01557 331645.
Open mid-Mar–Oct daily 10–5.30 (to 6pm Apr–Aug).

TOUR 4

i Horsemarket, Ladyacre Road, Lanark. Tel: 01555 661661.

i 155 High Street, Biggar (seasonal). Tel: 01899 221066.

i Service Area, Junction 13, M74 northbound, Abington. Tel: 01864 502436.

i Service Area, M74 northbound, Hamilton. Tel: 01698 285590.

❶ New Lanark
New Lanark Visitor Centre
Tel: 01555 661345.
Open daily 11–5.

❷ Biggar
Biggar Gasworks Museum
Gasworks Road. Tel: 01899 221050.
Open Jun–Sep daily 2–5.
Gladstone Court Museum
Entrance by 113 High Street. Tel: 01899 221050.
Open Easter–mid-Oct Mon–Sat 11–4.30, Sun 2–4.30.
Moat Park Heritage Centre
Kirkstyle. Tel: 01899 221050.
Open Apr–Oct Mon–Sat 10.30–5, Sun 2–5; Nov–Feb weekdays only, during normal office hours.

❸ Wanlockhead
Museum of Leadmining
At the north end of the Mennock Pass. Tel: 01659 74387.
Open Apr–Oct daily 10–4.30.

❹ Sanquhar
Sanquhar Castle
Open at all times.
Tolbooth Museum
High Street. Tel: 01659 50186.
Open Apr–Sep, Tue–Sat 10–1 & 2–5, Sun 2–5.

❻ Strathaven
John Hastie Museum
Threestanes Road.
Tel: 01357 521257.
Open Apr–Sep daily 12.30–4.30.

❼ Hamilton
Low Parks Museum
129 Muir Street. Tel: 01698 328232.
Open Mon–Sat 10–5, Sun noon–5.
Hamilton Mausoleum
Tours available from Low Parks Museum only.

Tours Sat, Sun & Wed, summer 3pm; winter 2pm.
Cadzow Castle Ruins
Hamilton Hyde Park.
Open at all times.

❽ Blantyre
David Livingstone Centre
165 Station Road.
Tel: 01698 823140.
Open Mon–Sat 10–5, Sun 12.30–5 (restricted winter opening).

❾ Bothwell Castle
Castle Avenue, Uddingston.
Tel: 01698 816894.
Open Apr–Sep daily 9.30–6.30; Oct–Mar 9.30–4.30 (closed Thu afternoon, all day Fri & Sun morning).

❿ Craignethan Castle
5 miles (8km) west of Lanark off A72. Tel: 01555 860364.
Open Apr–Sep, daily 9.30–6.30; Nov–Mar Sat 9.30–4.30, Sun 2–4.30.

For Children
Discover Carmichael Visitor Centre
Carmichael. Tel: 01899 308169.
Open late Mar–early Jan daily 9–5.
Biggar Little Theatre (International Purves Puppets)
Broughton Road.
Tel: 01899 220631.
Open on certain days only.
Strathclyde Country Park
Hamilton Road, Motherwell. Tel: 01698 266155.
Always accessible.
M & D's Theme Park
Strathclyde Country Park.
Tel: 01698 333777.
Open daily, 10am–10.30pm, outdoor rides noon–10pm.

Back to Nature
Chatelherault
Ferniegair, southeast of Hamilton on A72.
Tel: 01698 426213.
Open: house Mon–Thu & Sat 10–5, Sun noon–5; Visitor Centre Mon–Sat 10–5, Sun 2–5.

TOUR 5

i Churchgate, Moffat (seasonal).
Tel: 01683 220620.

Practical information

ⓘ Tourist Information Office
⑫ Number on tour

ⓘ High Street, Peebles.
Tel: 0870 608 0404.

ⓘ 3 St John Street,
Galashiels (seasonal).
Tel: 0870 608 0404

**❶ Dawyck Botanic
Garden**
Stobo. Tel: 01721 760254.
*Open Mar–mid-Nov daily
9.30–6.*

❷ Broughton
John Buchan Centre
Tel: 01899 221050.
*Open Easter & May–mid-
Oct daily 2–5.*
Broughton Gallery
North on A701. Tel: 01899
830234.
*Open Apr–Sep & mid-Nov–
mid-Dec 10.30–6 (closed
Wed).*

❹ Peebles
Tweeddale Museum
Chambers Institute, High
Street. Tel: 01721 724820.
*Open Mon–Fri 10–noon,
2–5; Easter–Oct also Sat
10–1 & 2–4.*
**Cornice Museum of
Ornamental Plasterwork**
Innerleithen Road.
Tel: 01721 720212.
*Open Mon–Fri 10–12 &
2–4.30.*
Old Cross Kirk
Off High Street.
*Open daily (pm only on Sun);
Jan–Mar apply to keykeeper.*
Neidpath Castle
1 mile (1.6km) west..
Tel: 01721 720333.
*Open Easter & Jun–Sep
Mon–Sat 10.30–4.30, Sun
12.30–4.30.*
Kailzie Gardens
2½ miles (4km) south on
B7062. Tel: 01721 720007.
*Open late Mar–Oct daily;
call for winter opening.*

❺ Innerleithen
Robert Smail's Printing
Works
7–9 High Street. Tel: 01896
830206.
*Open Easter & Jun–Sep
Thu–Mon noon–5 (Sun
1–5).*
Traquair House
Traquair, south on B709.
Tel: 01896 830323.
Open Apr–Oct daily .

❻ Galashiels
Lochcarron Cashmere
Wool of Scotland Visitor
Centre
Waverley Mill, Huddersfield
Street. Tel: 01896 752091.
*Open all year Mon–Sat 9–5;
Jun–Sep also Sun 12–5;
guided tours Mon–Thu at
10.30, 11.30, 1.30 & 2.30
(morning only on Fri).*
**Old Gala House and
Christopher Boyd Gallery**
Scott Crescent. Tel: 01750
20096.
*Open Easter–Sep Tue–Sat
10–4; Jul–Aug also Sun 2–4
& Mon 10–4; Oct Tue–Sat
1–4.*

❼ Yarrowford
Bowhill House and
Country Park
3 miles (4.8km) west of
Selkirk. Tel: 01750 22204.
*Open Jul daily 1–4.30; coun-
try park late Apr–Aug daily
12–5, closed Fri ex Jul.*

TOUR 6

Telephone enquiries for
tourist information in the
area should be directed to
tel: 0870 608 0404.
Information for personal
callers is available at:

ⓘ Abbey House, Abbey
Street, Melrose (seasonal).

ⓘ Murray's Green,
Jedburgh.

ⓘ Drumlanrig's Tower,
Tower Knowe, Hawick
(seasonal).

ⓘ Halliwell's House,
Selkirk (seasonal).

❶ Dryburgh Abbey
Dryburgh. Tel: 01835
822381.
*Open daily 9.30–6.30 (to
4.30pm Oct–Mar, Sun
2–4.30).*
Smailholm Tower
Northwest of Dryburgh
Abbey on B6404.
Tel: 01573 460565.
*Open Apr–Sep 9.30–6.30;
Oct–Mar Sat–Sun only.*

❷ Jedburgh
Jedburgh Castle Jail and
Museum
Castlegate. Tel: 01835
863254.

*Open Easter–Oct Mon–Sat
10–4.30, Sun 1–4.*
Jedburgh Abbey
Tel: 01835 863925.
*Open Apr–Sep daily 9.30–
6.30; Oct–Mar Mon–Sat
9.30–4.30, Sun 2–4.30.*
**Mary, Queen of Scots'
House**
Queen Street. Tel: 01835
863331.
*Open Mar–Nov Mon–Sat
10–4.30, Sun noon–4.30*

❸ Hawick
Peter Scott Woollen Mill
11 Buccleuch Street.
Tel: 01450 372311.
*Open all year Mon–Fri
10–5, Sat 10–4.*
**Wrights of Trowmill
Weaving Flat**
2½ miles (4km) NW on
A698. Tel: 01450 372555.
*Open Mon–Thu 9–4, Fri
9–11.30; shop daily 9/10–5.*
**Hawick Museum and
Scott Art Gallery**
Wilton Lodge Park.
Tel: 01450 373457.
*Open Apr–Sep Mon–Fri
10–noon & 1–4.45, Sat &
Sun 2–4.45; Oct–Mar
Mon–Fri 1–4, Sun 2–4.*

❹ Hermitage Castle
Tel: 01387 376222.
*Open Apr–Sep daily
9.30–6.30.*

❺ Eskdalemuir
Kagyu Samye Ling
Monastery
B709 NE of Langholm.
Tel: 013873 73232.
Open all year daily 9–6.

❼ Ettrick
James Hogg Exhibition &
Aikwood Tower
On B7009. Tel: 01750 52253.
*Open Easter Sun & May–
Sep Tue, Thu & Sun 2–5.*

❽ Selkirk
Sir Walter Scott's
Courtroom
Market Place. Tel: 01750
20096.
*Open Apr–Sep Mon–Sat
10–4 (from 1pm in Oct);
Jun–Aug also Sun 2–4.*
Halliwell's House Museum
Market Place. Tel: 01750
20096.
*Open Easter–Oct Mon–Sat
10–5, Sun 2–4 (to 5pm
Jul–Aug).*

❾ Abbotsford
Tel: 01896 752043.
*Open mid-Mar–May & Oct
Mon–Sat 9.30–5, Sun 2–5;
Jun–Sep daily 9.30–5.*

For History Buffs
Trimontium Exhibition
Ormiston Institute, The
Square, Melrose. Tel: 01896
822651 or 822463.
*Open Apr–Oct daily
10.30–4.30.*

Back to Nature
Harestanes Countryside
Visitor Centre
Harestanes, Ancrum, 3
miles (5km) north of
Jedburgh off A68.
Tel: 01835 830306.
Open Apr–Oct daily 10–5.
Priorwood Garden
Adjacent to Melrose
Abbey. Tel: 01896 822493.
*Open Apr–24 Dec Mon–Sat
10–5.30, Sun 1.30–5.30 (to
4pm Oct–24 Dec).*
Harmony Garden
St Mary's Road, Melrose.
Tel: 01721 722502.
*Open Apr–Sep Mon–Sat
10–5.30, Sun 1.30–5.30.*

For Children
Jedforest Deer and Farm
Park
Mervinslaw Estate, Jed-
burgh. Tel: 01835 840364.
*Open May–Aug 10–5.30;
Sep–Oct 11–4.30.*

For History Buffs
Drumlanrig's Tower
Tower Knowe, Hawick.
Tel: 01450 373457.
*Open 1 Apr–Oct Mon–Sat
10–5 (to 6 Jul–Aug), also Sun
1–4 Easter–Sep (to 5
Jul–Aug).*

TOUR 7

ⓘ 3 Princes Street,
Edinburgh. Tel: 0131
473 3800.

ⓘ Scottish Mining
Museum, Lady Victoria
Colliery, Newtongrange.
Tel: 0131 663 4262.

ⓘ Quality Street, North
Berwick. Tel: 01620
892197.

ⓘ 143 High Street,
Dunbar. Tel: 01368
863353.

ⓘ Auld Kirk, Manse Road, Eyemouth (seasonal). Tel: 0870 608 0404.

ⓘ Town Hall, High Street, Coldstream (seasonal). Tel: 0870 608 0404.

ⓘ Town House, The Square, Kelso. Tel: 0870 608 0404.

❶ Gullane
Dirleton Castle and Gardens
Dirleton. Tel: 01620 850330.
Open Apr–Sep daily 9.30–6.30; Oct–Mar Mon–Sat 9.30–4.30, Sun 2–4.30.

❸ Tantallon Castle
3 miles (5km) east of North Berwick off A198.
Tel: 01620 892727.
Open Mon–Sat 9.30–6.30, Sun 2–4.30 (closes 4.30 Oct–Mar when also closed Thu pm, Fri & Sun).

❹ Preston
Preston Mill and Phantassie Doocot
East Linton. Tel: 01620 860426.
Open Apr–Sep Thu–Mon noon–5 (Sun 1–5).

❼ St Abbs
Coldingham Priory
Open May–Sep Wed 2–5, Sun all year for services, noon.

❽ Eyemouth
Eyemouth Museum
Auld Kirk. Tel: 018907 50678.
Open Apr–Jun & Sep Mon–Sat 10–5, Sun 11.30–4.30; Jul–Aug Mon–Sat 9.30–5.30, Sun 11.30–4.30; Oct Mon–Sat 10–4, closed Sun.

❾ Duns
Jim Clark Room
44 Newtown Street.
Tel: 01361 883960.
Open Easter–Sep Mon–Sat 10.30–1 & 2–4.30, Sun 2–4; Oct Mon–Sat 1–4.

Manderston
A6105, 2 miles (3km) east.
Tel: 01361 883450.
Open mid-May–Sep, Thu, Sun & bank hol 2–5.

🔟 Coldstream
Coldstream Museum
12 Market Square.

Tel: 01890 882630.
Open Easter–Sep Mon–Sat 10–4, Sun 2–4; Oct Mon–Sat 1–4.
The Hirsel
Tel: 01890 882834.
Open Mon–Fri 10–5, Sat & Sun noon–5; grounds daily.

⓫ Kelso
Floors Castle
Tel: 01573 223333.
Open Apr–Oct daily 10–4.30.
Kelso Abbey
Tel: 0131 668 8800.
Open Apr–Oct daily (Sun pm only).
Mellerstain House
Gordon. Tel: 01573 410225.
Open Easter & May–Sep daily (ex Tue & Sat) 12.30–5.

⓫ Lauder
Thirlestane Castle
Off A68. Tel: 01578 722430.
Open Easter & May–Sep daily (except Sat) 10.30–4.30.

⓭ Crichton Castle
Tel: 01875 320017.
Open Apr–Sep daily 9.30–6.30.

For History Buffs
Scottish Mining Museum
Lady Victoria Colliery, Newtongrange. Tel: 0131 663 7519.
Open Mar–Oct daily 10–5.

For History Buffs
Roslin Chapel
Roslin. Tel: 0131 440 2159.
Open all year daily, Mon–Sat 10–5, Sun 12–4.45.

Back to Nature
St Abbs Head National Nature Reserve
Tel: 01890 771443.
Open all year; Reserve Centre Apr–Oct daily 10–5.

For Children
Scottish Seabird Centre
North Berwick. Tel: 01620 890202.
Open Apr–Oct daily 10–6; Nov–Mar Mon–Fri 10–4 (5 Feb & Mar), Sat–Sun 10–5.30.

TOUR 8

ⓘ Albany Street, Oban.
Tel: 01631 563122.

ⓘ Lochnell Street, Lochgilphead (seasonal).
Tel: 01546 602344.

ⓘ Front Street, Inveraray.
Tel: 01499 302063.

ⓘ NTS Visitor Centre, Glen Coe (seasonal).
Tel: 01855 811307.

ⓘ Albert Road, Ballachulish (seasonal).
Tel: 01855 811866.

❶ Easdale
Easdale Island Folk Museum
Tel: 01852 300370.
Open Apr–Oct daily 10.30–5.30.

❷ Kilmartin
Kilmartin House Centre for Archaeology & Landscape Interpretation
Tel: 01546 510278.
Open all year daily 10–5.30.
Carnassarie Castle
North, beside A816.
Open at all times.

❹ Lochgilphead
Highbank Pottery
Highbank Industrial Estate.
Tel: 01546 602044.
Open Mon–Fri 9–5, Sat 10–5.

❺ Crarae Garden
On A83 near Minard. Tel: 01546 886614.
Open daily during daylight hours.

❻ Auchindrain Township Open Air Museum
On A83 6 miles (10km) southwest of Inveraray.
Tel: 01499 500235.
Open Apr–Sep daily 10–5.

❼ Inveraray
Inveraray Jail Museum
Church Square. Tel: 01499 302381.
Open Apr–Oct daily 9.30–6; Nov–Mar daily 10–5.
Arctic Penguin
The Pier. Tel: 01499 302213.
Open daily 10–5 (to 6pm Apr–Sep).
Inveraray Castle
Northern edge of town, on A83. Tel: 01499 302203.
Open Apr–Oct Mon–Thu & Sat 10–1 & 2–5.45, Sun

1–5.45 (also Fri Jul–Aug, when there are no lunchtime closures).

❽ Loch Awe
Cruachan Power Station
Dalmally. Tel: 01866 822618.
Open Easter–Nov daily 9.30–6.
Kilchurn Castle
Head of Locha Awe, south off A85.
Open at all times.

❾ Glen Coe
Glen Coe Visitor Centre
Tel: 01855 811307.
Open Apr–Oct daily 10–5 (9.30–5.30 mid-May–Aug).
Glen Coe and North Lorn Folk Museum
Tel: 01855 811314.
Open Easter–Sep Mon–Sat 10–5.

🔟 Scottish Sea Life Sanctuary
Barcaldine. Tel: 01631 720386.
Open daily 10–5 (to 6pm in high season).

⓬ Loch Etive
Bonawe Iron Furnace
Bonawe. Tel: 01866 822432.
Open Apr–Sep daily 9.30–6.30.

For Children
Oban Rare Breeds Farm Park
New Barran, Oban.
Tel: 01631 770608.
Open Apr–Oct daily 10–6.
Argyll Wildlife Park
Inveraray. Tel: 01499 302264.
Open daily 10–5.

For History Buffs
Dunadd Fort
1 mile (1.6km) west of Kilmichael Glassary.
Open at all times.

TOUR 9

ⓘ Glasgow International Airport, Paisley. Tel: 0141 848 4440.

ⓘ Milton, A82 northbound, Dumbarton.
Tel: 01389 742306.

ⓘ Clock Tower, The Pier, Helensburgh (seasonal).
Tel: 01436 672642.

Practical information

ⓘ Tourist Information Office
⓬ Number on tour

ⓘ Harbour Street,
Tarbert. Tel: 01880 820429.

ⓘ 7 Alexandra Parade,
Dunoon. Tel: 01369
703785.

❶ Dumbarton
Dumbarton Castle
Tel: 01389 732167.
*Open 9.30–6.30 (to 4.30pm
Oct–Mar, and closed Thu pm
& Fri).*

❷ Helensburgh
Hill House
Upper Colquhoun Street.
Tel: 01436 673900.
*Open Apr–Oct daily
1.30–5.30.*

❹ Lochgoilhead
Carrick Castle
On west side of Loch Goil.
Open at all times.

❺ Loch Fyne
Strachur Smiddy
The Clachan. Tel: 01369
860565.
Open Easter–Sep daily 1–4.

❼ Dunoon
Castle House Museum
Castle Gardens. Tel: 01369
701422.
Cowal Bird Garden
Lochan Wood, Sandbank
Road. Tel: 01369 707999.
*Open Easter–Oct daily
10.30–6.*
Dunoon Ceramics
Hamilton Street. Tel: 01369
704360.
*Open Mon–Fri 9–12.30 &
1–4.30 (3 on Fri); shop
9–3.30.*
Younger Botanic Garden
Benmore. Tel: 01369
706261.
Open Mar–Oct 9.30–6.

❽ Greenock
Custom House Museum
Custom House Quay,
Greenock. Tel: 01475
881452.
Open Mon–Fri 10–4.
**McLean Museum and Art
Gallery**
15 Kelly Street, Greenock.
Tel: 01475 715624.
Open Mon–Sat 10–5.
Newark Castle
On the A8, Port Glasgow.
Tel: 01475 741858.
*Open Apr–Sep Mon–Sat
9.30–6.30, Sun 2–6.30.*

❷ Kilbarchan
Weaver's Cottage
The Cross. Tel: 01505
705588
*Open Easter–Sep daily
1.30–5.30; Oct weekends.*

For Children
Helensburgh Pier
Pier Car Park, West Clyde
Street. Tel: 01436 671552.
*Open Apr–May & Sep
weekends, Jun–Aug daily
1.30–10.*

For History Buffs
Castle Toward
End of the A815 south of
Dunoon.
Open at all times.

Special To...
PS *Waverley* cruises
Anderston Quay, Glasgow.
Tel: 0845 130 4647.
Cruises Jul–Aug daily.

TOUR 10

ⓘ 11 George Square,
Glasgow. Tel: 0141 204
4400.

ⓘ Drymen Library, The
Square, Drymen
(seasonal). Tel: 01360
660068.

ⓘ Breadalbane Folklore
Centre, Falls of Dochart,
Killin (seasonal). Tel: 01567
820254.

ⓘ The Square, Aberfeldy.
Tel: 01887 820276.

ⓘ High Street, Crieff.
Tel: 01764 652578.

ⓘ Rob Roy and Trossachs
Visitor Centre, Ancaster
Square, Callander.
Tel: 01877 330342.

ⓘ Trossachs Discovery
Centre, Main Street,
Aberfoyle (seasonal).
Tel: 01877 382352.

❶ Gartocharn
**Balloch Castle Country
Park**
Old Station, Balloch Road,
Balloch. Tel: 01389 758216.
*Open all year 8–dusk; visitor
centre Apr–Oct daily
10–5.45.*

❷ Luss
National Park Centre
Tel: 01301 702785.

Open daily.
Thistle Bagpipe Works
Tel: 01436 860250.
*Open daily 9–5.30 (later in
summer).*

❸ Killin
Ben Lawers Visitor Centre
Lynedoch, Main Street.
Tel: 01567 820397.
*Open Apr–Sep daily 10–5
(may close for lunch).*
**Breadalbane Folklore
Centre**
St Fillan's Mill. Tel: 01567
820254.
*Open Mar–May & Oct daily
10–5; Jun & Sep daily 10–6;
Jul–Aug daily 9.30–6.30.*

❺ Aberfeldy
Watermill
Mill Street. Tel: 01887
820803.
Call for information.
Castle Menzies
Weem. Tel: 01887 820982.
*Open Apr–mid-Oct week-
days 10.30–5, Sun 2–5.*

❻ Crieff
Thistle Pottery
Visitor Centre, Muthill
Road. Tel: 01764 654014.
*Open all year daily Apr–Oct
9–5.30; Nov–Mar 10–4.*
Glenturret Distillery
Northwest off the A85.
Tel: 01764 656565.
*Open Feb–Dec Mon–Sat
9.30–6, Sun 12–6 (last tour
4.30); Jan, Mon–Fri 11.30–4
(last tour 2.30).*

❽ Callander
**Rob Roy and Trossachs
Visitor Centre**
Ancaster Square. Tel: 01887
330342.
*Open Jan–Feb weekends
11–4.30; Mar–May &
Oct–Dec daily 10–5; Jun
daily 9.30–6, Jul–Aug daily
9–8; Sep daily 10–6.*

❾ Loch Katrine
Sir Walter Scott cruises
Trossachs Pier, by Callander.
Tel: 01877 376316.
*Open Apr–Oct daily, sailings
11, 1.45 & 3.15.*

❿ Aberfoyle
Scottish Wool Centre
Off Main Street. Tel: 01877
382850.
*Open all year daily 9.30–
5.30 (to 6pm on Sat & Sun).*

Recommended Walks
**Queen Elizabeth Forest
Park Visitor Centre**
North of Aberfoyle on the
A821. Tel: 01877 382258.
*Open daily, Easter–Oct
10–6; Nov–Dec 11–4.*

For History Buffs
Inchmahome Priory
Accessible by ferry from
Port of Menteith.
Tel: 01877 385294.
*Open Apr–Sep daily
9.30–6.30.*

TOUR 11

ⓘ 41 Dumbarton Road,
Stirling. Tel: 01786 475019

ⓘ Royal Burgh of Stirling
Visitor Centre, Castle
Esplanade, Stirling. Tel:
01786 479901

ⓘ Pirnhall Motorway
Service Area, M9/M80 Junc
9 (seasonal). Tel: 01786
814111

ⓘ Stirling Road, Dunblane
(seasonal). Tel: 01786
824428

ⓘ Mill Trail Visitor Centre,
West Stirling Street, Alva.
Tel: 01259 769696

ⓘ 1 High Street,
Dunfermline (seasonal).
Tel: 01383 720999

ⓘ Burgh Halls, The Cross,
Linlithgow (seasonal).
Tel: 01506 844600

ⓘ Car Park, Seaview
Place, Bo'ness (seasonal).
Tel: 01506 826626

ⓘ NTS Visitor Centre,
Bannockburn. Tel: 01786
812664

❶ Causewayhead
Wallace Monument
Abbey Craig. Tel: 01786
472140.
Open all year daily.

❷ Dunblane
Doune Castle
Tel: 01786 841742.
*Open Apr–Sep daily 9.30–
6.30; Oct–Mar 9.30–4.30
closed Thu afternoon, all day
Fri & Sun morning.*
Dunblane Museum
The Cross. Tel: 01786
826591.

Practical information

Open early May– early Oct,
Mon–Sat 10.30–4.30.

3 Dollar
Castle Campbell
Off A91 at head of Dollar
Glen. Tel: 01259 742408.
Open daily 9.30–6.30 (to
4.30pm Oct–Mar, closed Thu
pm, Fri, & Sun am).
Mill Trail Visitor Centre
Glentana Mill, Alva.
Tel: 01259 769696.
Open all year daily.

4 Culross
Culross Palace, Town
House and The Study
West Green House.
Tel: 01383 880359.
Open Apr–Sep daily noon–5;
Town House & Study open
at 1.30, and are open week-
ends in Oct noon–5.

5 Dunfermline
Dunfermline Abbey
Pittencrieff Park. Tel: 01383
739026.
Open Mon–Sat 9.30–6.30,
Sun 2–6.30 (to 4.30pm Oct–
Mar, closed Thu pm).
Abbot House Museum
The Maygate. Tel: 01383
733266.
Open all year daily 10–5.
Pittencrieff House
Museum and Art Gallery
Pittencrieff Park. Tel: 01383
722935 & 313838.
Open all year daily 11–4 or 5.
Andrew Carnegie
Birthplace Museum
Moodie Street. Tel: 01383
723638.
Open Apr–Oct Mon–Sat
11–5 (from 10am Jun–Aug),
Sun 2–5.

6 Blackness
Blackness Castle
Tel: 01506 834807.
Open Apr–Sep Mon–Sat
9.30–6.30, Sun 2–6.30;
Oct–Mar 9.30–4.30 closed
Thu afternoon, all day Fri &
Sun morning).

7 Linlithgow
Linlithgow Palace
Tel: 01506 842896.
Open Mon–Sat 9.30–6.30,
Sun 2–6.30 (4.30 Oct–Mar).
Burgh Halls Visitor Centre
The Cross. Tel: 01506
844600.
Open Easter–Oct daily
10–5.

House of the Binns
Tel: 01506 834255.
Open May–Sep daily (ex
Fri) 1.30–5.30; parkland
Apr–Oct daily 10–7;
Nov–Mar 10–4.
The Linlithgow Story
High Street. Tel: 01506
670677.
Open mid-Apr–Oct daily
10–5 (1–4 on Sun).
Canal Museum
Manse Road Basin.
Tel: 01506 842125.
Open Easter–Oct weekends
2–5 (daily Jul–Aug).

8 Bo'ness
Bo'ness & Kinneil Railway
and Birkhill Clay Mine
Bo'ness Station, Union
Street. Tel: 01506 822298.
Open Apr–Oct weekends &
bank hols; Jul–Aug daily ex
Mon.

9 Bannockburn
Heritage Centre
Glasgow Road, Stirling.
Tel: 01786 812664.
Heritage Centre: open Mar
& Nov–23 Dec daily
11–4.30; Apr–Oct daily
10–5.30; the site is open all
year daily.

For Children
Blair Drummond Safari
and Leisure Park
Blair Drummond.
Tel: 01786 841456.
Open late Apr–early Oct
daily 10–5.30.

i Lower City Mills, West
Mill Street, Perth. Tel: 01738
450600.

i Caithness Glass,
Inveralmond, by the A9.
Tel: 01738 492320.

i The Cross, Dunkeld.
Tel: 01350 727688.

i 26 Wellmeadow,
Blairgowrie. Tel: 01250
872960.

i Brechin Castle Centre,
Haughmuir, Brechin
(seasonal). Tel: 01356
623050.

i Bridge Street,
Montrose (seasonal).
Tel: 01674 672000.

i Market Place, Arbroath.
Tel: 01241 872609.

i 1B High Street,
Carnoustie (seasonal).
Tel: 01241 852258.

i 21 Castle Street,
Dundee. Tel: 01382 527527.

1 Dunkeld
The Ell Shop
The Cross. Tel: 01350
727460.
Open Apr–Sep Mon–Sat
10.30–5.30 (also Sun from
12.30 Jun–Aug); Oct–23
Dec Mon–Sat 10–4.30.

3 Meigle
Sculptured Stone Museum
Tel: 01828 640612.
Open daily 9.30–6.30 (to
4.30pm Oct–Nov); may
close for lunch on weekdays.

4 Glamis
Glamis Castle
Tel: 01307 840393.
Open late Mar–late Oct
10–6 (last admission 4.30).
Angus Folk Museum
Kirkwynd, Glamis.
Tel: 01307 840288.
Open Easter & May–Sep
Sat–Wed noon–5.

6 House of Dun
Montrose. Tel: 01674
810264.
Open Easter & May–Sep
Fri–Tue 12.30–5; grounds all
year 9.30–sunset.

10 Dundee
Discovery Point Visitor
Centre
Discovery Quay, Riverside
Drive. Tel: 01382 201245.
Open Mon–Sat 10–6, Sun
11–6 (up to 5pm Nov–Mar).
Frigate *Unicorn*
Victoria Dock. Tel: 01382
200900.
Open Easter–Oct daily
10–5; Nov–Easter Mon–Fri
10–4.
McManus Galleries
Albert Square. Tel: 01382
432084.
Open Mon–Sat 10.30–5 (to
7pm on Thu), Sun 12.30–4.
Broughty Castle Museum
Castle Approach, Broughty
Ferry. Tel: 01382 436916.
Open Mon–Sat 10–4, Sun
12.30–4 (closed Mon
Oct–Mar).

Back to Nature
Loch of the Lowes Visitor
Centre
Dunkeld. Tel: 01350
727337.
Open Apr–Sep daily 10–5.

i 70 Market Street,
St Andrews. Tel: 01334
472021.

i Museum and Heritage
Centre, Crail (seasonal).
Tel: 01333 450869

i Scottish Fisheries
Museum, Harbourhead,
Anstruther (seasonal). Tel:
01333 311073.

i Kinross Service Area,
off Junc 6, M90. Tel: 01577
863680.

1 Crail
Museum and Heritage
Centre
62–4 Marketgate.
Tel: 01333 450869.
Open May Sat–Sun 10–1,
2–5; Jun–Sep Mon–Sat
10–1, 2–5, Sun 2–5.
Crail Pottery
75 Nethergate. Tel: 01333
451212.
Open Mon–Fri 9–5, Sat &
Sun 10–5.

2 Anstruther
Scottish Fisheries Museum
St Ayles, Harbourhead.
Tel: 01333 310628.
Open Mon–Sat 10–4.30,
Sun 11–4.
Scotland's Secret Bunker
4 miles (6km) north on
B940. Tel: 01333 310301.
Open Apr–Oct daily 10–5.

3 Pittenweem
St Fillan's Cave
Tel: 01333 311495.
Open all year (get key from
9 High Street).
Kellie Castle
3 miles (5km) northwest
of Pittenweem. Tel: 01333
720271.
Open Easter & Jun–Sep
daily 1–5; weekends in Oct
1.30–5.30; grounds all year
daily 9.30–sunset.

4 St Monans
St Monans Windmill
Tel: 01333 412934.

Practical information

Open late Jun–Sep daily noon–4.

6 Falkland
Falkland Palace
Tel: 01337 857397.
Open Apr–Oct Mon–Sat 11–5.30, Sun 1.30–5.30.

8 Kinross
Loch Leven Castle
Ferry from Kirkgate Park.
Tel: 07778 040483.
Open Apr–Oct from 9.30 (last ferry off the island departs at 6pm, or 4pm in Oct). Closed Tue, Fri in Oct..
Kinross House Gardens
Tel: 01577 863467.
Open Apr–Sep daily.

10 Cupar
Hill of Tarvit
Ceres. Tel: 01334 653127.
Open Apr–Sep daily 1–5, Oct Sat–Sun 1–5.
Scotstarvit Tower
Ceres.
Open Apr–Oct daily noon–5 (key from Hill of Tarvit).

For Children
Scottish Deer Centre and Raptor World
Rankeilour Park, Bow of Fife, by Cupar. Tel: 01337 810391 (Deer); 07976 227699 (Raptors).
Open daily from 10am; closes at 5 or 6, depending on the season.

TOUR 14

i Castle Wynd, Inverness.
Tel: 01463 234353.

i 62 King Street, Nairn (seasonal). Tel: 01667 452753.

i 116 High Street, Forres (seasonal). Tel: 01309 672938.

i 54 High Street, Grantown-on-Spey (seasonal). Tel: 01479 872773.

i Picnic Area, Daviot Wood, on the A9, by Inverness (seasonal). Tel: 01463 772203.

1 Fort George
11 miles (18km) northeast of Inverness. Tel: 01667 462777.

Open daily Apr–Sep 9.30–6.30; Oct–Mar daily 9.30–4.30.

2 Cawdor Castle
Tel: 01667 404401.
Open May–mid-Oct daily 10–5.30.
Kilravock Castle
6 miles (10km) south of Nairn off B9090. Tel: 01667 493258.
Open by appointment only.

3 Nairn
Nairn Museum
Viewfield House. Tel: 01667 456791.
Open late Mar–Oct daily 1–4.30; Nov Sat–Sun 1–4.30.

4 Brodie Castle
Brodie, near Forres.
Tel: 01309 641371.
Open Apr & Jul–Aug daily noon–4; May–Jun & Sep Sun–Thu noon–4; grounds: all year daily 9.30–sunset.

5 Forres
Falconer Museum
Tolbooth Street. Tel: 01309 673701.
Open Apr–Oct Mon–Sat 10–5; Nov–Mar Mon–Thu 11–12.30, 1–3.30.
Sueno's Stone
Findhorn Road, east of Forres. Tel: 01667 460232.
Open at all times.

7 Grantown-on-Spey
Grantown Museum & Heritage Trust
Burnfield House, Burnfield Avenue. Tel: 01479 872478.
Open Mar–Dec, Mon–Sat 10–4.

8 Carrbridge
Landmark Highland Heritage and Adventure Park
Tel: 0800 731 3446.
Open late Mar–Oct daily.

9 Culloden
Battlefield and Visitor Centre
Culloden Moor. Tel: 01463 790607.
Site always accessible; visitor centre open Feb–Dec daily 10–4; (9–6 Apr–Oct).
Clava Cairns
On B9006. Tel: 0131 668 8800.
Open at all times.

Special To...
Speyside Heather Centre
Skye of Curr, Dulnain Bridge. Tel: 01479 851359.
Open Feb–Dec daily 9–6.

TOUR 15

i 17 High Street, Elgin.
Tel: 01343 542666/ 543388.

i Clock Tower, The Square, Dufftown (seasonal). Tel: 01340 820501.

1 Lossiemouth
Lossiemouth Fisheries and Community Museum
Bitgavney Quay. Tel: 01343 813772.
Open Easter–Oct, Mon–Sat 10.30–5.
Palace of Spynie
2 miles (3km) north of Elgin off A941. Tel: 01343 546358.
Open Apr–Sep daily 9.30–6.30; Oct Sat–Wed 9.30–4.30; Nov–Dec Sat–Sun 9.30–4.30; Jan–Mar daily 9.30–4.30, (pm only Sat–Sun).

2 Fochabers
Baxters Factory Tours and Visitor Centre
1 mile (1.6km) west of Fochabers on A96. Tel: 01343 820666.
Open all year.
Fochabers Folk Museum
High Street. Tel: 01343 821204.
Open May–Sep daily 10.30–4.

3 Spey Bay
Tugnet Ice-House Museum
Tugnet. Tel: 01309 673701.
Open Apr–Sep daily 1–5 (to 7pm Jul–Aug).
Moray Firth Wildlife Centre
Tugnet. Tel: 01343 820339.
Open Apr–Oct daily 10.30–5; Feb–Mar Sat–Sun 10.30–5.

4 Buckie
Buckie Drifter Maritime Heritage Centre
Freuchny Road. Tel: 01542 834646.
Open Apr–Oct Mon–Sat 10–5, Sun 12–5.

---

i Tourist Information Office
12 Number on tour

5 Cullen
Findlater Castle
By Sandend.
Open at all times.

6 Portsoy
Portsoy Marble Workshop
Shorehead. Tel: 01261 842404.
Open Fri & Sat afternoons.

7 Keith
Strathisla Distillery
Seafield Avenue. Tel: 01542 783044.
Open Apr–Oct Mon–Sat 10–4, Sun 12.30–4.

8 Dufftown
Keith & Dufftown Railway
Dufftown Station.
Tel: 01340 821181.
Open Easter–mid-Oct Sat–Sun 10–5.
Glenfiddich Distillery
Tel: 01340 820373.
Open all year Mon–Fri 9.30–4.30; also Sat 9.30–4.30, Sun 12–4.30 Easter–mid-Oct.
Balvenie Castle
Tel: 01340 820121.
Open Apr–Sep daily 9.30–6.30.

9 Rothes
Glen Grant Distillery
Elgin Road. Tel: 01542 783318.
Open Apr–Oct Mon–Sat 10–4, Sun 12.30–4.

Back to Nature
Dolphin Cruises
Shore Street Quay, Inverness. Tel: 01463 717900.
Open Mar–Oct daily.

Special To...
Speyside Cooperage
Dufftown Road, Craigellachie. Tel: 01340 871108.
Open all year Mon–Fri 9.30–4.

TOUR 16

i Collie Lodge, Banff (seasonal). Tel: 01261 812419.

i 3 Saltoun Square, Fraserburgh (seasonal). Tel: 01346 518315.

i 18 High Street, Inverurie. Tel: 01467 625800.

[i] 9A The Square, Huntly (seasonal). Tel: 01466 792255.

[4] Fraserburgh
Scotland's Lighthouse Museum
Kinnaird Head. Tel: 01346 511022.
Open all year, Mon–Sat 11–5 (to 6pm Jul–Aug; 4pm Nov–Mar), Sun noon–5 (to 6pm Jul–Aug; 4pm Nov–Mar).

[5] Peterhead
Maritime Heritage
The Lido, South Road.
Tel: 01779 473000.
Open Jun–Aug Mon–Sat 10.30–5, Sun 11.30–5.
Arbuthnot Museum and Art Gallery
St Peter Street. Tel: 01771 622906.
Open Mon–Sat 11–4.30 (to 1pm Wed; closed 1–2 Sun & public holidays).

[7] Ellon
Haddo House
Tel: 01651 851440.
Open, House: Jun Fri–Mon 11–4.30; Jul–Aug daily 11–4.30; Garden all year daily 9.30–6.

[8] Pitmedden Garden
On A920 1 mile (1.6km) west of Pitmedden village.
Tel: 01651 842352.
Open May–Sep daily 10–5.30.

[10] Inverurie
Archaeolink Prehistory Park
Oyne, off A96 8 miles (13km) northwest of Inverurie. Tel: 01464 851500.
Open Apr–Oct daily 10–5.

[11] Huntly
Huntly Castle
Tel: 01466 793191.
Open summer: daily; winter: closed Thu pm, Fri, Sun am.
Recommended Walks
Duff House
Banff. Tel: 01261 818181.
Open Apr–Oct daily 11–5; Nov–Mar Thu–Sun 11–4.

For Children
Northfield Farm Museum
New Pitsligo, Fraserburgh.

Tel: 01771 653504.
Open May–Sep daily 11–5.30.

Back to Nature
Sands of Forvie National Nature Reserve
Collieston. Tel: 01358 751330. *Open at all times.*

For History Buffs
Fyvie Castle
Fyvie. Tel: 01651 891266.
Open Apr–Jun & Sep Fri–Tue noon–5; Jul–Aug daily 11–5.

TOUR 17

[i] 22 Atholl Road, Pitlochry. Tel: 01796 472215/472751.

[i] NTS Visitor Centre, Killiecrankie (seasonal). Tel: 01796 473233.

[i] Ralia, on the A9 near Newtonmore (seasonal). Tel: 01540 673253.

[i] Grampian Road, Aviemore. Tel: 01479 810363.

[i] The Square, Tomintoul (seasonal). Tel: 01807 580770.

[i] Old Royal Station, Station Square, Ballater. Tel: 013397 55306.

[2] Blair Atholl
Blair Castle
Tel: 01796 481207.
Open Apr–Oct daily 9.30–4.30; Nov–Mar Tue 9.30–12.30.

[3] Dalwhinnie
Distillery
Tel: 01540 672219.
Open Mar–Dec Mon–Fri 9.30–4.30 (also Sat Jun–Oct; also Sun 12.30–4.30 Jul–Aug).

[4] Kingussie
Highland Folk Museum
Duke Street. Tel: 01540 661307.
Open Apr–Aug Mon–Sat 9.30–5.30; Sep–Oct Mon–Fri 9.30–4.30.
Ruthven Barracks
Open at all times.

[5] Kincraig
Highland Wildlife Park
3 miles (5km) south on B9152. Tel: 01540 651270.

Open daily 10–6 (to 7pm Jun–Aug; to 4pm Nov–Mar).

[6] Aviemore
Strathspey Steam Railway
Aviemore Speyside Station, Dalfaber Road.
Tel: 01479 810725.
Open 1 Apr–Oct (daily Jun–Sep), call talking timetable (01479 812220) for details.

[9] Tomintoul
Tomintoul Museum
The Square. Tel: 01309 673701.
Open Apr–Oct Mon–Fri 9.30–noon, 2–4 (to 4.30 Jun–Aug; also Sat Jun–Sep).
Glenlivet Distillery
Glenlivet, Ballindalloch.
Tel: 01542 783220.
Open mid-Mar–Oct Mon–Sat 10–4, Sun 12.30–4 (to 6pm Jul–Sep).

[10] The Lecht
Corgarff Castle
8 miles (13km) west of Strathdon on the A939.
Tel: 01975 651460.
Open daily in summer; weekends in winter.

[11] Ballater
Balmoral Castle
Tel: 013397 42334/5.
Open mid-Apr–Jul.

[12] Braemar
Braemar Castle
Tel: 013397 41219.
Open mid-Apr–Oct daily 10–6. Closed Fri, ex Jul–Aug.

TOUR 18

[i] Provost Ross's House, Shiprow, Aberdeen.
Tel: 01224 288828.

[i] 66 Allardice Street, Stonehaven (seasonal). Tel: 01569 762806.

[i] Bridge Street, Banchory. Tel: 01330 822000.

[i] Railway Museum, Station Yard, Alford (seasonal). Tel: 019755 62052.

[1] Stonehaven
Tolbooth Museum
The Harbour. Tel: 01771 622906.
Open May–Oct daily (ex Tue) 1.30–4.30.

Dunnottar Castle
2 miles (3km) south.
Tel: 01569 762173.
Open Easter–Oct Mon–Sat 9–6, Sun 2–5.

[2] Fettercairn
Fettercairn Distillery
Tel: 01561 340205.
Open May–Sep Mon–Sat 10–2.30.
Fasque House
Tel: 01561 340569.
Open May–Sep daily 11–5.30.

[3] Drum Castle
Drumoak. Tel: 01330 811204.
Open: castle Easter & May–Sep daily 1.30–5.30; Oct weekends; garden Easter & May–Sep daily 10–6; grounds all year 9.30–sunset.
Garlogie Mill Power House Museum
Garlogie, Skene. Tel: 01771 622906.
Open by appointment.

[4] Crathes Castle and Gardens
Crathes, by Banchory.
Tel: 01330 844525.
Open Apr–Oct daily 10.30–5.30; garden and grounds all year daily 9–sunset.

[5] Banchory
Banchory Museum
Bridge Street. Tel: 01771 622906.
Open Apr Sat 11–1, 2–4.30 May–Oct Mon–Sat 11–1, 2–4.30 (also Sun 2–4.30 Jul–Aug).

[8] Kildrummy Castle
Kildrummy. Tel: 01975 571331.
Open Apr–Sep daily 9.30–6.30.

[9] Alford
Grampian Transport Museum
Tel: 019755 62292.
Open Apr–Oct daily 10–5.
Alford Valley Railway
Alford Station. Tel: 019755 62811.
Open Apr–May & Sep Sat & Sun 1–5; Jun–Aug daily 1–5; Dec (phone for details).
Haughton House Country Park
Tel: 019755 62453.
Open all year dawn–dusk.

Practical information

Alford Heritage Centre
Mart Road. Tel: 019755
62906.
*Open Apr–Oct Mon–Sat
10–5, Sun 1–5.*

[11] Castle Fraser
Sauchen, Inverurie.
Tel: 01330 833463.
*Open Apr–Sep Fri–Tue
noon–5.30 (Jun–Aug daily
from 11); grounds open all
year daily 9.30–sunset.*

Back to Nature
Fowlsheugh RSPB Seabird
Colony
Crawton, by Stonehaven.
Tel: 01224 624824.
Open at all times.

For Children
Stratosphere
The Tramsheds, 179
Constitution Street,
Aberdeen. Tel: 01224
640340.
Storybook Glen
Maryculter. Tel: 01224
732941.
*Open all year, Mar–Oct daily
10–6, Nov–Feb Sat & Sun
11–4.*
Doonies Farm
Nigg, Aberdeen. Tel: 01224
875879.
Open all year 10–4.

TOUR 19

[i] Cameron Centre,
Cameron Square, Fort
William. Tel: 01397
703781.

[i] NTS Visitor Centre,
Glenfinnan (seasonal).
Tel: 01397 722250.

[i] Pier Road, Kilchoan
(seasonal). Tel: 01972
510222.

[i] Strontian (seasonal).
Tel: 01967 402381.

[1] Banavie
Inverlochy Castle
On Fort William road.
Open at all times.

Treasures of the Earth
On A830, Corpach.
Tel: 01397 772283.
*Open daily, summer 9.30–7;
winter 10–5.*

[2] Glenfinnan
Glenfinnan Monument
and NTS Visitor Centre

Tel: 01397 722250.
*Open all year; visitor centre
Apr–Oct daily 10–5
(9.30–6 mid-May–Aug).*
Railway Museum
Glenfinnan Railway Station.
Tel: 01397 722295.
Open Jun–Sep daily.

[5] Mallaig
Marine World Aquarium
The Harbour. Tel: 01687
462292.
Open daily 9–6 (or later).
Heritage Centre
Station Road. Tel: 01687
462085.
*Open Easter–Nov and
Christmas/New Year daily.*

[8] Acharacle
Castle Tioram
4 miles (6km) north.
Always open, subject to tides.

[9] Glenbeg
RSPB Glenborrodale
One mile (1.5km) south-
east of Glenbeg off B8007.
Open all year daily.

[11] Strontian
Ariundle Oakwood
Nature Reserve
Tel: 01967 402279.
Open all year daily.

[12] Lochaline
Ardtornish House
Gardens
Tel: 01967 421643.
*Open Apr–Oct daily (ex Tue)
10–5.*

For Children
Lochaber Leisure Centre
Belford Road, Fort William.
Tel: 01397 704359.
Open all year daily.

TOUR 20

[i] Car Park, Fort
Augustus (seasonal).
Tel: 01320 366367.

[i] Car Park, Kyle of
Lochalsh (seasonal).
Tel: 01599 534276.

[i] Main Street, Lochcarron
(seasonal). Tel: 01520
722357.

[i] NTS Centre, Torridon
(seasonal). Tel: 01445
791221.

[i] Achtercairn, Gairloch
(seasonal). Tel: 01445
712130.

[i] NTS Centre, Inverewe
(seasonal). Tel: 01445
781200.

[i] The Square,
Strathpeffer (seasonal).
Tel: 01997 421415.

[1] Invergarry
Invergarry Castle
Invergarry Castle Hotel.
Tel: 01809 501254.
Open at all times.

[2] Shiel Bridge
Eilean Donan Castle
Dornie. Tel: 01599 555202.
*Open Apr–Oct daily
10–5.30.*

[3] Kyle of Lochalsh
Balmacara Estate and
Lochalsh House
Woodland Garden
Tel: 01599 566325.
Open all year daily 9–sunset.

[5] Lochcarron
Strome Castle
4 miles (6km) southwest,
off A896.
Open all year daily.

[8] Torridon
NTS Countryside Centre
and Deer Museum
The Mains. Tel: 01445
791221.
*Open Easter–Sep daily
10–6; estate park and deer
museum all year daily.*

[9] Kinlochewe
Aultroy Visitor Centre
and Beinn Eighe National
Nature Reserve
Tel: 01445 760254.
*Open May–Sep daily 10–5;
nature reserve always open.*

[10] Gairloch
Gairloch Heritage
Museum
Auchtercairn. Tel: 01445
712287.
*Open Easter–Sep Mon–Sat
10–5; Oct Mon–Sat
10–1.30.*

[11] Inverewe Gardens
Poolewe. Tel: 01445
781200.
*Open daily 9.30–5 (to 9pm
mid-Mar–Oct).*

[14] Beauly
Beauly Priory
Tel: 01667 460232.
*Open mid-Jun–Sep daily
9.30–6.30.*

Moniack Castle
On the A862. Tel: 01463
831283.
*Open all year, Mon–Sat,
summer 11–5; winter 11–4.*

[16] Drumnadrochit
Official Loch Ness 2000
Tel: 01456 450573.
Open all year daily.
The Original Loch Ness
Visitor Centre
Loch Ness Lodge Hotel.
Tel: 01456 450342.
Open all year daily.
Urquhart Castle
On the A82. Tel: 01456
450551.
Open all year daily.

For Children
Gairloch Leisure Centre
Gairloch. Tel: 01445
712345.
Open all year daily.

TOUR 21

[i] Kirk Lane, Lochinver
(seasonal). Tel: 01571
844330.

[i] Ferrycroft Countryside
Centre, Lairg (seasonal).
Tel: 01549 402160.

[1] Knockan Cliff
Inverpolly National
Nature Reserve
Off A835.
Open May–Sep most days.

[2] Inchnadamph
Ardvreck Castle
Loch Assynt, Lochinver.
Open at all times.

[3] Lochinver
Assynt Visitor Centre
Kirk Lane. Tel: 01571
844330.
*Open Easter–Oct Mon–Sat
10–5 (longer hours Jun–Aug);
also Sun 11–4 in Aug.*
Highland Stoneware
Assynt. Tel: 01571 844376.
*Open all year Mon–Fri 9–6;
also Sat 9–5 Easter–Oct.*

[7] Lairg
Ferrycroft Countryside
Centre
Tel: 01549 402160.
*Open Apr–Oct daily 10–5
(to 4pm on Sun).*
Falls of Shin Visitor
Centre
Achany. Tel: 01549 402231.
Open Mar–Dec daily.

i Tourist Information Office
12 Number on tour

TOUR 22

i The Square, Dornoch.
Tel: 01862 810400.

i Durine, Durness
(seasonal). Tel: 01971
511259.

i Clachan, Bettyhill
(seasonal). Tel: 01641
521342.

i Riverside, Thurso
(seasonal). Tel: 01847
892371.

i County Road, John
o'Groats (seasonal).
Tel: 01955 611373.

i Whitechapel Road,
Wick. Tel: 01955
602596.

3 Durness
Balnakeil Craft Village
Tel: 01971 511277.
Open Apr–Oct daily 10–6.

4 Bettyhill
Strathnaver Museum
Tel: 01641 521418.
*Open Apr–Oct Mon–Sat
10–1 & 2–5.*
Invernaver Nature Reserve
Tel: 01847 821531.
Open at all times.

5 Reay
UKAEA Exhibition Centre
Dounreay. Tel: 01847
802233 or 802572.
Open Apr–Oct daily 10–4.

6 Thurso
Thurso Heritage Museum
Town Hall. Tel: 01847
892692.
*Open Jun–Sep Mon–Sat
10–1 & 2–5.*
Castle of Mey
Tel: 01847 851473.
*Open mid-May–Jul and mid-
Aug–Sep Tue–Sat 11–4.30,
Sun 2–5 (dates may vary).*

8 Wick
Castle of Old Wick
*Open at all times, unless
adjoining rifle range is in use.*
Wick Heritage Centre
Tel: 01955 605393.
*Open Jun–Sep Mon–Sat
10–5.*

10 Dunbeath
Heritage Centre
Old School. Tel: 01593
731233.

*Open Easter–Oct daily
10–5.*
Laidhay Croft Museum
1 mile (1.6km) north on
the A9. Tel: 01593 731244.
*Open Easter–Oct daily
10–6.*

11 Helmsdale
Timespan Heritage
Centre
Dunrobin Street. Tel: 01431
821327.
*Open Apr–Oct Mon–Sat
9.30–5, Sun noon–5.*

12 Brora
Clynelish Distillery
Tel: 01408 623000.
*Open Easter–Sep Mon–Fri
10–5; Oct 11–4;
Nov–Easter by appointment.*

13 Golspie
Orcadian Stone Company
Main Street. Tel: 01408
633483.
*Open Easter–Oct Mon–Sat
9–5.30.*
Dunrobin Castle and
Gardens
Tel: 01408 633177.
*Open Apr–mid-Oct daily
(ex Sun am) 10.30–4.30.*

TOUR 23

i The Square, Dornoch.
Tel: 01862 810400.

1 Evanton
Storehouse of Foulis
Foulis Ferry Point.
Tel: 01349 830000.
*Open Mar–Oct 10–5;
Nov–Feb 11–4.*

2 Tain
Tain Through Time
Tower Street. Tel: 01862
894089.
*Open Apr–Oct daily 10–6;
Nov–Mar Sat noon–4 (daily
towards end of Mar). Closed
over Christmas and New
Year.*
Glenmorangie Distillery
Outskirts of Tain. Tel: 01862
892477.
Open all year daily.

5 Cromarty
Cromarty Courthouse
Museum
Church Street. Tel: 01381
600418.
Open all year daily.

Hugh Miller's Cottage
Church Street. Tel: 01381
600245.
*Open Easter–Oct daily
noon–5 (closed Mon–Tue in
Oct).*

6 Rosemarkie
Groam House Museum
Tel: 01381 620961.
*Open May–Sep daily;
Oct–Apr weekend after-
noons.*

TOUR 24

i The Car Park,
Broadford (seasonal).
Tel: 01471 822361.

i Bayfield House, Bayfield
Road, Portree. Tel: 01478
612137.

i Ferry Terminal, Uig
(seasonal). Tel: 01470
542404.

i 2 Lochside, Dunvegan
(seasonal). Tel: 01470
521581.

6 Kilmuir
Museum of Island Life
Tel: 01470 552206.
*Open Apr–Oct, Mon–Sat
(phone for times).*

8 Dunvegan Castle
Tel: 01470 521206.
*Open all year, late Mar–Oct
Mon–Sat 10–5.30, Sun
1–5.30 (gardens open from
10.30am); Nov–Mar daily
11–4*

9 Colbost
Croft Museum
Next to the Three
Chimneys, near Dunvegan.
Tel: 01470 521296.
*Open Easter–Oct daily
9.30–6.*

10 Carbost
Talisker Distillery
Tel: 01478 614308.
*Open Apr–Oct Mon–Fri
9–4.30 (also Sat in
Jul–Aug); Nov–Mar
Mon–Fri 2–4.30.*

15 Armadale
Clan Donald Centre and
Armadale Castle
Tel: 01471 844305.
*Open Apr–Oct daily
9.30–5.30.*

TOUR 25

i The Pier, Main Street,
Tobermory (seasonal).
Tel: 01688 302182.

1 Craignure
Torosay Castle and
Gardens
Tel: 01680 812421.
*Open Easter–Oct daily
10.30–5; gardens open all
year.*
Mull & West Highland
Narrow Gauge Railway
Craignure (Old Pier)
Station. Tel: 01680 812494
(in season) or 300389.
*Open Easter–mid Oct daily
11–5.*
Duart Castle
Tel: 01680 812309.
*Open May–mid-Oct daily
10.30–6.*

3 Iona
Iona Abbey
Tel: 01828 640411.
Open all year, at all times.
Iona Heritage Centre
Tel: 01681 700576.
*Open Apr–Oct Mon–Sat
10.30–4.30.*

7 Dervaig
Old Byre Heritage Centre
Tel: 01688 400229.
*Open late Mar–late Oct
daily 10.30–6.30.*

Opening times
The opening times of
museums and other
attractions are subject
to change and, in
addition to opening and
closing times given in
the text, are usually
closed on some public
holidays. Some may be
open by appointment
outside the stated
times. Visitors are
advised to check
locally to avoid
disappointment.

INDEX

Index & Acknowledgements

The Automobile Association
wishes to thank the following libraries and photographers for their assistance
in the preparation of this book.

PICTURES COLOUR LIBRARY 4
SPECTRUM COLOUR LIBRARY 5, 131

The remaining photographs are held in the Association's own photo library (AA PHOTO LIBRARY) and were taken by
the following photographers:
M ALEXANDER 6, 12, 22, 30B, 36B, 40, 41, 42, 44B, 45, 46A, 47, 50A, 50B, 76B; A BAKER 67A, 82; J BEAZLEY 10, 16, 17,
19, 20, 24/5, 26A, 26B, 30A, 42/3, 46B, 51, 61A, 61B, 77, 87B, 88, 109, 128; J CARNIE 7, 33, 56B, 62, 62/3, 64, 67B, 71B,
78, 90, 104, 107B, 120, 212A, 121B, 144; D CORRANCE i34, 38, 65, 75A, 76A, 118; S DAY 52, 57B, 58, 59A, 66, 68, 70, 72,
73A, 73B, 75B, 79, 83B, 85, 86, 105A, 119A, 119B, 122; E ELLINGTON 87A, 93, 94/5, 97, 98A, 99, 103A, 110, 113, 115, 125,
132/3, 136B, 139A, 139B, 147A, 148, 154; R ELLIOTT 48, 53, 117A, 123, 126/7; D FORSS 55A, 55B, 157; S GIBSON
PHOTOGRAPHY 14, 28, 29, 60; A GREELEY 150B; D HARDLEY 57A, 116; J HENDERSON 36A, 89, 106A, 107A, 111B,
114B, 132, 134A, 140, 142, 143, 150A, 151, 153; C LEES 25, 35, 44A; S & O MATTHEWS 18/9;
K PATTERSON 8, 11, 21, 32, 37, 49A, 49B, 56A, 69, 81, 84, 111A, 112, 130B, 145A, 145B;
P SHARPE 9, 13, 23, 31, 59B, 92; J SMITH 124; M TAYLOR 74, 83A, 101B, 103B, 130A, 134B, 136A, 138, 146, 147B; R
WEIR 80, 91, 96/7, 100, 101A, 102, 105B, 108, 112/3, 114A, 135, 137, 141, 149, 152, 155A, 156; H WILLIAMS 27, 39, 106B.

Contributors
Verifier: Hugh Taylor   **Copy editor:** Dilys Jones   **Indexer:** Marie Lorimer